Blackaby

February 1961

THE MORAL POINT OF VIEW:

A Rational Basis of Ethics

CONTEMPORARY PHILOSOPHY

General Editor
Max Black, Cornell University

The Moral Point of View

A RATIONAL BASIS OF ETHICS

By Kurt Baier

PROFESSOR OF PHILOSOPHY

UNIVERSITY OF PITTSBURGH

Cornell University Press

ITHACA AND LONDON

First published 1958 by Cornell University Press
Seventh printing 1974

Published in the United Kingdom by Cornell University Press Ltd., 2-4 Brook Street, London W1Y 1AA.

This work has been brought to publication with the assistance of a grant from the Ford Foundation.

International Standard Book Number 0-8014-0025-2

Printed in the United States of America by Valley Offset, Inc.

Preface

SOONER or later controversies in ethics always encounter the problem of our knowledge of right and wrong. The scandal is that the principal traditional theories cannot provide a satisfactory solution to this problem. They construe moral judgments on the model of other kinds of utterance and are, therefore, unable to accommodate all the four main logical features of moral judgments: (a) that moral judgments can be mutually contradictory; (b) that moral judgments are capable of guiding a moral agent in search of the morally right thing to do; (c) that there must be good reasons why any and every moral agent should do the morally right thing rather than the opposite; (d) that we often know whether a course of action is right or wrong even though obviously we cannot perceive it by means of one of our senses.

As I have said, none of the principal traditional ethical theories can accommodate all these logical features of moral judgments. The so-called emotive theory (which maintains that moral judgments express the speaker's feelings and attitudes and tend to arouse the same in the listener) is incompatible with (a). That theory has indeed an explanation why one single person (logically) cannot claim that a given act is both wrong and not wrong, but no explanation why it is logically impossible that two persons, respectively, should correctly make these contradictory claims, and it must therefore deny the obvious fact that this is logically impossible.

The theories according to which moral judgments simply state facts, whether "natural" or "nonnatural" facts, cannot accommodate (b). For a fact by itself is logically compatible with any sort of behavior: it cannot therefore by itself guide a moral agent to do one thing rather than another.

Those theories which regard morality as a sort of ideal law are incompatible with (c). For the main reason we have for obeying (or disobeying) a law is that disobedience (or obedience) would be morally wrong. But if doing wrong were itself simply disobeying a special kind of law, then we would never have a reason for being moral, that is, for obeying this special kind of law.

All other theories stumble over (d).

The view propounded in this book does justice to all these logical features. On this view, judgments to the effect that a certain course of action is morally right or morally wrong express "natural," if complicated facts. They state that the course of action in question has the weight of moral reasons behind or against it. Since this theory belongs in the group which construes moral judgments as fact-stating, the main task confronting this view is to explain how such facts can guide a moral agent in his conduct. The answer is that knowledge of the fact that a certain course of action is morally right or morally wrong can guide a moral agent, because by 'moral agent' we mean a person who is already determined to do whatever is morally right and to refrain from doing whatever is morally wrong. The real difficulty is therefore transferred from feature (b) to feature (c). If my case is to be more than an empty definition of 'moral agent,' I must mention a reason why any and every agent *should be* a moral and not an immoral agent, why everybody should do what has the weight of moral reasons behind it and refrain from doing what has the weight of moral reasons against it. The reason is that a general acceptance of a system of merely self-interested reasons would lead to conditions of life well described by Hobbes as "poor, nasty, brutish, and short." These unattractive living conditions can be improved by the general adoption of a system of reasoning in which reasons of self-interest are overruled, roughly speaking, when following them would tend to harm others. Such reasons are what we call "moral reasons," and we rightly regard them as overruling reasons of self-interest, because the acceptance of self-interested reasons as overruling moral ones would lead to the undesirable state of affairs described by Hobbes. This is the reason why moral reasons must be regarded as superior to self-interested reasons and why everyone has an excellent reason for so regarding them.

Lastly, this theory can accommodate point (d). On this view, we are in a position to tell whether a given course of action is right or wrong by examining whether it has the weight of moral reasons behind or against it. This explains why we can often tell immediately (as if by a moral sense or by intuition) whether a given course of action is right or wrong: because we can often tell immediately whether it has the weight of moral reasons behind or against it, whether it is in accordance with or contrary to well-known moral rules such as 'Thou shalt not kill,' 'Thou shalt not steal,' 'Thou shalt not lie,' and so forth. Yet,

Preface

at the same time, we do not of course tell this by the use of one of our senses. We do so by our reason, by subsuming a given course of action under a given principle.

The views expressed in this book are closest to those of Stephen Toulmin, without whose help and encouragement I could not have written this book. I have also benefited greatly from discussions with Gilbert Ryle, Max Black, Peter Herbst, Douglas and Betty Gasking, Cameron Jackson, Dan Taylor, Richard Hare, Don Brown, Michael Scriven, George Paul, and Don Gunner, who may well recognize some of their points incorporated here. I hope they will accept this general tribute as a sufficient compensation for having their ideas used (and, no doubt, often distorted) without individual acknowledgment. I am, at any rate, unable to be more specific, since I cannot now remember what I took from whom and what I contributed myself. Of the many others who have assisted me I should mention in particular Dr. W. D. Falk, whose unyielding opposition has often persuaded me to abandon a point or to modify it beyond recognition. I am also deeply indebted to Otto van der Sprenkel and Bruce Benjamin, both of Canberra University College, and to Miss Barbara Taylor of the Australian National University, who have read parts of the manuscript and have saved me from many obscurities and mistakes. I also wish to thank the Editor of the *Australasian Journal of Philosophy* for permission to incorporate material contained in my article "The Point of View of Morality," which appeared in that journal in 1954.

K. B.

Canberra University College
September 1957

Contents

Contents

Two: Value Judgments 47

Three: The Best Thing to Do 85

Four: Individual Rules of Reason 107

Contents

Contents

THE MORAL POINT OF VIEW:

A Rational Basis of Ethics

Introduction

MORAL talk is often rather repugnant. Leveling moral accusations, expressing moral indignation, passing moral judgment, allotting the blame, administering moral reproof, justifying oneself, and, above all, moralizing—who can enjoy such talk? And who can like or trust those addicted to it? The most outspoken critics of their neighbors' morals are usually men (or women) who wish to ensure that nobody should enjoy the good things in life which they themselves have missed and men who confuse the right and the good with their own advancement. When challenged, they can substantiate their charges only by fine phrases. Yet there can be no doubt that the very best reasons are required, for it is an outstanding characteristic of morality that it demands substantial sacrifices. It is therefore not unreasonable to ask for an assurance that they are really necessary and justifiable. After all, what *is* wrong with gambling if one has enough money left to look after one's dependents? What *is* wrong with having several wives if they can all get along to-

1

gether? What *is* wrong with suicide if one finds nothing to live for in life—if one has nobody to keep?

Suppose it is granted that sacrifices are necessary. Who is to say which individual or group ought to make them? Everyone is busily demanding that others should shoulder a burden, deny themselves this indulgence, or suffer that hardship, but let someone ask why a certain person should make a given sacrifice and usually he will be offered only bogus reasons. 'You must do what your society demands of you, if you want to get on in life.' But there are many people who get on very well and who do not even trouble to conceal their contempt for the morality of their society. And what if one does not particularly want to get on? 'You must obey these commandments to please God.' But how can one be sure that such conduct will please God? And if one does not particularly want to please God? Moreover, why should anyone, society or God, impose such hardships or sacrifices? What could be the justification for frightening people into obeying certain rules if the required types of behavior have nothing to recommend them in themselves?

As a last resort, we are offered pious platitudes. Some authorities will recommend the purifying flame of pain, the serene joys of self-denial, the searing ecstasies of renunciation, the spiritual raptures of chastity, and all the wholesome joys of the life of virtue; others will speak highly of the pride in having played the game, the contentment that follows upon placing another man's good above one's own, or the strengthening of the character that results from doing the decent thing; they will probably point to the humiliation of letting down one's side, the shame of failing to pull one's weight; or they will condemn the coarseness and grossness of sensual pleasures, ultimately so unsatisfying, things merely of the moment that yield forever diminishing returns.

But, really, how crude, how beside the point, how unconvincing all this is—particularly, when we compare it with the precision and the certainty of the natural sciences. It is difficult to resist the conclusion that by comparison with natural science, morality is a primitive, outmoded, inexact sort of enterprise. Its continuing popularity seems to be based largely on people's disappointment at being less well equipped than their neighbors, on envy of others who have succeeded where they have failed, on the instinct of revenge, and on superstitious hopes and fears that the Lazaruses of this world will be in the bosom of Abraham, while the men successful on earth will be tormented in hell.

It would seem, then, that there is no case for morality unless it can be turned into a science. But here the greatest disappointment awaits us: morality appears to be incapable of such a transformation. It seems logically impossible to introduce into moral discourse the careful definition of terms employed, the very high standards of checking and testing hypotheses, the prodigious use of experiment, which are the marks of a science. As soon as we import the mathematico-experimental method into morality, we thereby automatically transform it into something different. We are not then doing better what we did before, but doing another thing.

What, then, is left to reassure our moral skeptics, if we admit that the most persistent users of moral language are highly suspect, that morality itself cannot be made respectable and reliable by the introduction of scientific method? How shall we meet the Glaucons and Adeimantuses of today? What are their most fundamental questions and what answer can we give them? Behind all the many doubts and objections just mentioned there stand the three fundamental questions of ethics requiring unequivocal and reassuring answers:

(a) Should anyone do what is right when doing so is not to his advantage and if so why?

(b) Does anyone do what is right when doing so is not to his advantage and if so why?

(c) Can anyone know what is right and if so how?

If we could affirm that we know what is right and wrong, and if we could explain the method by which we know, we could then remove the perennial uncertainty about what exactly it is that a person of good will is supposed to do. If we could affirm that people do what is right and refrain from doing what is wrong, and could show why they do it, we could set at rest that feeling of resentment aroused by the suspicion that our good will only serves to promote the advantage of unscrupulous men. And if we could prove that we really *should* do what is right and refrain from doing what is wrong by pointing to a good reason why we should, we could remove the most serious of all our doubts, the doubt whether morality is indeed a sensible "game," a practice worth preserving and worth conforming to.

In Chapter One, I shall try to show as briefly as possible that the various traditional answers to all three fundamental questions of ethics are inadequate. It must, of course, be understood that in an introductory chapter it is impossible to do justice to the subtleties and complexities of the many and often highly ingenious theories of the past. In most cases the mention of one good reason will have to suffice. In several cases, the full force of my reasons against one or the other of the traditional answers will not be clear until later chapters have been read. It might, therefore, be best if those not well acquainted with moral theories would turn immediately to Chapter Two, and come back to Chapter One after they have read the remainder of the book.

One

The Fundamental
Questions of Ethics

THE three questions—(a) Should anyone do what is right
when doing so is not to his advantage and if so why? (b) Does
anyone do what is right when doing so is not to his advantage
and if so why? (c) Can anyone know what is right and if so
how?—are of course connected. In giving an answer to any one
of them we must bear in mind how this will affect the others.
We cannot, for instance, say, in answer to our first question,
that we know what is right by a special moral sense and, in
answer to our second question, that men do what is right because doing what is right is always to one's advantage, or in
answer to our third question, that people really should do what
is right because doing so is always to one's advantage. For if we
have a special moral sense that tells us which courses of action
are right and which wrong, it might well turn out that there is
a conflict between what is right and what is to one's advantage.

The Moral Point of View

Bearing this in mind, we can now turn to what is probably the most natural and most persistent doubt about morality—whether, and if so why, we *should* do what is right and refrain from doing wrong, even when doing so is not to our advantage. This question is naturally asked by people who have little doubt about the correctness of their moral convictions but serious doubts about the worth-whileness of acting on them. They suspect that it would be better, wiser, more sensible, to do what one likes, what one enjoys doing, what one thinks worth while doing, even when this is in conflict with the demands of morality.

1 WHY SHOULD WE DO WHAT IS RIGHT?

Perhaps the most serious candidate for the position of justifier of morality is self-interest. This candidate's eminence is, of course, due to his unrivaled popularity with the public. What better recommendation could there be for morality than the fact (if indeed it is a fact) that it pays to be moral? Many people even feel that unless it pays the moral agent in some way to be moral, morality can have no justification; and if it has none, it would be foolish to be moral when it appears disadvantageous to be so. Unless we have a guarantee that in some way, perhaps in the long run, perhaps in the afterlife, it will pay us to do what is morally required, why should we not rather do what appears to be in our interest? If a proof can be given that doing what is right and shunning what is wrong will always work out to our advantage, then we need not examine whether a particular line of conduct is likely to be to our advantage or not. We can go ahead and do what is right in the assurance that what we are doing is in accordance with reason.

There are various ways of attempting such a proof. One rests on the simple view that what is right *must* be advantageous, because by 'right' we *mean* 'whatever is advantageous.' However,

6

this view, known as ethical egoism, is plainly false. This is not what 'right' means. We ordinarily use the words 'right' and 'wrong' in such a way that there is no contradiction in saying 'It would be wrong to do that (say, kill Aunt Martha who has left me a legacy) although it would be more advantageous to me than any other course open at the moment.[1]

Could it be that what is right always "happens" to be what is advantageous because the world has been so arranged, either by our society, or by God, that the man who does what is right also always "happens" at the same time to do what is to his advantage? We can neglect the first alternative, for clearly no society has so perfectly arranged its system of meting out justice that it will not be possible, for some people often and for all people sometimes, to do better for themselves by doing wrong than by doing what is morally right. The second alternative, however, must be considered, for God's machinery of retribution might be flawless.

There is a serious objection to the view that we should do what is right because God has so arranged the afterlife that doing what is right is always in our best interest in the long run. The objection is that this could not be the main or basic reason why we ought to do what is right, but at most a subsidiary, supplementary reason. Let us see why this is so.

It will be admitted that we have a reason for giving up smoking, because smokers run the risk of contracting lung cancer. This constitutes a reason, because, in a world of brute fact, lung cancer is the effect of smoking. In a God-governed world, we have an analogous reason if God has declared smoking morally wrong and punishes it by eternal hell-fire. But this consideration gives rise to a dilemma. We must say either that God had no reason why he thus outlawed and penalized smoking or that he

---

[1] For a more detailed refutation of ethical egoism, see below, Chapter Eight, section 1.

7

had a reason. We cannot say that God has no reason, because that would assimilate the workings of a just God to the workings of blind Nature, the penalties *for* smoking to the penalties *of* smoking. God's sanctions would then be indistinguishable from the regularities of nature. Moreover, doing the right thing would be tantamount to serving the most powerful and most capricious being, since right would be that type of conduct which is commanded, wrong that type which is forbidden, by God, whatever it is he commands or forbids. Such a view is repugnant not only because it fails to conform to our idea of the nature of God, but also because it does violence to our notion of morality. It is not inconceivable that the world should be governed by an all-powerful but wicked being. If it were so governed, morality would require us sometimes to disobey his commandments, though self-interest might counsel us always to obey them.

On the other hand, we cannot say that God might have had a reason for declaring certain types of conduct right or wrong. For if he had a reason for declaring them wrong, then that reason is *eo ipso* the reason why these things are wrong and why we ought not to do them. That God attaches sanctions to these types of conduct is merely an additional, self-interested, and purely extraneous reason for not doing them.

It might be asked why God could not have declared something wrong for a reason which was a reason for him but not for us. In that case, though he would have had a reason for giving his command, we would have no reason for obeying them. But then his reason would have to be one of self-interest in conflict with ours. If God for instance declared the eating of pork sinful, because he wanted to eat all the pork himself, or if he declared pride a sin, because he wished men to fall on their knees before him and worship him, then there might be a conflict of interest and God's reasons for declaring something wrong might not be reasons for us to obey him. But it is obvious that such commandments cannot come from a benevolent God and that they cannot correctly represent what is right and what is wrong.[2]

Another method of persuading us that we ought to do the right thing because it pays us to do so is by way of a psychological argument. It is said, for example by Plato, that doing what is right and shunning what is wrong makes us happier than any other principle of living. But this is surely contingent and depends on what morality requires of us, and we know that its requirements vary from age to age, from society to society, and even from one profession to another. Morality will require different things from a Catholic priest, a Moslem prince, a medieval knight, a Quaker business man, an Indian untouchable, a temple prostitute, a nun, an Aztec warrior, and so on. Whether the satisfaction of the demands made on him by morality makes the agent happy will depend on what these demands are, and on what sort of person the agent is. It is surely possible that by neglecting some of the demands of morality a certain man would be made much happier than by complying with them.

Kant has given a different justification for doing the morally right thing. He claims that wrongdoing is acting in a way contrary to reason. He arrives at this conclusion by way of the categorical imperative. Doing what is right is obeying the categorical imperative; doing what is wrong is disobeying it. In disobeying it, one is acting contrary to reason, for one is then acting on a maxim which one cannot, without contradiction, will to become a universal law; but it is contrary to reason to act on such maxims.

I do not think that this is so, but whether it is or not, we shall presently show [3] that a morality based on the categor-

---

[2] See also below, Chapter Seven, section 1.

[3] See below, Chapter One, section 3.23, p. 25.

ical imperative is useless for it rejects as immoral only self-contradictory and self-frustrating maxims. If we take good care not to act on those (but it is logically impossible to act on the first and very difficult to find instances of the second), we could do anything else we liked, including killing, stealing, maiming, lying, and hurting others, without involving ourselves in self-contradiction. Such a code can hardly be described as a morality.

In recent years, Prichard, in a famous paper,[4] declared that the search for a justification of morality was altogether misguided. He argued that 'Why should I be moral?' was an improper question. He claimed that 'Why should I be moral?' was a request for a proof of the moral convictions which people held without proof.[5] In other words, Prichard takes 'Why should I be moral?' to mean 'How do I know what is right and what is wrong?' and claims that the latter question is illegitimate because it involves an infinite vicious regress. We are not satisfied that we know *immediately*, without proof, that A is B. We require a criterion of knowledge, a way of telling whether our supposed knowledge that A is B is really knowledge. But there must be an end to criteria. "If, in order really to know that A is B, we must first know that we knew it, then really to know that we knew it, we must first know that we knew that we knew it." [6] And so on. We cannot ask for a proof of all our beliefs, our moral convictions included. For proof can only be a derivation of our beliefs from some which we know without proof.

In my opinion, this argument is unsound. We may admit that whenever anyone can claim to know something it must be possible to ask, 'How do you know?'; that it must be possible

---

[4] H. A. Prichard, *Moral Obligation* (Oxford: Clarendon Press, 1949), p. 1.
[5] *Ibid.*, p. 14.   [6] *Ibid.*, p. 14.

to ask for his grounds for saying so; that to say, 'I *just*]
is to show that one does not understand the meaning o. ...
word 'know.' But this is perfectly compatible with Prichard's
point that the number of grounds or criteria must be finite,
for it is possible that one cannot go on to ask how one knows
the grounds, and the grounds of the grounds, and so forth. 'John
and Mary have become engaged, secretly.' 'How do you know?'
'I found John's letter in Mary's writing desk.' 'How do you
know it was John's letter?' 'I know his handwriting.' 'How do
you know his handwriting?' 'I have seen many of his letters.'
'How do you know you have seen many of his letters?' 'Well,
we have been in correspondence for some time.' 'How do you
know that?' 'For heaven's sake, how could I be mistaken about
that?' At some stage, the question 'How do you know?' loses
its bite. We do not necessarily have to parry it with 'I *just* know.'
On the contrary, there comes a stage when we may reject the
question as unnecessary or inappropriate. And where it is inappropriate to ask, 'How do you know?' it may there be inappropriate to claim that one knows.

However, let us, for argument's sake, admit Prichard's point.
It is still possible to deny that it applies to morality. Some
utilitarians might well agree with Prichard that there are some
things which we "just" know and yet they would argue that we
do not "just know" what is right and what wrong, but that we
work it out on the basis of some other facts (what is for the
greatest happiness of the greatest number), some of which we
perhaps "just know."

At any rate, Prichard later gave a different interpretation of
the question 'Why should I be moral?' and declared that so
interpreted it also was illegitimate.[7] He claimed that both Plato

---

[7] H. A. Prichard, *Duty and Interest* (Oxford: Clarendon Press, 1928),
p. 21.

and the Sophists held a certain psychological theory about human behavior. They held that all men are essentially selfish, that is, that no man deliberately acts in a way he thinks contrary to his interests. Hence they thought that, if people were to be induced to act in certain ways, these ways must be made palatable to them. If we wish to persuade rational men to be moral, we must offer them incentives. We must show that doing right will be advantageous to them. Both Plato and the Sophists believed that advantageousness is a criterion of moral behavior. They differed only on one point: whether the currently accepted morality was in fact advantageous to the moral agent. Plato held that it was, the Sophists that it was not. Plato therefore supported, the Sophists rejected, current morality.

Prichard accepts the factual claims of the Sophists. He agrees that being moral is often disadvantageous to the moral agent. But he maintains that this is ethically irrelevant.[8] Human beings are not essentially selfish. Many people have a sense of duty, that is, a desire to do what is right for its own sake, even when this means making genuine sacrifices.[9] When we realize this, we no longer want to ask, 'Why should I be moral?' We see why we should be. We are no longer puzzled. Just as we are able to pick up the apple in front of us when we see it and because we desire to eat it, so we are able to do our duty as soon as we know what it is and *because* we desire to do whatever is our duty.

All this may very well be true, but it is not an answer to our question. 'Why should I be moral?' is not a request for an explanation. It does not mean 'How is it that I can be moral, that I can do what is right, even though it is not to my advantage?' If that were the question, then the fact that we have a desire to do our duty would indeed be an answer to it.

It is easy to see that this cannot be an answer to our original demand for a justification of being moral. If we have a desire to

---

[8] *Ibid.*, p. 10.　　　　[9] *Ibid.*, pp. 27, 28.

do our duty, it must be either irresistible or resistible. If it is irresistible, then the question arises whether we should not consult a psychiatrist to rid us of our psychological chains. If the desire is resistible, then we must ask ourselves whether to satisfy *it* or satisfy some other desire instead, for example, one that may be in conflict with our duty but to our advantage.

Some people seem indeed to be irresistibly in the grip of their desire to do right. They hunger and thirst after righteousness as others do after food and sex. They are moral automata, in the clutches of their superegos. Like Luther, they have to say, 'Here I stand and can do no other.' Plato's auxiliaries were to be drilled in this way. Tempered like steel, they should be unable to do anything except what they had been taught was right. Hamlet felt himself to be similarly afflicted; hence he claimed that conscience doth make cowards of us all. A man in this condition is not free. He is the slave of his conscience, under the thumb of his superego, a mere product of his moral upbringing. Because a man could not help acting rightly, he could never act *morally*. He is a mere imitation of the moral man, just as a robot is an imitation of a real man.

If people have an irresistible desire to do what is right, this explains why they do what they do: the reason is that they cannot help themselves. But none of this throws any light on the very different question 'Why should I be moral?' which can be asked only when the agent has a choice before him. This question arises only when the agent is able to do what is right and also to refrain from so doing.

Prichard might admit all this. He might say, "I accept your distinction between explanation and justification. But even if 'Why should I be moral?' is a request for a justification and not for an explanation, it is still illegitimate. For how could there be such a justification? It cannot be a justification in terms of self-interest, for it must be admitted that morality does not necessarily pay. Nor can it be in terms of moral reasons, for we are now talking *about*, not *within* morality. 'Why should I be moral?' cannot mean 'Does being moral pay?' or 'Is there a moral reason for being moral?' But it cannot mean anything else either, for there are no other types of reason. Hence it is an illegitimate question." This seems to me a powerful argument and I have nowhere seen a satisfactory reply.[10]

2 WHY DO WE DO WHAT IS RIGHT?

The second question asked by moral skeptics arises because of their very general doubts about man's ability to satisfy the demands of morality. Many people believe, on general grounds, that all human conduct is causally determined. If so, they argue, a man would not be able to enter on a given course of action just because he recognized it to be the right course, but only if, at the same time, all those conditions were satisfied which are the necessary and sufficient conditions (the *cause*) of the course of action which he recognizes as right. Whether he is able to satisfy the demands of morality will, therefore, depend on his education and training as well as on his natural impulses and inclinations. Again, it is held, on general grounds, that all men always seek their greatest pleasure, their greatest happiness, or their greatest advantage, and that they can do the right thing only when they believe, rightly or wrongly, that these things coincide.

We have already examined and rejected one such answer: that we do what is right because it pays. This answer owes its persistence to the prevalence of certain fallacious but persuasive psychological theories of motivation, for example, that human beings can act only from a desire for the greatest possible advantage to themselves, or for their greatest possible happiness, or the greatest amount of pleasure. It is now generally admitted that there is no truth in such theories and we have therefore no

---

[10] For a full treatment of this problem, see Chapter Twelve, section 2.

reason to believe that we do what is right only because or when we think it pays us or will make us happy. Skeptics cannot, therefore, derive any legitimate support from such theories.

There is, however, another more serious view which has contributed to skepticism, the view that reason can have nothing to contribute to the establishment of moral judgments. Hume, as is well known, argued that morality was not a matter either of empirical fact or of relations between ideas, but a matter of taste. It is natural to draw the conclusion that there are no objectively establishable moral judgments. Hume argued that "reason being cool and disengaged, was no motive to action, and directs only the impulse received from appetite or inclination, by showing us the means of attaining happiness or avoiding misery." [11] Thus the source of action can never be reason, for reason alone can never be a motive to any action of the will and can never oppose passion in directing the will. The primary source or spring or motive of action is not reason, but taste. For taste, "as it gives pleasure and pain, and thereby constitutes happiness or misery, becomes a motive to action, and is the first spring or impulse to desire and volition." Hume concluded from this that there could never be any conflict between reason and desire, that reason was, and ought only to be, the slave of the passions.

It has often been argued that this view is untenable. There can be no doubt that conflicts between reason and desire frequently occur. Reason tells us one thing: desire demands another. If Hume means by 'reason' what we ordinarily mean, his view is plainly false: there are too many obvious cases of conflict of this sort for us to be in any doubt about it. And if he does not mean the same by 'reason' as we ordinarily mean, then he has no contribution to make to answering our question.

Kant took seriously the common-sense view that there can

---

[11] David Hume, *An Enquiry concerning the Principles of Morals*, ed. by L. A. Selby-Bigge (Oxford: Clarendon Press, 1894), app. I, p. 294.

be, and frequently is, conflict between reason and desire, holding that reason frequently is but never ought to be the slave of the passions. He took the view that we know by reason what is right and what is wrong and also that reason frequently determines our conduct. Like Hume, he thought of reason as an inner organ or faculty but, unlike Hume, as capable of moving us to action. He conceived of it as a causality in its own right. Men, he claimed, lived in two different realms or worlds, the world of phenomena and the world of noumena, and they were capable of action because their limbs could be moved by their will. Human wills were subject to two forms of causation: causation by the desires and causation by reason. Hence there existed the possibility of conflict between reason and desire. Only beings whose wills are subject to this dual causation can have obligations. Purely rational creatures, that is, creatures with a holy will, are not subject to obligation, because for them there can be no conflict between what reason commands and something else: without having to resist any other force, they do what is commanded by reason. Nor can animals be subject to obligation, for they are not rational. They are subject merely to the causation of their desires. Human beings are subject to both types of causation and are said to be free when they follow reason rather than desire, that is, when their reason is *stronger than* their desires or when their will is *under the control of* reason rather than desire.

The objections to this view are well known. If reason is one of the forces acting on the will, then the question whether a person is free is itself a question of causality. A person will be free simply if his reason is stronger than his desires, and this is just a matter of the relative strengths of the two forces, reason and desire. The balance will necessarily vary from person to person, for even if the force of reason is the same in everyone, the strength of desires varies from one person to another. Hence, whether a person is free or not will depend on his natural endowment. Such a view cannot provide the required metaphysical guarantee of free will for all men.

Among those who claim that we do what is right (when we do it) because we have a desire to do what is right—a conscience or sense of duty which drives us to do what is right and avoid what is wrong—there is disagreement about whether this desire is innate or acquired, implanted in our nature or inculcated by education and environment.

Philosophers who claim that we are prompted by an innate conscience or sense of duty to do what is right and shun what is wrong mean that, although on occasion we may have inclinations not only to do what is right but also to do what is wrong, we would nevertheless always do what is right if only "we followed Nature," that is, our strongest natural, unconditioned desire. This view has been denied by other philosophers and psychologists. Their view is that our conscience is the product of upbringing, embodying the precepts learned from our parents and teachers as well as the guilt feelings acquired as the result of suffering the consequences of disobedience in the home, for example, loss of love, nagging by the parents, corporal punishment, reprobations, and so on. It is impossible, at this stage, to do justice to the complexities of these issues. It must suffice to say that though an excellent case has been made for the view that environment plays an important role in modifying the individual's conscience (that is, both his opinions about, and his propensities to do, what is right), no conclusive proof has been given either of the view that individuals are, or of the view that they are not, born with propensities leading to right conduct.[12]

Our cursory review of answers to the second fundamental question in ethics shows that often it is not adequately distinguished from our first and third questions and that none of the

---

[12] For a full discussion of this topic see below, Chapter Eleven.

suggested answers has been satisfactorily established. In particular, the respective roles of reason and desire, of innate disposition and environmental conditioning, have not been clearly delineated. Nothing has, therefore, been said to silence the skeptics who doubt whether we are capable of satisfying the demands of morality.

3 HOW DO WE KNOW WHAT IS RIGHT?

More fundamental, however, than both the questions so far discussed is our third question, how we know what is right and what is wrong, an answer to which is presupposed by the other two. If we do not know what is right, there is no need to ask ourselves why we do or ought to do it. The complete failure of moral philosophers to give a satisfactory answer to this fundamental epistemological question is probably the main reason for continued skepticism in ethics.

This third question arises very naturally. We are all taught the moral convictions of our group, but we also notice that other groups accept very different teachings. Accordingly, we desire to be acquainted with the methods by which we can make sure whether our group convictions are right or mistaken.

The received theories in this field fall into four main types which I shall call "law theories," "moral fact theories," "response theories," and "the emotive theory." Law theories are those which conceive of morality as a system of commands, rules, or laws issuing from some venerable or frightening authority. Such a conception of morality is very natural since it would seem to account for the outstanding fact about morality, namely, that it requires of us certain kinds of behavior just as commands, rules, or laws do. This conception of morality enables us to give a simple answer to our first question. It implies that we know what is right in the same way as we know what is required of us by statute law. If morality is a certain sort of command, rule,

d only consider the word of the moral commander,
ɔr legislator.

ɪne second main type (the "moral fact theory") conceives
of morality as a system of facts, namely, moral facts, which are
stated more or less correctly and accurately in the moral convictions of this or that group. The two main subgroups of this
type of view are naturalist and nonnaturalist theories.

Naturalists hold that there is nothing special about moral
facts. Words such as 'right' and 'wrong,' 'good' and 'bad,'
'wicked' and 'virtuous,' state ordinary though complex properties
of conduct and people. All we have to do is to give a definition
of these words by means of other simpler words. From this conception of morality there follows a very straightforward answer
to our first question: we know what is right and what is wrong in
the same way in which we know everything else, namely, by our
senses. All we need to do is to find out exactly what the moral
terms mean and, with this definition in hand, look and see
whether this or that course of action, this or that person, possesses the moral property in question.

Nonnaturalist theories, on the other hand, maintain that
moral facts are of a very special sort. They consist not in the possession of an ordinary, natural property like 'yellowness,' which
can be perceived by our senses, but of a peculiar, nonnatural
property like 'rightness' or 'goodness,' which cannot be so perceived. This view implies a different answer to our third question: we know what is right and what is wrong by virtue of a
special moral sense, an eye of the soul, intuition, the light of
reason, or some such faculty or power.

The third main type of theory (the "response theory") de-
picts morality as a system of responses to certain sorts of behavior. It underlines the plain fact that various types of behavior
arouse in the people affected, or even in unaffected bystanders,
certain favorable or unfavorable feelings, responses, or attitudes;

19

and it regards morality as in one way or another located in, o. concerned with, these responses and not with the persons or the behavior which arouses them. The response theory could also be classed as a naturalist theory because it believes that our moral convictions state ordinary, natural, empirical facts. It differs from other forms of naturalism only in its insistence that moral utterances are not about the conduct or the people which they seem to be about, but are really about the responses produced in one person by the conduct of others. This view returns to our first question the same answers as naturalism, with the difference that it locates the evidence in people's responses to the world rather than in the world itself.

The fourth main type of theory (the "emotive theory"), on the other hand, marks a radical departure from all previous theories. While emphasizing the same facts, and looking for the evidence in the same place, as the response theory, it makes the novel claim that moral utterances are not characteristically *about* anything, do not characteristically *assert anything of anything*, but express certain characteristically moral feelings aroused in the speaker by people and their conduct. The emotivist answer to our third question is, therefore, that it cannot arise. Since moral utterances cannot be true or false, there is nothing to know. Hence there is no epistemological problem in ethics. The reason why philosophers have not been able to find an answer to our third question is simply that there is nothing to find.

I now turn to a brief discussion of these four types of view.

3.1 The "law theory"

This theory is probably the one most widely held among philosophical laymen and the most easily refuted. Commands, rules, and laws require an imponent, who gives the commands, imposes the rules, lays down the laws. This confronts us with a dilemma: either we know the imponent or we do not. If he is known, as our earthly rulers and legislators are, then, though there will be no difficulty in discovering what his commands or laws are, his word, like theirs, may be fallible. How could we possibly tell, on this view, whether his word was correct or incorrect? If morality is the word of ordinary legislators, then we can never know what is right and wrong, but only what they command us to do. And if we say that morality is the command, rule, or law of a *perfect* being, then, though there will be no doubt about the correctness of *his* word, we can never tell whether any given set of commandments, rules, or laws really was issued by that *perfect* being. We can never know whether the voice from the mountain is God's or the Devil's.

It is, moreover, quite absurd to say that what is right or wrong has been made so by someone's fiat. No one, not even an omnipotent being, can say, 'I shall abolish the moral law against killing' or 'I have introduced a moral law against eating' or 'Yesterday I exempted Cretans from the moral law against lying.' [13]

3.2 The "moral fact theory"

It is unnecessary to enumerate the formidable difficulties which a naturalist theory of ethics has to overcome. The works of G. E. Moore and Sir David Ross are sufficiently well known to make such an enumeration otiose. It must suffice to say, quite dogmatically, that none of the proposed definitions of the key moral terms 'right' and 'good' can stand up to the nonnaturalist attacks. However, nonnaturalism itself can hardly be said to fare any better. Naturalism would have no difficulty in answering our third question if only it could find the correct definitions of 'right' and 'good.' But nonnaturalism, in rejecting the naturalist claim that we know what is right and

---

[13] For further details, see Chapter Seven, section 1, pp. 177–179.

what is wrong by sense perception, is confronted by insuperable epistemological difficulties. The most popular solutions of this problem are that we know moral facts by a special moral sense, by intuition, or by reason. However, none of these can provide a satisfactory answer to the question how we know what is right.

3.21 The *moral sense theory* attempts to overcome the difficulty by the claim that we have a special moral sense, a sort of inner eye, which enables us to see the rightness or wrongness of certain sorts of action. The absolutely fatal objection to this view is that there is no such moral sense, no such inner eye. There is no part of a man's body whose removal or injury would specifically affect his knowledge of the rightness or wrongness of certain types or courses of action, as the removal or injury of our eyes or ears would affect our knowledge of what color a thing has or what sounds it produces. We cannot, for example, test people for "moral blindness" as we test them for color blindness. But if there were such a thing as a moral sense or moral organ, we would have to be able to do that. Otherwise we would risk being unfair to those who, because of their "moral blindness," are unable to "see" and, therefore, to do what is right. Before a person is issued a driving license, he must pass a test for color blindness because, if he were color blind, he could not be blamed for not stopping at a red light. How much more important would be a test of people for "moral blindness" before allowing them to marry, to educate their children, and to go into business or politics. We are, however, quite certain that being able to tell the difference between right and wrong does not require such a special moral sense or organ.

3.22 *Intuitionism* can overcome some of the difficulties caused by the term 'moral sense,' for the view that it is our intuition or our conscience which tells us what is right and what is wrong does not imply that we have a special sense yielding characteristic sensations of rightness and wrongness, as the eyes do of color. Mrs. Jones's intuition does indeed work *like* a sixth sense, in that she can tell, before he has said or done anything, that her husband is in a bad mood. But that is all we mean when we speak of her intuition. We do not mean that she has additional sensory organs or extra faculties, but only that she is more observant, or more perceptive, than other people and knows her husband so well that she can "read him like a book."

Moreover, Mrs. Jones can be said to know her husband's mood by intuition only because ordinary ways of knowing his mood are also available to us. We conclude that there are some things (such as her husband's moods) which she knows by intuition and does not merely guess rightly because we are able to confirm or refute her claims and because they are almost always confirmed rather than refuted. But the confirmation of her claims has to be effected in ordinary ways, not by intuition. I could not claim to know complicated mathematical truths by intuition, as mathematical prodigies do, if my special powers consisted merely in the ability to give immediate answers to questions such as 'How much is $6{,}534.897 \times 9{,}143.682$?' I am a mathematical prodigy only if I can give immediate and correct answers to such questions. But whether they are correct answers must, of course, be established by ordinary multiplication, not by asking other mathematical prodigies. In order to be able to tell that a person knows certain things by intuition, we must make certain that his claims about them usually turn out to be true and are not just unfounded assertions. At some point we must be able to establish by ordinary methods that the claimant possesses the *power of intuiting.*[14]

---

[14] This point was made very clearly by S. E. Toulmin, "Knowledge of

Hence intuition in moral matters, if admissible at all, can only be of secondary importance. For moral intuitions, like all other kinds, presuppose corresponding techniques of confirmation which, if more pedestrian, are more reliable. If there is to be moral intuition by anybody, there must be a method of moral verification open to all. Perhaps great moral reformers know by intuition what is right. But if we are to tell whether they are moral teachers or mere humbugs, we must be able to verify their intuitive insights. How can this be done? Are we to say that "inspired seers" are those whose intuitions have stood the test of time, and so distinguish them from would-be prophets whose claims are now forgotten? But what importance can we attach to the fact that some intuitions have stood the test of time while others have not? Is the mere fact of survival to be decisive? Surely superstitions can be as hardy as truth. In any event, the one test which is clearly inadmissible is the use of one intuition to validate another.

3.23 By *rationalism* (the third variant of nonnaturalist theories) I mean the view that we know by reason what is right and what is wrong. One of its forms, calculative rationalism, maintains that the ordinary meaning of 'right' is 'means to an end' and that reason enables us to tell what is right by working out what is a means to our end. Obviously this theory will be tenable only if it can find a satisfactory answer to the question 'How do we determine what is a proper end for us to aim at?'

Calculative rationalism therefore manages to overcome the epistemological problem in connection with rightness only at the cost of shifting it to another field. Although it tells us how we know what is right and what is wrong, it can do so only by deriving this knowledge from a knowledge of what is a

Right and Wrong," in *Proceedings of the Aristotelian Society* (London: Harrison and Sons, 1950), L (1949–1950), 146–149.

proper end to aim at, but it cannot tell us how we know the latter.

Categorical rationalism (a view propounded by Kant) asserts that reason can tell us what are proper ends to aim at as well as what are the best means thereunto. Hypothetical imperatives (of the form, 'If you want x, you ought to do y') are commands of reason informing us that y is the best means to x, and commanding us to do y if we want to attain x. Categorical imperatives (of the form, 'You ought to bring about y') are commands of reason informing us that y is an end-in-itself, that is, a proper end to aim at, and commanding us to aim at it. The objection to Kant's view is obvious. Categorical imperatives are almost wholly empty. They do not order us to do this thing or another but merely to act in accordance with a very highly general principle: 'Act only on that maxim which thou canst at the same time will to become a universal law of nature.' Taken literally, this principle excludes only self-contradictory maxims such as 'Lie and don't lie' and self-frustrating maxims such as 'Ask for help when you are in trouble, but refuse other people help when they are.' It does not exclude maxims such as 'Don't ever help another man when he is in trouble,' for such maxims can be willed to become universal laws of nature. One cannot will it to become a universal law of nature *both* that everyone should ask for help when he is in trouble *and* that no one should give help to another when asked for it, because the second half frustrates what is obviously the point of the first half: to get help.[15] But there is nothing self-contradictory or self-frustrating in making into a universal law of nature the maxim 'Don't ever help another man when he is in trouble.' Mutual co-operation is one possible system of human behavior; everyone for him-

---

[15] For a more detailed discussion of self-contradictory and self-frustrating principles, see below, Chapter Eight, section 3, pp. 196–197.

self is another. The first is probably better than the second, but either is possible.[16]

3.3 The "response theory"

If the response theory were true, then we could give an answer to our third fundamental ethical question 'How do we know what is right and what is wrong?' for then moral judgments such as 'That was wrong' would be analogous to remarks such as 'That was depressing' except that the feeling, response, or attitude would have to be the characteristically moral one. We could therefore ascertain whether something was wrong by ascertaining whether the relevant person had the characteristic moral feeling, response, or attitude.

This theory faces two insuperable difficulties. The first is to find a method whereby to single out those feelings and so on which are characteristically moral. After all, they come without an identifying label, and even if they did come with such a label, this would be no guarantee against mistakes in the labeling department. The second insuperable difficulty is to solve the question *whose* feelings, responses, or attitudes should count when there are differences among people. The second of these two difficulties need concern us only if the first can be met. For it is only if the rightness of an act consists in its power to produce a certain characteristically moral response in some person (or persons) that we need to concern ourselves with the question of his (or their) identity. I shall therefore concentrate on the first difficulty which, as we shall see below, is also encountered by the emotive theory.

A follower of the response theory might retort that everyone knows very well what the characteristic moral feelings, responses, or attitudes are: they are moral approval and disapproval. 'I disapprove of *x*' implies '*x* is wrong' and vice versa;

---

[16] For further details on this point, see below, Chapter Eight, section 1.

'I disapprove of this but it is not morally wrong' and 'This is morally wrong but I do not disapprove of it' are self-contradictory remarks.

However, this reply seems adequate only because it ignores the distinction between moral and nonmoral approval. If the response theory analyzes 'x is morally right' as 'I (morally or nonmorally) approve of x,' then the analysis is untenable and the response theory false. For there is simply no logical connection between moral rightness and nonmoral approval, between moral wrongness and nonmoral disapproval. I may disapprove of your color scheme without thinking it morally wrong or without regarding you as a scoundrel for selecting it. Mussolini may have approved of Count Ciano as a son-in-law without thinking that Ciano was a man of moral merit or that, in marrying, his daughter and Ciano were doing the morally right thing.

On the other hand, if the response theory confines its analysis of rightness and wrongness to moral approval and disapproval, then, though it avoids the first pitfall, it throws away the epistemological advantages which make it attractive. There is indeed some logical connection between 'x is morally wrong' and 'I morally disapprove of x,' but this substitution is no help toward solving our epistemological problem, 'How do we know what is morally right and what is morally wrong?' While it may be comparatively easy to tell that a given person nonmorally approves or disapproves, it is difficult to tell whether he does so morally. For morally approving and disapproving is being for or against something on *moral* grounds: it is nonsense to say 'I morally disapprove of war though I have only selfish reasons for my disapproval.' Hence the answer to our epistemological problem presupposes a knowledge of moral reasons, but the response theory has no light to shed on what are moral, as opposed to other, reasons.

The Moral Point of View

Some followers of the response theory would, of course, maintain that moral approval is not the attitude of being in favor of something on moral grounds, but is a certain characteristic feeling or response. But what is the *characteristic* of this feeling or response? How do we make sure that it is *characteristically moral?* Plainly we cannot tell in the way in which we tell that a particular feeling we now have is a tickle rather than pins and needles. Feelings such as these are indeed immediately recognizable by their characteristic "feel"; they are caused by something; we can suddenly find ourselves experiencing them without knowing what caused them, and we may try to discover their causes. Since they are *felt* occurrences, we may like or dislike having them and may on their account take steps to terminate them and prevent their recurrence in the future, or to prolong and renew them. Moral approval and disapproval, however, are not such feelings. It would be quite absurd to say, 'I wonder what is causing that moral disapproval of war of mine' or 'I must do something to experience again that moral approval of keeping promises' or 'I suddenly found myself having that feeling of moral approval of kindness.'

Moral approval and disapproval are not even feelings such as anger, fear, and depression, or dispositions such as belief. It is possible that we cannot help feeling angry when we think of what Jones did or afraid when the gun is pointed at us, even though we must admit that we have absolutely no reason to be angry (Jones does not mean to insult us) or to be afraid (the gun is not loaded). But it is simply nonsense to say that we cannot help feeling moral approval even though we must admit that there are no moral reasons for it whatsoever. There is in these feelings and dispositions a stubborn, uncontrollable element which is causally determined: we can have irrational fears and beliefs even after we have seen them to be irrational. There is no such irrational element in moral approval. Feelings such as anger and dispositions such as belief are only partly reason-guided; moral approval is wholly so. Of course, people may morally approve for bad moral reasons, but not *after* they have come to think them bad. A man may still *feel sympathy* for conscientious objectors and may even stand up for them, after he has been convinced that pacifism is morally wrong, but he cannot say, 'I still morally approve of pacifism though I no longer consider it morally right.'

It is also incorrect to think that moral approval and disapproval are "adopted at will" or "deliberately taken" in the way certain responses or attitudes are. They are indeed completely under one's control, as feelings and dispositions are not, but a person cannot deliberately and capriciously approve or disapprove morally of a person, as he can deliberately and capriciously be hostile or charming to him. This may easily be overlooked if we do not carefully distinguish between approval and its expression. One may indeed, capriciously and contrary to one's reasons, express moral approval and disapproval, but this is possible only because 'expressing approval' does not entail 'expressing *one's* approval'; because 'Jones expressed approval' does not entail 'Jones expressed *his* approval' or 'Jones approved.'

'Do I morally approve of this?' is not therefore a question like 'Am I having pins and needles now?' or like 'Am I being nasty to old Jones?' It is neither a question about what is now *going on* in my mind or what I am now *experiencing*, nor a question about what it is I am now *doing* in response to something. It is rather like the question 'Do I have the tendency or disposition to be in favor of something?' But it differs from this in requiring an answer based on what I take to be the best moral reasons—even if they are not the best and even if I have difficulty in formulating them.

We can now say why an answer to the question whether I in

fact now morally approve of something can never settle the question whether it is morally right. To say that I now morally approve of x only tells us that I have a certain disposition to be in favor of something. But this gives rise to the question how I came to have this disposition, to which there are only two answers: either it was inculcated in me by my environment or I adopted it independently. In the first case, I now have this disposition because of the moral convictions of my group. In the second case, I have made up my own mind independently. Neither possibility is of any use, for the response theory was supposed to give me a way of checking on my moral convictions or on those of my group. Instead I am merely referred to the fact that I have moral convictions and that I have derived them either from those of my group or have arrived at them independently, but not how. The epistemological problem has simply been side-stepped. Revealing the ancestry of my beliefs is not proving them.

There remains, furthermore, a general doubt about the analysis of 'x is morally wrong.' Followers of the response theory are right in claiming that the remark 'I morally disapprove of x, but x is not morally wrong' is absurd, but they are wrong in thinking that it is absurd because 'I morally disapprove of x' entails 'x is morally wrong.' The truth is that by *saying* 'I morally disapprove of x' the speaker implies [17] that he believes x to be morally wrong. There is no absurdity in saying, 'Jones morally disapproves of x, but x is not morally wrong,' because in saying that Jones disapproves, the speaker does not imply that he (the speaker) disapproves; hence he implies only that Jones believes x wrong, not that he (the speaker) believes x wrong. In other words, we can claim only that it is logically

---

[17] In a sense fully discussed by G. E. Moore, for instance, in *The Philosophy of G. E. Moore*, ed. by P. A. Schilpp (Evanston: Northwestern University, 1942), pp. 540–544.

impossible for a person morally to disapprove of something and at the same time not to believe it to be morally wrong. However, as many philosophers have pointed out, from the fact that a man cannot morally disapprove of a course of action without *believing* it to be morally wrong, it does not follow that a person cannot morally disapprove of it without its *being* wrong. Thus, even if it were possible to ascertain, without a knowledge of moral reasons, whether a person morally disapproves of something, it would still not help us to solve our epistemological problem, for we cannot infer from the fact that a person morally disapproves of something that it is morally wrong.

How, then, is it possible that this childishly simple point has been overlooked or denied? The reason is that there are two quite different purposes for which sentences such as 'This is wrong' or 'This is blue' can be used—either to make a factual assertion or to state an established fact—and that these two uses have been confused. Philosophers thought that in showing the logical equivalence of 'I morally disapprove of *x*' to '*x* is morally wrong' in one of these uses they had also shown this equivalence for the other use.

What are these two uses? Asked about Joan's eyes, I reply, 'They are blue.' This is doubted by someone and, after seeing her again, I repeat, 'They are blue.' In the first case, I made merely an assertion, perhaps entirely without basis, perhaps based on casual observations in the past, perhaps on hearsay. In the second case, my claim is based on careful, deliberate observations made for the purpose of verifying or disproving my first claim. In the first case, I make a claim which I realize may be true or false, though I believe it to be true. In the second case, I make a claim after having established the fact. My first remark states an unestablished, possible fact; my second an established fact.

The Moral Point of View

The sentence 'This is morally wrong' can be used in either of these ways: the sentence 'I morally disapprove of this' only in the first way, namely, to claim the unestablished, possible fact that this is wrong. 'I morally disapprove of this' is therefore quite useless for epistemological purposes. It can never amount to more than an unestablished claim to the effect that something is wrong. It cannot help us to establish that moral claim. When I assert that she has blue eyes, my friend may retort, 'You say so, but is it a fact?' After I have seen her again and specially looked at her eyes to make sure about their color, I can meet my friend's challenge by saying, 'Yes, it is a fact; I made sure this morning.' When I say, 'His conduct was morally wrong,' my friend may voice similar doubts, 'I know you say so, but was it *really* wrong?' If I have a way of establishing its wrongness, I can then meet his challenge by the retort, 'Yes, it really was wrong, for these and these reasons.' I can never meet the same challenge by saying 'Yes, I really disapprove of it, for these and these reasons.' Such a "proof" would never do, for my friend could always answer, 'I now see that you really disapprove of it, but *ought* you to?' Proving that I really disapprove of x shows that I really think x wrong, but it cannot show that I ought to disapprove of x, that x really *is* wrong.

It might now be objected that this account identifies 'I morally disapprove of x' with 'I think x morally wrong' although these two remarks are clearly different: a person may think lying morally wrong without morally disapproving of it. The substance of this objection must be admitted. From the fact that A sincerely says or believes that x is morally wrong it does not follow that A morally disapproves of x, for A may not be a man of good will. Men of good will are resolved to act in accordance with the best moral reasons and never contrary to them, hence resolved to be against, to disapprove of, what is morally wrong, that is, contrary to the best moral reasons. All men can in principle work out what is morally wrong, but only those of good will are resolved to refrain from doing wrong. Hence the fact that a man believes a certain course of action to be morally wrong does not entail that he will morally disapprove of, be against, it. He may know that the best moral reasons are against a certain course, and yet be for it.

The response theory cannot, therefore, give an answer to our third fundamental ethical question, 'How do we know what is right and what is wrong?' For its analysis of rightness and wrongness in terms of approval and disapproval, even if correct, is epistemologically helpful only if approval is taken to mean nonmoral approval. Only then have we been shown a way of proving moral judgments true or false. However, an analysis of rightness in terms of nonmoral approval has not even initial plausibility and must therefore be rejected outright. An analysis of rightness in terms of moral approval has initial plausibility, but it cannot help to solve our epistemological problem. Knowing that someone morally disapproves of something involves knowing that he is against it on *moral* grounds, and the response theory has no answer to the question what are specifically *moral* grounds. Even if we could tell somehow what are moral grounds and, therefore, when a person morally disapproves of something, there would still be another insuperable hurdle. For the statement that one morally disapproves of x is no more than an unestablished assertion to the effect that x is morally wrong. It is never tantamount to a statement of the established fact. The response theory mentions no method whereby we can transform this unestablished assertion into the established fact. It is therefore unable to answer our third fundamental question of ethics 'How do we know what is right and what is wrong?'

3.4 The "emotive theory"

This theory differs from all those previously discussed by the radical manner in which it deals with our fundamental epistemological problem 'How do we know what is right and what is wrong?' Unlike the others, it does not attempt to solve it: it denies its existence. It distinguishes sharply between two functions of language, the fact-stating or "descriptive" and the dynamic or "emotive." Scientific discourse, it argues, belongs in the first, moral in the second, category. Moral judgments do not serve to state facts, to describe the world, or to relate what is happening; they serve to influence or guide people and to intervene in what is happening. Supporters of the emotive theory admit that moral judgments make factual claims, but maintain that they do not do so always and, when they do, only incidentally so. In telling someone that a course of action is wrong, we are therefore not describing that course of action; we are not telling him that it possesses a certain property: we are expressing our feelings or attitudes toward that course of action and, by expressing them, tending to arouse in him similar feelings and attitudes, that is, tending to influence him in the direction of conformity with the feelings and attitudes expressed and to direct and guide him along certain courses of action. According to the emotive theory, remarks such as 'Jones's conduct was wrong,' insofar as they are intended as moral judgments, are primarily dynamic or imperatival and have primarily emotive or prescriptive meaning; that is to say, they serve primarily the function of expressing the speaker's feelings and attitudes and of arousing or causing similar feelings and attitudes in the listener.

Although in some of the versions of the emotive theory great stress is laid on the fact that certain occurrences or actions tend to arouse in an observer certain emotional responses, the idea common to all versions of this theory is that making a moral judgment amounts to an active intervention in the course of events. All versions of the emotive theory stress that moral judgments are not primarily descriptions, records of what is going on, statements of fact, but are essentially verbal ways of throwing one's weight about. Some supporters of the emotive theory would indeed admit that what moral agents see and hear causes them to make moral utterances, but they would all agree that the crucial feature of moral utterances lies in their effects rather than in their causes; in their aim, purpose, or function rather than in their origin. They all agree that in wielding moral judgments, man is engaged not in giving information to others, but in influencing, guiding, or directing them.

The emotive theory can succeed in eliminating our fundamental epistemological problem only if it manages to prove that there can never be a question of the legitimacy, validity, acceptability, correctness—or otherwise—of moral judgments. For as soon as this kind of question is allowed, it is possible to ask for an account of *how* the legitimacy or illegitimacy, and so on, of a moral judgment is proved; how, in other words, we move from the unestablished moral assertion to the conclusively established fact.

As will be shown presently, the emotive theory fails in this task. It is worth pointing out the two reasons why its failure is so widely overlooked. The first is that the magnitude of the task is not understood. It is quite generally, though falsely, believed that no epistemological problem can arise if moral judgments are not verifiable or the reverse by looking, listening, touching, tasting, or smelling. This is a simple-minded blunder, as will be shown in greater detail later on.[18] Here it must suffice to say this. Even simple empirical questions, such as whether a certain theater contains 500 or 501 seats or whether the Pygmy in front of us is a tall Pygmy, cannot be answered simply by looking: in the first case, we must employ a *procedure, counting;* in the second we must be familiar with the *standard of tallness* for Pygmies. Even if moral judgments were in no sense empirically verifiable, there might still be a problem exactly analogous to that of finding the truth of a statement, namely, that

---

[18] See below, Chapter Two, section 3.

of finding its correctness or validity or legitimacy (and their opposites)—or whatever are the appropriate terms to characterize this sort of distinction in the case of moral judgments.

It is plain enough that moral judgments are not verifiable by looking in the way that color judgments are. It may even be true that they are not correctly describable as true or false. Nevertheless, a person saying that there is nothing morally wrong with murder may be making a moral judgment which is faulty, whereas a man who says that murder is morally wrong is making one which is not. If we can so distinguish between two contradictory moral judgments, then there is an epistemological problem (or a problem exactly analogous to an epistemological one), namely, how we characterize this distinction, what are the criteria of the distinction, and what are the methods of eliminating mistakes.

The second reason why the failure of the emotive theory is not noticed is that there are two different versions, each of which can deal with some difficulties but not with others, and which are confused with each other, thus giving the impression of one single theory which can cope with all problems. The cruder version, which I call "the impact theory," can consistently maintain that the epistemological problem does not arise, but it gives an account of moral judgments which is plainly false. The more sophisticated version, which I call "the imperatival theory," is less obviously false, but it cannot consistently maintain that there is no epistemological problem in ethics.

3.41 The *impact theory* maintains that, in ethics, no epistemological problem exists, because there can be no moral questions, properly speaking, and because, where there is nothing to ask, there is nothing to answer, hence nothing to know.[19]

[19] C. L. Stevenson, *Ethics and Language* (New Haven: Yale University Press, 1944), p. vii.

Fundamental Questions

Why, on this view, can there be no moral questions? When I ask, 'Has Joan blue eyes?' I demand an utterance which would constitute an answer, namely, 'Joan has blue eyes' or 'Joan does not have blue eyes.' Hence I am raising a genuine question, for both these remarks are factual assertions that can be verified or shown false. Factual questions are genuine since they are requests for factual assertions. But when I ask a moral question, I am not requesting a factual assertion. 'Jones's conduct was wrong' is not a factual assertion; it is merely the expression of my feelings or attitudes, with the aim and the effect of arousing similar feelings and attitudes in my listener. Accordingly, if I ask 'Was Jones's action wrong?' I am not asking a genuine question. For the "answer" to this "question" would have to be either 'Yes, Jones's conduct was wrong' or 'No, Jones's conduct was not wrong,' neither of which is a factual assertion. In asking a moral question, I request merely a moral reply, that is, the expression by my listener of his feelings or attitudes. I ask for this in order to be influenced by my listener's feelings and attitudes. Why? Because I myself have as yet no feelings or attitudes, or only conflicting ones. The impact theory thus maintains that moral "questions" can be "asked" only when the speaker has no clear feeling or attitude toward a certain course of action (either because he has none at all or because he has conflicting ones), that such "questions" express the speaker's indecision and request the listener to express his feelings and attitudes in order thereby correspondingly to influence the speaker and to terminate his indecision.

It must be admitted that the impact theory emphasizes an important feature of moral judgments: their tendency to influence hearers in certain comparatively uniform ways. It must also be admitted that certain other types of utterance, such as descriptive or narrative or scientific utterances, do not have this tendency. However, it does not follow from this that while the function of descriptive utterances is to say something, to make assertions or claims, to say what can be true or false, correct or incorrect, and so on, the function of moral judgments is none of these, but merely to produce in others certain effects, namely, to arouse certain feelings and attitudes.

This distinction between the function of descriptive and of moral utterances would be plausible if it were the case that factual remarks only made assertions, but did not have any effects on hearers, did not arouse feelings and attitudes in them. However, factual remarks, too, tend to influence hearers. If I tell someone that the forecast is for rain, he will be disposed to take his raincoat or his umbrella, or to stay home, or to cancel his weekend trip.

Stevenson admits that both descriptive and moral utterances have an influence on hearers but attempts to overcome this difficulty by distinguishing between two different kinds of influence, "cognitive" and "affective-conative." He claims that descriptive utterances are characterized by descriptive meaning, that is, by their tendency to arouse in hearers certain cognitive dispositions, whereas moral utterances are characterized by emotive meaning, that is, their tendency to arouse in hearers affective-conative dispositions. Both cognitive and dynamic dispositions consist, on Stevenson's view, in dispositions to behave and feel in certain ways. But Stevenson is quite unable to point to any distinguishing marks between them.[20]

This is not surprising, for the distinction is bogus. It is not true that the function of some kinds of remark is to produce a certain influence on hearers while the function of others is to say something; or of some kinds of remark to produce cognitive, and of others to produce emotive, dispositions in the hearer. The truth is that both kinds of remark have a meaning, that

---

[20] *Ibid*, pp. 60, 66–67.

in as far as they can be said to have a function at all it is their function to convey that meaning, and that both kinds of remark produce certain effects, but what effects they produce will vary from person to person and from situation to situation.

We must in all cases distinguish between *what* I say or mean, *why* I said it, and *what effect* it will have on my listener. In mentioning the forecast, I may merely wish to tell my listener, or I may wish to achieve a certain effect which I expect the telling will have. 'The forecast is for rain' always has the same sense, whether I merely aimed at giving him my opinion or whether perhaps I hoped it would cause him to cancel his weekend trip, and whether or not it had the intended effect. Similarly, the remark 'Joan's conduct was wicked' always has the same sense, whether I merely intend to give him my opinion, or whether I desire to cause my friend to break off his engagement with Joan, and whether or not my remark has the intended effect.

The facts emphasized by the impact theory are important, but while they may show that moral judgments tend to influence hearers more often and in a more uniform way than do other types of remark, they do not show that, in addition to 'What was the effect of Robert's moral judgment on Jones?' we may not ask the further question 'Was *what* Robert said correct?' I conclude that the impact theory cannot make good its main contention that no epistemological problem exists in ethics. It cannot prove that the function of moral judgments is not to *say something* but merely to evince emotions and feelings and thereby to influence hearers. Hence it can offer no reason for saying that in ethics there is nothing to ask and nothing to answer, hence nothing to know, and therefore no epistemological problem.

3.42 The *imperatival theory* reiterates the claim that the function of moral judgments is not to describe things or state facts or say anything capable of being true or false.[21] However, it correctly distinguishes between what a remark means or says and the influence it has or tends to have on those who hear it. Instead of distinguishing between conveying information and influencing hearers, as does the impact theory, it distinguishes between *what* a person says (the content) and the effect which his saying it has on a hearer, on the one hand; and on the other, between two ways of saying something, between telling someone what is the case and telling someone to do something. On the imperatival theory, moral remarks are not merely ways of *influencing someone:* they are characteristic ways of *saying something,* though not ways of conveying information (of telling someone certain facts) but of commanding or requesting someone, of telling him to act in a certain way. Therefore, there are genuine moral questions and they are of the same kind as the question 'What shall I do?' and moral judgments are of the same kind as answers to that question, namely, commands such as 'Do this.'

I shall show in greater detail that moral questions are not requests to be commanded to do something.[22] Here it must suffice to say that even if this analysis were correct, it could not be used to solve our epistemological problem. For the admission of genuine moral questions poses a dilemma for the imperatival theory, namely, whether or not to allow the existence of moral reasons bearing on the answers to moral questions. If such moral reasons are disallowed, then the imperativalist analysis of moral questions renders them meaningless, thereby making the imperatival indistinguishable from the impact

---

[21] This claim was also made by the impact theory. See above, section 3.41, p. 37.

[22] See below, Chapter Two, section 2, and Chapter Three, sections 2 and 3.

theory. If, on the other hand, we admit the existence of such moral reasons, then the old epistemological problem arises again.

Embracing the first horn of the dilemma, let us say that there are no moral reasons that bear on the answers to moral questions. When I say, 'Jones's conduct was wrong,' then, on the imperatival theory, I am expressing my disapproval and am "prescribing" to my listener to do the same. But what is Roberts doing when he asks Richards a moral question, let us say, 'Was Jones's conduct wrong?' A question is always a request for an answer, that is, for a remark which would constitute an answer. In our case, this would be either 'Jones's conduct was wrong' or 'Jones's conduct was not wrong,' that is to say, Richards' expression of his disapproval or approval of Jones's conduct together with Richards' command to Roberts to do the same as he, Richards. But this would turn Roberts' moral question into a request addressed to Richards to express his approval or disapproval and to command Roberts to do the same as Richards. In other words, the questioner is commanding the listener to command the questioner to do the same as the listener. But if no listener can give reasons for his command, why should any questioner wish to be commanded? What point could there be in asking anyone for such a service? Why should a man rather wish to obey the command of a man whom he had commanded to command him something than simply to make up his own mind? Asking a moral question in that case would be no different from tossing a coin, for in tossing a coin I resolve to obey "the command" of the coin which I have forced to give me "a command." But this is to do what the impact theory does: it is to make moral questions into requests to be helped to terminate one's indecision. We have already seen reason to reject this view.

Even odder than the above is the analysis of Roberts' question 'Was Jones's conduct wrong?' when addressed to himself. For when addressed to himself it becomes a command to himself to command himself to do the same as himself. But what can one make of this? If Roberts does not yet approve or disapprove of Jones's conduct, he cannot ask himself whether his conduct was wrong, for if he does not yet have a feeling or attitude he cannot command himself to command himself to do the same. But surely a person will often ask himself the question 'Was Jones's conduct wrong?' when he has not yet got an opinion. And if a person already has an opinion, then the question 'Was Jones's conduct wrong?' can never lead to a truer view than he already has because, in asking it, he is merely commanding himself to command himself to do the same as himself. Surely this is all nonsense.

Let us then try the other horn of the dilemma, and let us say that there are moral reasons relevant to the answers to moral questions. But this fatally weakens the case for saying that there is no epistemological problem in ethics. For if reasons are admitted at all, there can and will be cases of sufficient or conclusive reasons. Where there are conclusive reasons, there are knowledge and error. If, for example, there are conclusive reasons for saying that Jones killed his wife, then he who has them can and does know that Jones killed his wife. And if there are conclusive reasons for saying that Jones's action was wrong, then he who has them can know that Jones's action was wrong. If I can adduce reasons for having a feeling of disapproval of what Jones did, it becomes at least possible for me to have conclusive reasons for my feeling. And if so, then I have conclusive reasons for saying that what Jones did was wrong. But then I can and do *know* that what he did was wrong.

It might be objected that the emotive theory uses the word 'reason' in a special sense, namely, the sense in which a command can be supported by reasons, and that, therefore, this conclusion does not follow. Stevenson, for instance, claims that a reason for or against a moral judgment is "*any* statement about *any* matter of fact which *any* speaker considers likely to alter attitudes, whether or not this statement will actually make any difference to the attitudes of the hearer." [23] So defined, "reasons" which support or controvert moral judgments are related to them psychologically, but not logically. It follows that by whatever combination of reasons a moral judgment is supported, a person rejecting that moral judgment need never be guilty of an error of fact or of logic. The giving of such "reasons" does not serve the same purpose as the giving of proofs or disproofs. Its only function is to intensify and render more permanent the influence on attitudes which the emotive meaning of words can often no more than begin. Giving reasons is one way of imparting the speaker's attitude to someone else. The use of moral and other words with emotive meaning is another way of achieving the same end. On this view, giving reasons is mentioning facts which *one thinks* will move the listeners. Giving conclusive reasons is giving reasons which *actually will* move the person in the desired way.

From this special sense of 'reason,' none of the conclusions follow which I have drawn above. For to say in this special sense that I have "conclusive reason" for my opinion that Jones's conduct was morally wrong is not to imply that it is thereby proved that Jones's conduct was morally wrong, that I now know that it was wrong, that anyone rejecting this would be guilty of an error of fact or of logic. It only means that I am in possession of facts which I know will move a certain person or persons to agree with me.

It is perhaps worth pointing out that this is not the ordinary use of 'reason.' As we normally use the word, we may have, and

---

[23] Stevenson, *op. cit.* pp. 114–115. For further statements on this point see also *ibid.*, pp. 30–31, 36, 113.

offer to someone, conclusive reasons for holding an opinion, and yet that person might not be convinced. The mere fact that a person is not convinced does not prove, as Stevenson maintains it does, that the reason was not conclusive. But, contrary to what Stevenson says, it does follow that if a hearer does not accept a proposition that is supported by conclusive reasons, then he is in the wrong, "is guilty of an error of logic." [24]

This departure from the ordinary use of the word 'reason' is no real gain. It can confuse the reader into thinking that the emotive theory has solved our fundamental epistemological problem, but it has not really done so. It is, of course, true that with the admission of "reasons" (in this special sense) we avoid the consequence which is fatal to the emotive theory (that the surveying of moral reasons makes it possible to know some moral judgments to be correct and to be mistaken in regard to others), but the consequence desired by the emotive theory (that one should be able to ask genuine moral questions) does not follow either.

Why does this consequence not follow? The admission of "relevant moral reasons" in this special sense amounts to very little. To know that when we ask a moral question such as 'Would this course of action be wrong?' we can survey "relevant moral reasons" is to know merely a hypothetical proposition, namely, that *if* we dwell on certain facts there will be certain effects on us, whereas *if* we dwell on other facts there will be quite different effects. But this is only putting off the evil day. The question still remains: which facts should we dwell on; which effects should we try to produce in us by dwelling on which facts? Normally, the surveying of relevant reasons helps

---

[24] For further details of the ordinary use of 'reason,' see below, Chapter Three, sections 4–6, pp. 93–105, and Chapter Six, sections 2–4, pp. 150–168.

us to settle this sort of question. "Reasons," in this special sense, only postpone settlement.

If we say, 'Dwell on those facts which will most quickly and effectively settle your indecision *one way or the other*,' we are back to the impact theory. For then our question 'Would this course of action be wrong?' is not a genuine question; it is merely a request to be helped to end our indecision one way or the other. If we reject this, then we must find *some* reason for choosing to dwell on certain facts ("reasons") rather than others. And this in turn could only lead to further "reasons" which would influence us one way or the other. And why should we dwell on those that would influence us this way rather than on those that would influence us that way? There is no way out of this infinite regress.

It seems to me clear, therefore, that this view of 'reason' makes the imperatival theory indistinguishable from the impact theory. But no other view of the nature of reason is open to the emotive theory.

4 THE CRUCIAL QUESTION

The picture that emerges from this preliminary discussion is clear enough: none of the three fundamental questions of ethics has so far been satisfactorily answered. It is also apparent that our first two questions cannot be properly tackled until after the third has been answered, for we cannot tell why we should do what is right, or why we in fact do it, if we do not already know what is right. However, the state of our knowledge in this field is particularly disheartening. Neither the various attempts to solve the epistemological problems in ethics nor the attempt to dismiss them as pseudo problems have succeeded. They are therefore still with us and unsolved. How are we to overcome this impasse?

The Moral Point of View

It is plain that the main difficulty lies in the double nature of moral judgments. They are obviously designed to guide us, hence the plausibility of the emotive theory. But they are also meant to tell us something, not merely to influence us, hence the attractiveness of the various traditional theories which maintain that there is something to know in morality. The crucial moral question, for our purposes, will therefore be the agent's question 'What ought I to do?' asked before acting, asked in order to obtain guidance by moral reasons, asked in order to be put in a position to decide on what is the morally right thing to do. This will be the crucial question because the answers to it must have the dual features which, in the past, have been regarded as incompatible by moral philosophers: the ability to give guidance and the ability to be correct or incorrect.

This question, as will be shown presently, is equivalent to the question 'What is the best thing to do, morally speaking?' or 'What is the course supported by the best moral reasons?' These are obviously of the same general nature as evaluative questions such as 'What is the best hotel in town?' In asking this question, the agent is attempting to evaluate in a certain way the various courses of action open to him. If we wish to understand the crucial moral question, we must be clear about value judgments. This, therefore, will be our first task.

Two

Value Judgments

IN recent years, there has grown up, both in philosophy and in sociology, a doctrine which has relegated value judgments to the realm of personal idiosyncrasies. On this view, utterances are divided into two kinds, statements of fact and judgments of value. The former occur characteristically in scientific discourse which is concerned to state the facts, to describe and explain the world, to say how things are, were, and will be, or would be in certain conditions, and to say what makes them the way they are. Value judgments, on the other hand, direct our feelings, attitudes, and behavior. Scientific discourse is objective, precise, capable of being true or false, empirically verifiable or the reverse. Value judgments are subjective, vague, ambiguous, unverifiable by the senses. The problem is to show whether, and if so how, statements of fact can be relevant to value judgments. The problem is, to borrow the title of a well-known book, to find "the place of value in a world of facts."

More precisely, the commonly accepted doctrine maintains

that, unlike statements of fact, judgments of value can be neither empirically verified or disproved, nor deduced from any statements of fact. It is of course felt that such a doctrine is paradoxical, and so philosophers attempt to explain away this paradox. I have already mentioned the two leading theories in the field: Moore's ideal utilitarianism and the emotive theory. Enough has been said in the previous chapter and by many contemporary writers [1] to exhibit the inadequacy of these explanations. Fortunately, we need not examine these controversies in detail, for there is no call for such theories. It is unnecessary to explain why English girls are not passionate, for many are. Similarly, we are not called upon to explain why value judgments cannot be proved true or false and why statements of fact have no logical bearing on them, for many of them are verifiable or the reverse and many statements of fact have logical bearing on them. This is what I wish to show first.

1 JUDGMENTS

Well, what exactly are value judgments? In philosophical and sociological writings this expression is usually intended to cover all judgments in which the words 'good,' 'better,' 'best,' and 'bad,' 'worse,' 'worst' are used, as well as all other judgments which are logically equivalent to these. Wide though it is, this use nevertheless excludes a good many utterances which are listed by philosophers and social scientists as instances of value judgments, for it allows only *judgments* proper. 'I suppose Eclipse is a good horse since Wisdom is betting on it' is not a judgment but a conjecture; 'Hmmm, that was a good meal!' is (frequently, at any rate) not a judgment, but merely the expression of the speaker's appreciation or enjoyment; 'Good,

---

[1] For example, S. E. Toulmin, *The Place of Reason in Ethics* (Cambridge: Cambridge University Press, 1950), or P. H. Nowell-Smith, *Ethics* (Pelican ser.; Melbourne, London, Baltimore: Penguin Books, 1954).

Value Judgments

let's go then!' is not a judgment, but the speaker's signification of assent.

Not all kinds of utterance are judgments. Contrast judgments with utterances such as observations, verbatim reports, meter readings, descriptions, narrative, and so on. These are essentially *verbal reproductions or pictures,* verbal substitutes for witnessing. Verbatim reports reproduce a verbal performance; meter readings the position of an indicator on a scale; observations an observed fact, that is, the possession by something of a property or the existence of a certain relation between two things; and narrative a series of occurrences. Descriptions are word pictures of something, usually for the purpose of enabling someone to identify the thing when he comes across it. Judgments, on the other hand, are in no way verbal pictures or reproductions. Wittgenstein's early view that a proposition is a picture of a fact is not plausible for judgments, though it is true or nearly true for all the types of utterance I have just mentioned.

But though judgments are not pictures drawn from life, they are not shots in the dark either. Judgments must be distinguished from guesses, conjectures, hunches, hypotheses, assumptions, suppositions, and the like, which are verbal pictures from the imagination. They aim at representing something without actually copying it. They are portraits without a sitter. They are like present-day paintings of Christ, likenesses attempted on the basis of reports of his appearance, his character, the impression he made on others, and so on. Such pictures may or may not in fact resemble him. To get at the truth by such methods is a matter of luck or genius, not of judgment.

Nor are judgments attempts to increase our knowledge by the trusted "armchair ways" of doing so. Scientists, sleuths, philosophers frequently have to get answers to some of their questions not by investigation, observation, or exploration, but

49

by sitting down quietly and thinking. To be good at these things, we need not be perceptive or observant, we need not have good eyes or ears. Nor good judgment. What we need is a good intellect and skill in the relevant technique of working out something. The results so obtained are reliable. These methods yield knowledge. Judgments, on the other hand, are not methods of *working something out*. They are not forms or outcomes of calculation, excogitation, or deduction.

Nor, of course, least of all, are judgments expressions of feelings, emotions, attitudes, and the like. For these are linguistic ways of showing one's response or reaction to something. Expressions of satisfaction or dissatisfaction, appreciation or resentment, approval or disapproval, surprise, disappointment, and so forth, are *responses* to occurrences, to expressed or implied opinions or intentions. Judgments are not ways of showing one's reactions or responses.

Note that, contrary to the prevalent view, statements are much more like expressions of attitudes than judgments are. For both statements and expressions of attitudes are indications of where the speaker stands in relation to something that has gone before. Expressions of attitude indicate the speaker's intentions and eventual response, irrespective of whether or not they are spontaneous, genuine, or sincere. Statements also indicate where the speaker stands, but they are carefully considered, worded, studied. They do, and are intended to, commit the speaker, or the people whose spokesman he is. Statements are made by company directors, union officials, Foreign Office spokesmen, and the like. In a statement, every word counts, for the person making it is committed to all he says, implies, or suggests in it. We can later take him up on any particular word he used. To say, 'He stated the following . . .' is to draw attention to precisely what he said, precisely what he committed himself to.

Value Judgments

Contentions, assertions, claims, and the like, in which the emphasis is on *the contentious claim* or issue, where the important question is, 'Is this *right* or not?' must be distinguished from statements, expressions of attitude, and so on, where the emphasis is on what *the speaker* believes, feels, or intends to do, where the important question is 'Where does *he* stand?' Contrary to the prevalent view, judgments belong to the first, statements to the second group. When someone judges the distance from one place to another, or judges a bathing belle or a bull, or a work of art, the important question is, 'Is he right or wrong?' and not 'Where exactly does he stand?' Some writers have claimed that what is important about moral and aesthetic judgments is that they indicate where the speaker stands.[2] By means of them, it is said, the speaker is making a moral stand. They contrast this with statements, in which, it is said, factual claims are made. The reverse is the case.

Of course, we must not exaggerate this point. All I am saying is that when we refer to a given utterance as a statement we are singling out that aspect of it which is stand-making, speaker-committing. I am not denying that there are other aspects. A Foreign Office spokesman may include many factual claims in his statement. But he may also include value judgments, moral judgments, explanations of the government's past actions and indications of its future policies. On the other hand, when we call an utterance a judgment, we refer to the claim-making rather than the stand-making aspect. This does not mean that there are not occasions when a judge judging, say, bathing belles has to stand up and be counted.

It might be objected that this is a very special and very

---

[2] Margaret Macdonald, "Natural Rights," in *Proceedings of the Aristotelian Society*, 1946–1947 (London: Harrison & Sons, 1947); Karl Popper, *The Open Society and Its Enemies* (London: George Routledge & Sons, 1945), vol. I, ch. v.

narrow use of the word 'statement,' that it derives from a wider use, and that philosophers have not had the narrow but the wider use in mind. I agree with the first two contentions but I reject the third.

I agree that there is another more general use of 'statement,' as in 'He stated the Weber-Fechner Law incorrectly' or 'Please state your amendment to the motion' or 'Can't you state your question more succinctly?' 'Stating' in this use means the same as 'formulating aloud.' In this use, a person who has "stated something" has not "made a statement," but has "given a statement *of* something"; he has not "stated *that* something is such and such," but has "stated *a something*: a theory, law, amendment, or view"; he has not made an assertion, contention, or claim, but has put something into words.

The difference between the two uses is this. In the wider use, we have merely put into words a certain sort of content, a proposition, and we have offered it as a certain sort of thing, a theory, law, amendment, motion, or view. We have not offered it as coming from a certain person. We have not involved anyone in the responsibility for putting forward this proposition as *his* theory, law, or amendment.

The second point is also true. Making a statement is a special case of stating something, namely, *one's own* position. But it is not merely stating one's own position, it is also declaring it to be one's own position. Making a statement is doing two quite different things. It is stating what is in fact one's position *and* letting it be known that it is one's position, taking responsibility for it.

It is, therefore, quite impossible that philosophers should have had the wider use in mind when they spoke of statements. For, in the first place, they have always meant by it something involving an assertion, a contention, a factual claim. And we have just seen that, in the wider use, 'statement' does not involve an assertion, that is, a speaker's being committed to his words.

Secondly, philosophers have always wished to contrast statements with expressions of attitudes, desires, wishes, or feelings. But such a contrast makes sense only when we mean 'statement' in the narrower use. In that use, there is indeed a contrast between statement and expression. They are two quite different ways of committing a person. Statement is explicit, direct; expression is implicit, indirect. The words 'I love you' both *state that* I have a certain feeling for you and *express* that feeling. The words 'My darling, my angel,' kisses, embraces, and so on merely express my feelings, they do not *state that* I have them. Nevertheless, they commit me in their own manner. The reproach 'If you did not love me, you should not have said those words to me, you should not have kissed me in that way, etc., etc.' may be perfectly justified. In the wider sense, on the other hand, there is no contrast at all. One can state attitudes, desires, wishes, intentions, emotions, even feelings, just as much as one can state theories, motions, amendments, laws, views, opinions, beliefs, or assumptions. As statements *of* these things, *none* can be true or false; they can only be correct or incorrect, accurate or inaccurate, succinct or rambling, neat or clumsy, and so on. But, of course, statements *that* I have certain feelings, can be true or false; expressions *of* these feelings can be neither.

Even less plausible is the view, recently advocated,[3] that judgments are so-called performatory utterances. Judgments are different from verbal exercises of authority such as deciding, consenting, permitting, approving, acceding to, and agreeing or refusing, forbidding, declining, and so on. It is unfortunate

---

[3] See H. L. A. Hart, "The Ascription of Responsibility and Rights," reprinted in *Essays on Logic and Language*, ed. by A. G. N. Flew (Oxford: Basil Blackwell, 1951), pp. 157 ff.; Margaret Macdonald, "Ethics and the Ceremonial Use of Language," in *Philosophical Analysis*, ed. by Max Black (Ithaca, N.Y.: Cornell University Press, 1950).

that the most obvious paradigm of judgment, the judge's verdict, is not only right or wrong, but also an exercise of authority. The judge plays a dual role. He not only judges what is the law, he also decides what shall be done. He is a solicitor in authority. When making up his mind whether or not a person has committed a breach of the law, he is performing the same job as a solicitor. When giving the verdict, the legal opinion therein expressed has final, decisive authority. True, he might sleep throughout the proceedings, never know what the whole case is about, toss a coin, and then pronounce the accused guilty because it was heads. We would still have to say that the judge had judged the accused guilty. But this can be called judgment only "ex officio." It would be true and important to claim that in such a case he had not really *judged* the man guilty, for he has not heard the case. Judging cannot, therefore, be essentially the exercise of authority, but must be the giving of an informed opinion on some issue.

Still, it might be urged, judgments are from their very nature unverifiable. For when they seem to be verifiable, we are not dealing with judgments, but with empirical assertions or claims. A man who gets the color of a thing right is either guessing it or he is seeing it. In neither case is he judging. On the other hand, a man who awards the first prize to Aphrodite is judging her the best, the most beautiful, the best dressed, and so forth. And he does so not because he is either *guessing at* something he is not yet allowed to see or is *reading off* a feature which he is allowed to see. *He* is judging her. *He* likes her best in those and those respects. There *can* be no verification or disproof.

I shall take up this point more fully later on.[4] At this stage, let me say only that if this point were correct it could not be so because of the nature of judgment, but only because of the

---

nature of the special type of judgment considered. For there are judgments proper, in which verification is possible. A man may be a good judge of character, or of distance, or of speed. We say that he is a good judge of these things if he can usually judge these things correctly. And we say that he has this power if he can get correct results *under conditions other than optimum;* that is to say, when the pedestrian, reliable methods of verification have not yet been used, as when a person has to judge someone's character after a short acquaintance, or when he has to judge distances without being allowed to use a tape measure, or speeds without a speedometer. Judgment, then, involves giving correct answers under difficult conditions. It involves being able to give correct answers more quickly, in bad light, or without instruments when reliable answers cannot be given *without a special skill.*

2 THEORETICAL AND PRACTICAL JUDGMENTS

I now take it for granted that there is nothing in the nature of judgment that excludes empirical verification. Are there, then, some types of judgment which are not empirically verifiable, perhaps practical or value judgments? Let us first distinguish theoretical and practical judgments. Theoretical judgments are a type of fact-stating claim requiring special talents or skills, such as judging distances, speeds, and chances of success or failure at some enterprise. They differ from meter readings in not being made under optimum conditions, from workings out in not being arrived at by foolproof, easy methods; they differ from guesses, conjectures, or intuitions in being based on a skill or gift, about which we know enough to develop it by practice.

Practical judgments, on the other hand, are judgments with a direct logical bearing on what *should* be done. Judgments to the effect that something is legal or illegal, just or unjust, good or bad, right or wrong, are directly relevant to answering the question 'What shall I do?'

Commands, authoritative decisions, orders, and the like also directly bear on this question. Hence practical judgments have been identified, not to say confused, with them. Hare, for instance, says: "A statement, however loosely it is bound to the facts, cannot answer a question of the form, 'What shall I do?'; only *a command* can do this." [5] This view reveals a complete misunderstanding of the question 'What shall I do?' Hare and many others think that when we ask this question we are requesting to be commanded or to be told to do something. He says, for instance, "Telling someone to do something, is answering the question, 'What shall I do?' " [6] And again "Commands . . . like statements, are essentially intended for answering questions asked by rational agents." [7]

This is simply not true. Commands are not *essentially* intended for answering questions. They can and will usually be given when no questions have been asked. 'Attention,' 'Bring me the slippers,' 'Go to bed,' may be said out of the blue. They are not essentially replies. In fact, commands are only very exceptionally replies, namely, when children, employees, or subalterns are *asking for orders*. Commands may be, but are not essentially, used to answer questions of the form 'What shall I do?'

'What shall I do?' is frequently not asked in order to elicit a command or order. When I come for advice, I do not want to be commanded or ordered about. I do not even want to be requested or begged or pleaded with. I want to know what you think is the best thing for me to do. I need your knowledge,

---

[5] R. M. Hare, *The Language of Morals* (Oxford: Clarendon Press, 1952), p. 46.

[6] *Ibid.*, p. 15. [7] *Ibid.*, pp. 15–16.

not your authority. I want you to think, to deliberate on my behalf. I want to make use of your intelligence, your experience, your practical wisdom. I don't expect you to take responsibility. 'What shall I do?' may indeed mean 'Tell me what to do.' But then I expect you to tell me *what* to do, and not, as Mr. Hare says, "to tell me to do something." The first is answering a question, the second is giving orders. In the first case, 'What shall I do?' means 'What would you do in my place?'; in the second, it means 'What are your orders?'

Practical judgments are answers to the question 'What shall I do?' but it does not follow from this that they are commands. Practical judgments are indeed designed to guide us, but it does not follow from this that they cannot be true or false. Admittedly, authoritative decisions, orders, commands, prescriptions, prohibitions, and the like are *also* designed to guide us. Admittedly, they cannot, from their nature, be true or false. But not because they are designed to guide us. Practical judgments can guide us *and* they can be true or false. There is, moreover, no mystery in this. Being rational is being prepared, even determined, to be guided, not by someone's orders, commands, or laws whatever their content may be, but by the best judgments available. And, of course, none are better than true, correct ones. It will not always be possible to find out whether a judgment is correct or incorrect. We shall frequently have to make do with unverified ones. But then we often have to make do with unverified factual claims also.

3 FACTUAL COMPARISONS AND RANKINGS

I shall now try to show that value judgments, one sort of practical judgment, are empirically verifiable. Note first that they may be either comparisons or rankings—either assertions to the effect that one thing, event, state of affairs, person, or deed is better or worse than, or as good or bad as, another or assertions to the effect that one thing, event, etc., is good, bad, or just average.

Not all comparisons and rankings are value judgments. Moreover, there is no doubt that factual, that is, nonevaluative, comparisons and rankings are empirically verifiable. 'This man is taller than that' and 'She is a tall girl for her age' are ordinary empirical claims. If we are clear about the logic of empirical comparisons and rankings, we will be in a position to say whether what distinguishes evaluative from nonevaluative comparisons and rankings makes the former unverifiable in principle. It is my contention that the misunderstanding of the logic of empirical comparisons and rankings is, at least partly, responsible for the view that value judgments are not verifiable. An elucidation of factual comparisons and rankings will, in any case, throw a good deal of light on the nature of value judgments.

To say that one man is taller than another may be a judgment, for example, when one of them is sitting down and the other standing up. This can be verified by making both stand up, barefoot, back to back. Under these optimum conditions we can see which is the taller or whether they are equally tall. With more experience we learn to make correct claims of this sort even in difficult conditions, as when one has high-heeled shoes, or is sitting down, or is wearing a hat, and so on. Good judgment in this sort of thing is the ability to make correct claims of this kind in other than optimum conditions. We could not say of anyone that he had good judgment unless there were some way of *verifying* his judgments.

Not all comparisons are as simple as this one. Sometimes we compare things in respect of properties which are defined in terms of others. When I say that this house is *bigger* than that, I may base this claim on the possession to a higher degree of one or all of three *other* properties, that is, it is *longer*, *wider*, or *higher* than the other house. But these are not the only ones. We may also have in mind the possession of *more* rooms, or of *larger* rooms. These properties are the criteria of 'being bigger.' Criteria are properties, the possession of which to a higher degree (for instance, 'smaller') implies the possession of the other property to a higher degree (for instance, 'cheaper') or lower degree (for instance, 'less comfortable'). In our case we must say that the longer, the wider, the higher it is, the more rooms it has and the larger the rooms are, the bigger is the house.

This case is instructive because it shows how criteria may conflict. We have no way of deciding what we should say if one house were longer and wider but lower, or if it had more but smaller rooms, than the other. We have no way of *compounding* these criteria when they conflict. In such conflict cases, no clear answer can be given to the question 'Which is the bigger house?' Yet, there can be no doubt that the claim 'This house is bigger than that' is empirical, is capable of empirical verification or disproof. The mere fact that value comparisons may be based on criteria capable of conflicting can, therefore, have no tendency to show that they are not capable of verification.

It is often said that value judgments are vague. One of the things we mean by the vagueness of a claim is just this, that in a comparatively large number of cases it will be impossible to determine whether the claim is true or false, because the criteria on which it is based conflict. Vagueness is not incompatible with empirical verifiability.

In ranking something, we are not directly comparing *two* objects, but are concerned with only one. In comparing, we want to know which of *two* objects has a given property to a higher degree. In ranking we want to know *the* degree to which *one* object has the property in question. Nevertheless, rankings too are sorts of comparison, though more complex. When we rank a man as tall, we assign him the highest rank on a three-place scale, tall, medium, short. Knowing the meaning of 'tall' involves knowing the logical relationship between being tall, of medium height, and short. One must know the number, names, and order of the places on the scale. One must know that 'tall' means 'taller than of medium height and short,' that 'of medium height' means 'taller than short and shorter than tall,' and that 'short' means 'shorter than tall and of medium height.' It is not enough to know that 'tall' is the opposite of 'short'; for that would not enable us to distinguish between opposites such as 'dead' and 'alive,' which are not capable of degrees, and opposites such as 'tall' and 'short,' which are.

Knowing these things is enough to *understand* rankings, but it is not enough to verify them. For that, we need additional factual information, namely, the *standard* by which the object has been ranked. Every ranking implies such a standard. Though we do not know what the standard is and can, therefore, only understand what is *meant by* the claim 'This Pygmy is tall,' we could not even understand that claim unless we took *some* standard to be implied. There is, therefore, a sense in which claims such as 'This Pygmy is tall,' 'This man is tall,' 'This child is tall,' 'This horse is tall' are all making *the same claim* about different objects, and therefore a sense in which 'tall' *means the same* in all these cases. Yet the empirical verification of these claims involves a different factor every time, namely, *the appropriate standard* of tallness.

Remember the differences between criteria and standards. Standards are implied in all rankings but in no comparison. It would not make sense to say, 'He is tall,' 'This is hot,' and so on unless *some standard of tallness* or *hotness* were implied. For a tall Pygmy is a short man, and a hot bath would be merely a warm drink. On the other hand, it does not make sense to ask by what standard I judge one man taller than another, one drink colder than another. Criteria may, but need not, be involved in either ranking or comparing. I simply see that one man is tall, or taller than another. I simply feel that one bath is hot, or hotter than another. By contrast, 'This cup of tea has a temperature of 60 degrees F.' and 'This house is bigger than that' do involve criteria. The criterion of the first is the expansion of mercury in a thermometer, the criteria of the second are length, width, and height.

This discussion has brought to light two reasons why it is thought that value judgments cannot be verifiable by experience. The first is that philosophers had never examined comparisons and rankings and had never, therefore, considered the particular form of verification appropriate to them. The second and connected reason is that philosophers rely on a highly specialized model of empirical verification. They think of it as verification by looking, listening, touching, tasting, or sniffing. It should have occurred to philosophers that often a good deal more is involved than that. Thus, I may claim that the Union Theatre has 500 seats. But I cannot verify this by looking, listening, touching, tasting, or sniffing. It should, therefore, be declared not to be empirically verifiable. No one has ever objected to counting as a nonempirical way of verifying propositions. Nor, strangely enough, to measuring or weighing. Yet, these latter methods involve arbitrary standards and often criteria. But when value judgments are made, people claim that they are not verifiable because they involve criteria and standards.

4 VALUE COMPARISONS AND RANKINGS

Ah, it will be objected, but *value* judgments are different. Let us take a simple case first: 'John's was *a faster* mile than Richard's' and 'John's was *a better* mile than Richard's.' Do they come to the same thing? No, 'better' is obviously a more general expression than 'faster.' In 'better ship,' 'better razor,' 'better fountain pen,' 'better school,' 'better man,' it becomes increasingly less appropriate to replace 'better' by 'faster.' A man who knows the words 'fast' and 'mile' must know that, if the runners have started at the same time, then he who arrives at the milepost first has run the faster mile. In other words, he must know the criterion of 'running a faster mile.' But a man may know the words 'good' and 'mile,' and yet not know the criterion of 'running a *better* mile.' In order to know what is the criterion of 'running a *better* mile than . . .' one must in addition know the purpose of a race. If we know that races are competitions in which people are trying to run as fast as they can in order to win, we know what the purpose of races is. It is then also obvious that we must evaluate miles on the basis of speed.

It might, therefore, be said that 'faster mile' is a "more objective" or "more factual" expression than 'better mile.' If this merely means that the criterion of 'faster mile' is independent of, whereas that of 'better mile' is dependent on, *human purposes,* this is perfectly true. But since in many cases the purpose, point, or function of something can be quite objectively determined, the criteria of 'better' can, in these cases, also be quite objectively determined.

Take now a slightly more complicated case: 'A is a better miler than B.' Here, too, we are concerned with a competition, though on a somewhat larger scale, as it were. We are here calling someone the winner, not of a particular race, but of a competition made up of many races. Here, too, the purpose of the competition determines the criterion, namely, the number of wins. If A has always won, or won more often than he lost, or has run better times, or run equally good times but more often, or equally often but under more difficult conditions, then he has the greater number of "wins," the better record.

Value Judgments

Perhaps we are not satisfied to crown the winner merely of past competitions. When we say, 'A is a better miler than B,' we may have in mind all times, not only the past. We then include his potentialities. In such a case, verification will have to wait for future performances. Many value judgments contain references to the future and cannot, therefore, be "read off" now. Unduly preoccupied with propositions of the form 'This chair in front of me is brown,' many philosophers have felt that value judgments are not empirically verifiable because the goodness or badness of a thing cannot be "read off," as its brownness can.

No additional difficulties are introduced by value *rankings*. There is, of course, an implied standard, but that is irrelevant, for there were implied standards in the case of factual rankings also. Landy is a superb miler by world standards, I am a bad miler by any standard. But some boys are good milers by college or university or club, though not by world, standards. Obviously, standards of this sort can themselves be ranked as high, medium, or low. The higher the standard, the lower the ranking, and vice versa. A Cambridge IIB is a Tasmanian starred first.

"But," it will be said, "you are forgetting the obvious differences. These value judgments are based essentially on only one criterion: speed. What if there are several?" We have already seen that in factual rankings and comparisons there may be a multiplicity of criteria capable of conflicting with one another. In such a case there may be no clear answer to the question 'Which of the two has the required property to a higher degree?' But this has no bearing on empirical verifiability and has nothing to do with the specifically evaluative nature of value comparisons and rankings.

At any rate, there will be an enormous number of cases where value judgments can be verified or disproved. I once bought, from a street vendor, a fountain pen which he described as a Parker 51, imported duty-free. My friend warned me against buying it. He said it was no good. To cut a long and disappointing story short, it was not a Parker, and it was no good. It did not have a gold nib, or even a proper filling mechanism. When I bought it, I thought it was good, for I tried to write with it and it seemed to work. Later, I discovered that it wasn't any good, for it did not write and could not be filled. It did not satisfy any of the generally recognized criteria of a good fountain pen. There can be no doubt that in this case I *learned from experience*, no doubt that my friend's claim, that the pen was no good, was conclusively verified.

"This does not prove much," it will perhaps be objected. "I possess a Parker 51 and a Waterman. I have had them for many years, and I still do not know which is the better. And it is not as if I had not had the necessary time to try them out. Yet I shall never know." One explanation might be that they are equally good. When, after a long time of using a pen, one cannot discover which is the better, then it may well be that neither *is* better, but that they are equally good.

"But can we be certain whether they are equally good? Or can this never be settled?" It must be admitted that there are some subtleties about utensils such as fountain pens about which the average user will never be able to arrive at the truth for himself. I have no record of how often I have had my two pens repaired, nor do I possess the statistics for others; I do not know how well their iridium points have worn or how often I have had to fill the two or how long they will continue to be serviceable and so on. But experts may know; hence experts will be able to tell which is the better pen, even where I cannot. Experience with pens, expert knowledge, may be necessary to substantiate such a claim. Although value judgments may not always be empirically verifiable by laymen, it is still possible that they can be verified by experts.

Value Judgments

5 MATTERS OF OPINION AND MATTERS OF TASTE

"But you know as well as I do," it will be said, "that even experts differ. Some doctors recommend one brand of tooth paste or soap, others another. These things are simply matters of opinion." It is true that some such disagreements are matters of opinion, but not all. That Landy is a better miler than I, that Plato was a greater philosopher than Joad, that cars are now better than they were fifty years ago, that *Hamlet* is a greater play than *A Streetcar Named Desire*, that Gandhi was a better man than Stalin, are not matters of opinion, but are quite indubitably true. Anyone who maintained the opposite would have to be said not to know what he was talking about. That some value judgments are matters of opinion does not have any tendency to show that all are. If all were, then they would indeed be empirically unverifiable. For it is a characteristic of matters of opinion that they are unverifiable, because incurably open issues. But obviously not all value judgments are matters of opinion.

Moreover, many obviously factual issues are also matters of opinion: whether Hitler would have won the war if he had invaded England instead of attacking France; whether Churchill is more of an extrovert than Mussolini was; whether immigration is one of the main causes of inflation in Australia. Some people have been tempted to say that these are value judgments just because they are matters of opinion, that is, not conclusively verifiable or the reverse. Yet this is absurd, for there are other claims of exactly the same sort which are not matters of opinion, but plainly true: that Hitler would have won the war if Germany had not got herself involved with Russia and America; that Mussolini was more of an extrovert than Kafka; that the higher cost of imports is among the main causes of inflation in Australia.

It is equally absurd to claim that all value judgments are

matters of taste. True, when we are engaged in comparing or ranking pictures, cows, clothes, food, or drinks, there comes a point where further talk about the matter is no longer helpful in settling the disagreement. We simply agree to differ. We part peacefully in the knowledge that what separates us is merely a difference in taste. Nevertheless, it is obvious that a 1956 Bentley Continental is a better car than a 1927 Bentley, even if some lovers of vintage cars would rather own the latter. Even in disputes which are so largely matters of taste, such as the quality of a certain meal or someone's cooking, there are claims which are not matters of taste. It is obvious that the meal I recently had at the Florentino was vastly superior to the meal I cooked at home the night before, even if it were true that I liked my own cooking better. Nor can there be any doubt that the chef at the Florentino is a better cook than I, even if my friends prefer my plain T-bone steak to his elaborate Italian confections.

6 SCIENTIFIC PRECISION

"Well," my objector might say, "maybe you can get some sort of empirical verification of value judgments, but you can't get anything that is really important. What makes for greater certainty and more reliable information is the formulation of one's claims in the scientific manner. You won't find matters of opinion, let alone of taste, in the sciences. Scientists do indeed need their imagination, their hunches, their flair, and so on. But they need them only in order to think up new ideas; they don't need them when it comes to the verification or proof of these ideas."

This is perfectly true, but not as damaging as might be thought at first. For the same precision is possible in the field of value judgments also. Consider the following simple case. Jones is good at judging distances and lengths. He can say how long it will take a person to walk from one place to another, whether the dressing table or the carpet will fit into the bedroom, whether the tree to be felled would hit the house if it happened to fall that way, and so on. Normally, that he has good judgment could be confirmed only by waiting for the disputed event to take place.

Someone now hits on the idea of 'measuring in paces.' We find that if in walking along the carpet we take 13 paces one way and 14 paces the other, and if in walking from one wall of the room to the other we take 16 paces one way and 20 paces the other, the carpet fits easily into the room within several paces to spare. In this way, we can make pretty sure before actually trying it out whether the carpet will or will not fit into the bedroom. We have eliminated judgment and replaced it by measurement. Individual skill has been replaced by an ingenious method requiring practically no skill at all, only diligence.

There are many gains. We have now a way of stating lengths which is topic-neutral. We do not have to speak of the carpet *being smaller than* the room, or the tree being *too short* to hit the house, and so on. We can state objectively, that is, topic-neutrally, *how long it is*. We do not have to wait for the verifying event to happen before we can be sure of the truth of our claim. And the matter is easy, almost mechanical. Anyone can now work out for himself *how long* something is. We do not have to call in an expert.

Measuring is like comparing and ranking. It is like comparing in that it compares any given object to the standard length which is used as a measure. It introduces numbers into comparing by stating that a given length is a multiple of the standard length. It is like ranking in that it assigns to the object to be ranked a place on a scale consisting of the multiples of the unit or standard length. The method makes claims of length more objective, but also more arbitrary. It is obvious why the standard for the tallness of Pygmies differs from that for the tallness of Europeans: because their average height differs. A pace or foot or inch or meter, on the other hand, is totally unrelated to the lengths to be measured. Hence it is not true that empirical verification is made impossible by arbitrary standards or criteria. As long as they are *known*, verification is possible. I shall return to this point.

It is obvious how measuring by paces can be further improved, that is, made more objective. Different people take unequally long paces. The same person varies his pace from time to time. Concentration on the job, tiredness, moods, and the like will influence the length of his pace. The standard length should not vary from person to person, from occasion to occasion, from time to time, from mood to mood. A measuring rod will not have these defects.

All these changes are of the utmost importance, but they are not preconditions of verification, which was possible before their introduction. Their effect is merely to render the claims made capable of greater precision. It is comparatively easy to judge whether a carpet will fit into a room, but very difficult to judge whether it is 14 feet 3 inches or 14 feet 4 inches long. The new method enables us reliably to make these precise claims.

Something like this can also be done for value judgments. If we remember that measuring is a sort of comparing or ranking, composed of a standard unit and a scale made up of its multiples, we need only select an appropriate unit for the merit of something. Suppose we say that when we evaluate running performances we are attempting *to measure their "merit."* We shall say that running one mile in ten minutes measures 100 merits; two miles in ten minutes, 200 merits; a mile in twenty minutes, 50 merits; and so on. We can then always ask, 'How many merits were his race?' and we can always give a numerical answer.

"But this does not mean the same thing as before," it might be objected. The answer is "Of course not." When the thermometer was introduced, a new concept, 'temperature,' was introduced also. To say that it is hot in here, or that it is a hot day, or that the soup is hot, or that the bath is hot, is to say something different from saying that the room temperature is 80 degrees F., the air temperature is 100 degrees F., or the temperature of the soup is 94 degrees F. More obviously, the remark 'The temperature of the air is lower than the temperature of the soup' cannot mean the same as 'The day is not as hot as the soup,' for the latter does not even make sense. Thermometers enable us to compare in respect of a certain property, temperature, things which could not previously be compared in terms of 'colder than . . .' or 'hotter than. . . .' The introduction of measuring devices may therefore change the meaning of assertions. Prior to the introduction of the thermometer, a disagreement about hotness or coldness could not be settled. If everyone except me judges that the soup is hotter than the coffee, I have not been shown wrong—I am merely outnumbered. Now, the claim can be tested by putting a thermometer in. I may be the odd man out; nevertheless my tongue may be the only thermometrical one. Everyone else may be wrong. This shows that 'temperature' does not mean exactly the same as 'degree of hotness or coldness.'

Yet, no one would say that the invention of the thermometer had made a muddle of our ordinary claims. The new method is an improvement. It is extremely useful for all sorts of purposes. Though it does not matter whether the soup is hotter or colder than the bath, it does matter whether the temperature of the water in my radiator is or is not above 190 degrees F. It would be equally *legitimate* to introduce the system of measuring in "merits," if only there were any use for it. I can see none, but it would make one kind of value judgment as precise as some kinds of scientific measurement.

"But what of the cases where criteria conflict?" my tiring opponent might now inquire. Well, remember the case of judging one house bigger than another. Here, too, we could think of cases where the criteria might conflict. Yet, the introduction of the concept of volume helps to make even these cases decidable. We now say that one house is bigger than another if it has a greater volume, volume being defined as the product of the numerical values for its length, width, and height. Such a figure does not correspond to anything very much in our practice. It tells us which house would hold more water, but little else. It does not tell us anything about the number and size of rooms, or about the length, width, and height. The information is perfectly precise but very abstract, very general. We have achieved verifiability of previously unverifiable claims at the cost of no longer conveying the information we were looking for. The information we wanted cannot be given in terms of the concept of volume. Nor can it be given in terms of the concept 'bigger than . . .' because the criteria conflict. We have to say, for example, 'It's longer, *but* narrower and lower than the other house; and it's got more, *but* smaller rooms.'

The same is true for value judgments. When we look at the score chart in Motor Manual, we find two columns, one containing the average score, the other the score for the tested car. We find headings such as Styling, Bodywork, Interior, Instruments. Against each heading, there is a ranking *word*, for example, modern, attractive; well finished; neat; easy to read; and so on. And there is a score number, one for the average, one for the tested car. For instance, under Styling, we read: modern, attractive, 4 (for the average), 4 (for the tested car). That is to say, the tested car scores the same as the average. If we go through the whole score chart, we get a lot of information about the merits of the car under each of the headings listed. If we read only the total score, 100 for average, 104 for the car tested, we know very little about its merits. The case seems to me analogous to that of volume.

Still, it will be said, this introduction of numbers is most misleading. When you rank cars, or bathing belles, or students' essays, you draw up a list of criteria, and you *give* points under each of them, then you add them up. That looks like working out the volume, but it is not. For when the test driver gives the car 4 points for Styling, he does not arrive at that figure by measurement. He simply rates or ranks it as 4, and that is judgment, not measurement. Your introduction of numbers is a fraud.

There is some weight in this point. It is true that the introduction of numbers does not produce complete scientific objectivity. However, it has one justification: to make an overall judgment possible, where there would otherwise be no way of computing the partial merits due under each heading. The procedure is similar to that of introducing the concept of volume *as the product of* length, width, and height. This concept could not have been introduced if the "dimensions" of which it is made up had not already had numerical values. If I said that the house was as long as the fence, as wide as the river, and as high as the gum tree, then there would be no way of working out *the volume* as the product of these three dimensions. Similarly, if I say that the merit of the car as a whole is made up of the attractiveness of the body styling, the good finish of the bodywork, the neatness of the interior, and so on, no over-all rank can emerge. But if I allocate numbers to each item and add them up, I can arrive at an over-all result.

However, it will still be objected that in the case of length, width, and height we arrive at numerical values by *measure-*

ment, but in the case of the criteria of cars we do so by *allotting* a number. This is completely true, but as we have seen in evaluating running performances, we can introduce measuring devices where we wish. The same sort of device could be introduced for ranking body styling, body finish, and so on. Of course, such measuring devices are *arbitrary*. They do not mean quite the same as our original rankings. But then neither does 'greater volume' mean quite the same as 'bigger.' As long as we know how such measurements are arrived at and how such individual measurements are computed into over-all rankings, *the demand for objectivity* has been satisfied. We can then understand exactly what has been asserted (even if it is not the same as was asserted before the numerical methods are introduced) and we can verify this new and precise claim. Sometimes it will be impossible to render our original claims more precise and verifiable, but this is so equally in the scientific and in the evaluative cases.

7 VERIFICATION AND VALIDATION

"But now you have given the show away," our persistent objector will exclaim. "What you have said just now has suddenly illuminated for me that elusive difference between factual and value judgments which so many philosophers have tried to elucidate. You have proved to my satisfaction that value judgments can be transformed into unambiguous, precise, and empirically verifiable remarks. But in doing so, you have also shown, without meaning to, that by this transformation they become, *eo ipso*, something else. They not only come to *mean* something different, they become utterances of a different sort, they cease to be guides to behavior. They no longer provide reasons for us to do one thing rather than another. When we have made a value judgment unambiguous, precise, and verifiable, we have turned it into a factual judgment. It then no longer *guides us*, it merely describes something."

This objection is based on an important truth, but it is stated in a confused and misleading manner. The truth contained in it is this. Value judgments and factual claims serve different purposes. In factual comparisons and rankings, our normal purpose is to describe something, to say to what degree it has certain properties. The idea is to enable someone else to identify it, or to establish laws about it, that is, correlations of some of its properties with others, or correlations between variations in some of its properties and variations in others. When we make factual comparisons and rankings more precise by introducing devices such as measurement or weighing, we are sometimes introducing *new properties* as well. But this is of no importance as long as the new properties are more helpful in identifying the thing in question or in establishing correlations. With evaluative comparisons and rankings, our purpose is different, however. We are not concerned to describe a thing, so that people can identify it or can establish laws, but to give rational guidance. We are concerned not merely with the nature of the thing in question, but also with how well a thing of this nature can minister to our wants, desires, aims, needs, aspirations, ideals, and the like.

This has an important corollary. In the case of factual comparisons and rankings, a change in the criteria is of no great consequence. Of course, such a change might give rise to misunderstandings, if one party is unaware of it. You may be using 'being bigger than . . .' with the same criteria as 'having a greater volume than . . .' whereas I may be using it with the ordinary criteria. We may then appear to disagree about the size of a given house, whereas we have merely misunderstood each other's claims. When I say, 'Smith's house is bigger than

Gordon's,' I base this on the fact that Smith's house has more rooms, but when you say, 'No, they are equally big,' you base it on the fact that they have the same volume. When this difference between us is brought to light, however, our disagreement vanishes, for it is of no consequence in which of these two ways we use the expression 'bigger than. . . .'

But where value judgments are concerned, the discovery that we have been using different criteria does not end the disagreement. The real disagreement may only begin here. For while in nonevaluative comparisons and rankings we are simply concerned to state the degree to which a given thing satisfies given criteria, in value judgments we are concerned to say more. When, in nonevaluative judgments, we change the criteria, we are simply making a different nonevaluative claim, we are simply asserting the possession of a different property. In value judgments this is not so. Here we are concerned not merely to say something about the properties of the thing, but something about the *appropriateness* of certain lines of behavior in relation to a thing with such properties. Nothing follows about the appropriateness or otherwise of someone's behavior from saying either that the first house is bigger than the second or that it has a greater volume. Something does follow from saying that the first house is better than the second. It follows that, other things being equal, it would be contrary to reason to buy the second and in accordance with reason to buy the first. Hence a change of the criteria in the case of evaluative comparisons and rankings would *amount to giving different advice*. When we change criteria in factual comparisons and rankings, we are merely making different remarks about the things in question; hence people using different criteria *cannot* contradict each other, for they are no longer talking "on the same plane." When we use different criteria in value judgments, we *can* contradict each other, for we are still "talking on the same plane": we are saying that one thing is *better or worse than* another, that is, that there is a good reason for doing one thing rather than the other.

Value judgments, therefore, give rise to an additional question, which cannot arise in the case of factual ones, namely, 'Are these the *right* criteria?' Our proof that value judgments can be empirically verified is, therefore, not as far-reaching as it appeared at first. For what it amounts to is simply that, *if we agree on the criteria to be employed,* then value judgments can be empirically verified in exactly the same way as nonevaluative comparisons and rankings. However, even this insight is of some importance, for at least it shows how, *when* the criteria are agreed, as they are in very many cases, we can use our experience and our knowledge of facts to verify our value judgments.

All the same, the characteristic disagreement *in value,* as opposed to disagreements about fact, is the disagreement about the rightness of the criteria employed in ascertaining the "value" or "goodness" of the thing in question. We must, therefore, examine this sort of disagreement and find out whether it is capable of empirical settlement, and if so, how. Let us then distinguish between *verification* and *validation.* We have seen that value judgments can be verified just like factual claims, but that in value judgments we make claims that give rise to a further question, namely, whether the criteria employed are the right ones. Factual judgments are decisively confirmed if they are empirically verified. Value judgments, on the other hand, must be not only verified but also validated. It is not enough to show that, *if* certain criteria *are* employed, then a thing must be said to have a certain degree of "goodness"; we must also show that these criteria *ought* to be employed.

The important point contained in the above objection [8] is this, then: A remark ceases to be a value judgment and turns

8 P. 72.

into a factual claim as soon as the question of *the appropriateness of the criteria* is rejected as unnecessary or irrelevant. If I say that I once ran as well as Landy at his best because Landy ran a mile in four minutes, that is, his best run measured 250 "merits" (at the rate of 100 merits for a mile in ten minutes), and I once ran ten yards in one and a half seconds, amounting also to 250 "merits" (at the same rate), then I can be making an evaluative comparison only if I claim that my method of "measuring merits" *is appropriate*. If I do not claim that, my remark that I once ran *as well as Landy at his best* is not what it appears to be, an evaluative comparison of Landy and myself as runners, but an assessment of Landy's and my performances in terms of my novel (and highly misleading) points system.

The necessity of validating criteria is sometimes evaded by those who swear by ordinary usage. They speak as if the question of the appropriateness of the criteria, the validation of value judgments, could be answered merely by ascertaining whether the currently accepted criteria are employed or whether there has been a departure from ordinary usage. Thus, it might be said that in the case of 'having a greater volume than . . .' there has been a departure from the criteria used in 'being bigger than. . . .' Similarly, in the case of 'measuring the same merits as . . .' there has been a departure from the criteria used in 'being a better runner than. . . .' But while in the first case to say that the criteria are not the right ones is merely to say that they are not the ones currently accepted, in the second case this is not the only thing said. For even when I have shown that the criteria I have used are those currently accepted, I can still ask a further question, namely, whether they are the right criteria, whether they are those which are now rightly accepted.

Let us bear all this in mind, then. (i) Value judgments, on the one hand, and factual comparisons and rankings, on the other, differ in this respect: in the case of the former, but not the latter, we can ask whether the criteria used are the right or the wrong ones. (ii) If this is asked in the case of factual comparisons and rankings, it can only be a question about conformity with, or departure from, ordinary usage. (iii) Questions about whether or not the currently accepted criteria have been used are not unimportant when we wish to avoid misunderstandings, but they are irrelevant where *the truth or falsity, and not the meaning,* of a value judgment is concerned.

We must now return to our objection, which was, it will be remembered, that if a given remark is rendered empirically verifiable, unambiguous, or precise, then it (logically) cannot be a value judgment. This is completely wrong. As I have shown, the question of the verifiability, unambiguousness, and preciseness of a remark is quite independent of its being either evaluative or factual. Both evaluative and factual claims may be empirically verifiable or the reverse, comparatively unambiguous or ambiguous, precise or vague. It is not true that, of their nature, factual remarks are characterized by empirical verifiability, unambiguity, and preciseness, whereas value judgments are characterized by empirical unverifiability, ambiguity, and vagueness.[9] That a remark is evaluative does not entail that it is in principle unverifiable or the opposite, comparatively ambiguous, and vague. It does mean, however, that we can ask the question whether the criteria employed in verifying it are the right or the wrong ones, whereas this question cannot (literally) be asked when we are talking about nonevaluative comparisons and rankings.

8 VALUE JUDGMENTS ARE NOT COMMENDATIONS

I cannot forbear to mention one of those reasons which I think have contributed to the wide acceptance of the errone-

---

[9] Cf. C. L. Stevenson, *Ethics and Language* (New Haven: Yale University Press, 1944), p. 36.

ous opinion that empirical verification and value judgments are logically incompatible. I mean the view that value judgments are *commendations*. It is a case of the misunderstanding of the use of a word by a too ready reliance on pronouncements made in the Oxford Dictionary. Giving as his motto the following entry from the O.E.D., "Good. . . . The most general adjective of commendation, implying the existence in a high, or at least satisfactory, degree of characteristic qualities which are either admirable in themselves, or useful for some purpose . . ." [10] Mr. Hare goes on to say, "Almost every word in our language is capable of being used on occasion as a value-word (*that is, for commending or its opposite*); and usually it is by cross-examining a speaker that we can tell whether he is so using a word. The word 'brilliant' is a good example." [11] Hare believes that when we say of someone that he is brilliant we may be either describing or commending him, perhaps both. Insofar as we are describing him, what we say is verifiable or the reverse, but insofar as we are commending him, it is not. I suppose Hare would allow the possibility that someone might say on one occasion, 'Jones is a brilliant man' (thereby commending him), and on another occasion, 'Jones is not a brilliant man' (thereby describing him), without contradicting himself.

Be that as it may, Hare's point is, of course, perfectly true about commending. For commending someone is an *activity*, and a ritual one at that. It is patting someone on the back with words. It may be done with ritual words, for example, 'I hereby *commend* you for the work you have done throughout the year,' or with ordinary words as in 'What a nice party that was, Mrs. Charlesworth. It was very good of you to go to so much trouble,' etc., etc. Of course, only persons in the appropriate position can commend someone. I cannot commend my employer for being

[10] R. M. Hare, *op. cit.*, p. 79.　　　　[11] *Ibid.*, pp. 79–80.

so helpful to my brother and for having so generously promoted the interests of his employees, though *he* can commend
me for doing this. *I* can only express my gratitude or admira-
tion. Since commendations are verbal *performances*, not assertions, it is obvious that commendations cannot be true or false.
In commendations, words are used "performatorily," in Austin's
phrase.[12]

But value judgments are not commendations. When I say,
'The Bentley Continental is a better car than the Morris Minor'
or 'Landy is a better miler than I' or 'Jones is an excellent
salesman, a very capable organizer, and a most conscientious
worker,' I am not commending the Bentley, Landy, or Jones.
I am not in a position to do so, nor is there an occasion for doing
so, nor have they done anything to warrant commendation. I
may be praising them, though there is little pride in being a
better miler than I. But praising someone is not going through
a verbal ritual: it is purporting to enumerate the good points
of someone or something. And such enumerations can be true
or false. Suppose, in his kindness, my referee says the following
in a testimonial: "Baier is not only the most original, most
widely read, and best-informed philosopher I have ever met,
but also the most brilliant conversationalist, the most stimulat-
ing colleague, and the most conscientious teacher I have ever
had the good fortune to work with." He is then certainly praising and not commending me. But, obviously, what he says is
untrue.

If it is clear that value judgments are not commendations,
though they sometimes constitute praise or denigration, one
of the confusions responsible for the view that value judgment
and truth or verifiability are logically incompatible has been
cleared up.

---

[12] J. L. Austin, "Knowledge of Other Minds," reprinted in *Logic and
Language*, 2d ser., ed. by A. G. N. Flew (Oxford: Basil Blackwell, 1953).

9 THE TECHNIQUE OF VALIDATION

"All right," my imaginary opponent will reply, "value judgments *are* verifiable. But this is an empty triumph. What people meant to say was, of course, that they are incapable of what you now call validation. Value judgments differ from factual statements in just this, that they *require* to be validated, and that this is impossible, at least objectively. For to say that they are *valid* is to make another value judgment. And this in turn will require criteria and they in turn will have to be validated, and so on ad infinitum."

I do not wish to belittle the difficulties involved in validating value judgments, but there must be something wrong with this argument. For could anyone deny that 'Landy is the best miler in the world today' is capable of both verification and validation? Could anyone deny that, at any rate, the criteria mentioned for comparing and ranking milers are the right ones? Surely, Landy's record-breaking mile *is* the best mile ever run so far. Surely, the criterion, speed, is the right criterion to apply. Although it would not be true to say, literally, that 'the best mile' *means* 'the fastest mile,' yet since winning a race is running faster than any other competitor, speed is the proper criterion to use. Surely, here we have both verification and validation.

And what is true of this case is also true of all cases involving purposes. Roughly speaking, the proper criteria for evaluating cars, fountain pens, milers, and so on are determined by the purpose of the thing, activity, or enterprise in question. Knowing the purpose of the car enables us to see that speed, comfort, safety, and the like are proper criteria.

"But how are we enabled to *see* all this? How, for instance, do we know the purpose of cars? Is that something to know, anyway? Is it not something that *we give to* these things? And don't different people give different purposes to their cars? What purpose a car has is for its owner to decide, and to decide at will." It will be granted that we all know what cars are. And the fact that I know what a car is implies that I know the purpose of cars. For knowledge of what a car is, is more than the ability to recognize a car when it is parked in the street or in deserted country lanes or when it stands in a garage or in a showroom. The ability to do that amounts only to a knowledge of what cars look like. A Melanesian recently arrived in Melbourne and observing cars parked at night is told, in reply to his question, "These things are cars." This may be enough to enable him correctly to pick out cars. But even so he cannot be said to know what cars are, if he thinks that they are shelters for adolescents to pet in. He could not be said to know *the* purpose of cars, even though he has correctly guessed one of the purposes for which they can be and frequently are used by joy-riders.

Knowing the purpose of cars by itself is not enough to derive the appropriateness of criteria such as safety, comfort, or reliability. They can be derived from the purpose of cars only if taken together with a great many other more general human aims. Safety is a criterion not simply because cars have the purpose of serving as means of transportation, but because we want to live unhurt as long as possible. Of course, as I said before, if instead of them we wanted other things, then the criteria of excellence in cars would be different. It is, however, a plain fact that we do want these things. There is nothing arbitrary, subjective, personal about it. It would be absurd to claim that this was a matter of taste, opinion, personal preference, an idiosyncrasy, or what have you. On the contrary, anyone who claims that safety, reliability, comfort, and the like are *not* appropriate criteria of excellence in cars simply does not know what he is talking about, or is a little crazy, to say the least.

The real difficulty, however, does not lie in establishing that some criteria are objectively valid, but in drawing the line between those capable of objective validation and the others and, furthermore, where there are several criteria, in establishing which are the more important ones, and how much more important.

One way of extending the range of the capacity for objective validation is to narrow the basis of comparison. Instead of comparing or ranking cars, we may compare and rank racing cars or station wagons. Then the more specific purpose of the car determines objectively a narrower range and a clearer hierarchy of the criteria. Obviously speed is more important in a racing car than in a bus, and being able to carry a pay load is more important in a utility car than in a sports car. This method has corresponding disadvantages. It prevents me from saying that the Austin Healey is better than the Fargo, for one is a sports car, the other a truck. But this is not a very serious drawback, since there is little point in comparing the two anyway.

If we *insist* on comparing them, we can still do so by ranking each one on a scale appropriate to *it* and by comparing the respective ranks. Suppose the Austin Healey is an excellent sports car and the Fargo merely an average truck; then we can say that the Austin Healey is better than the Fargo, even though they have not been *directly* compared. What has been compared is merely the respective rank in their respective scales. What standards are appropriate for the ranking would depend on the purpose for which such a comparison was made.

Another thing we might do is to draw up a list of all criteria relevant to any type of car. We could then rank cars on the basis of each criterion, leaving it to everyone to determine for himself which criteria he regards as most important. In such a case only the selection of the criteria and the ranking for each are objective. No computation of all the partial rankings for the purpose of arriving at an over-all ranking or comparison is here attempted. The over-all rankings must be made by each individual on the basis of *his own* special purposes or aims. They are to that extent personal, but not purely subjective, since mistakes are possible even then: anyone having the same special purposes must obtain the same over-all ranking, *unless he has made a mistake.*

Alternatively, one might decide to compute such partial rankings conventionally. One might decide to rank, not on a three-place scale, good, average, bad, but on a numerical, say, ten-place scale. One has then made computation possible. The ranking is conventional, because all criteria are given the same importance. This sort of thing is done in the so-called score charts in motor journals. The person testing the car in question has a list of all the criteria he will consider, for example, Styling, Bodywork, Interior, Instruments, Comfort, Driving Position, and so on. For all these criteria, the road tester gives a rank by using one of the ordinary "grading labels" (in Mr. Urmson's useful terminology [13]), for example, attractive, well finished, neat, easy to read, good, excellent, good for short driver, and so forth. But he also gives a corresponding conventional number, say, 4, 4, 4, 4, 4, 5, 4. These numbers can be added up and provide an *over-all* evaluation. If we compare each ranking, and the over-all ranking, with the ranking for the average, we get a fairly clear idea of how good the car in question is.

I take it as established, then, that there are value judgments which can be empirically verified and also validated.

"But you can't leave it at that, surely," it will be said. "What about moral value judgments, what about aesthetic or economic value judgments, or so-called judgments of intrinsic value? You have selected the easiest type, the type no one has ever had any

---

[13] J. O. Urmson, "On Grading," reprinted in *Logic and Language*, 2d ser.

serious worries about. What about the philosophically interesting ones?" My main reason for talking about value judgments was not to elucidate these philosophically interesting value judgments, a task far beyond the scope of this book. My purpose was rather to show how value comparisons and rankings operate with criteria and standards. This had to be made clear because it is my main contention that all forms of so-called practical reasoning, including moral reasoning, are value comparisons of courses of action open to us. Practical reasoning is, roughly speaking, answering the value question 'Which is *the best* course open to me?' To this type of value judgment we must now turn.

Three

The Best Thing to Do

I HAVE already explained [1] that the question 'What shall I do?' is not normally or essentially a request for a command or order, but a question requiring an answer that can be correct or incorrect, true or false. In this chapter I want to show that 'What shall I do?' is a value question, that is, one requiring a value judgment for an answer. More exactly, 'What shall I do?' means the same as 'What is *the best* thing I can do?' That this is so is obvious from the reply 'I know this would be the best thing to do, but that is not what I want to know. I want to know, *what shall I do?*' A man who says this obviously does not know what he is asking. He may want to query the truth of what he is told, but he cannot claim that his question has yet to be answered.

[1] Chapter Two, p. 56.

The Moral Point of View

1 'WHAT SHALL I DO?' MEANS 'WHAT IS THE BEST THING TO DO?'

Some philosophers, such as Hare, would say that only a command, an order, or an imperative can answer, 'What shall I do?' For only imperatives tell persons to do something; indicatives tell them merely what is the case. 'What shall I do?' they would say is a request for guidance, for being told to do something, not for being told what is the case, because information about what is the case cannot guide anyone. But this is not true. I have already pointed out that there is a difference between asking to be told to do something and asking to be told what to do. The first is indeed a request for orders, but the second is a request for information.

"But there is a difference," it might be said, "between 'What *shall* I do?' or 'What *should* I do?' and 'What *ought* I to do?' You are talking about the latter, I am talking about the former." Well, if there is a difference, then philosophers like Hare do not build their case on this difference. On the contrary, they claim that remarks containing the words 'should' and 'ought' are commands or orders, because they can be given in reply to questions of the form 'What shall I do?' or 'What should I do?' or 'What ought I to do?' And I think that Hare is right on this point. There is no significant difference between these formulas. Of course, 'What shall I do?' may not be a request for advice, but for prediction, as in 'What shall I do, do you think, when I come out of the anesthetic—curse the doctor or be sick?'; though it would be better grammar to say 'What *will* I do, do you think . . . ?' The only difference between these questions that I can detect is that 'What ought I to do?' has a moral ring whereas 'What shall I do?' has not. Notwithstanding this, I can ask, 'What *ought* I to do, invite all wives, or only the Chancellor's and Vice-Chancellor's, or no wives at all?' which is not a moral matter, but a matter of etiquette. Conversely, I can ask, 'What shall I do, denounce him to the police or turn a blind eye on it all?' which may well be a moral matter requiring moral consideration.

2 'THE BEST THING TO DO' MEANS 'THE COURSE SUPPORTED BY THE BEST REASONS'

Granted, then, that 'What shall I do?' is a request for a value judgment, namely, 'What is the *best* thing to do?' we have to ask ourselves by what criteria we are supposed to judge which of the courses open to the agent is the best. It is natural to think that just as a manufactured article is judged by its power to serve the purpose for which it has been made, and for which it is normally used, so a line of action is judged by its ability to serve the purpose for which it is entered upon by the agent. But this is only a provisional judgment, for we can always ask whether what the agent is aiming at is the best thing to aim at. Frequently, when someone asks, 'What shall I do?' he is not merely asking which is the better course of action, *given a certain aim or end*, but which of several ends or aims is the best.

It is unfortunate that the means-end model has dominated philosophical thinking in this field. It has led some philosophers, maintaining (rightly) that we can ask which is the best thing to aim at in these circumstances, to conclude (wrongly) that there must be an *ultimate* aim or end, a *summum bonum*, to which all ordinary aims or ends are merely means. Hence, they claim, whether this or that is the better end to aim at must be judged by its serving the ultimate end or *summum bonum*. Other philosophers, maintaining (rightly) that there can be no such ultimate end or *summum bonum*, have concluded (wrongly) that we cannot ask which is the better end to aim at. They have claimed that reason can tell us only about what are the best means to given ends, but that ends themselves cannot be determined or judged by reason. However, 'being a good means to a certain end' is not the only criterion of the merit of a course of action.

The error which this means-end model of the evaluation of lines of action forces on us is this. It compels us to think that what is a reason for (or against) doing something is determined by what we are aiming at. Since different people aim at different things and since they frequently argue about what to aim at, either we are compelled to assume that there is one objectively determined end or aim which we must aim at if we are to follow reason, or, if we reject objective ends as absurd, we are compelled to renounce all reasoning about ends. However, it is not true that our ends determine what is a reason for doing something, but, on the contrary, reasons determine what we ought to, and frequently do, aim at. What is a reason for doing this, or against doing that, is independent of what this or that man is actually aiming at. The best course of action is not that course which most quickly, least painfully, least expensively, etc., leads to the gaining of our ends, but *it is the course of action which is supported by the best reasons.* And the best reasons may require us to abandon the aim we actually have set our heart on.

Our next question must, therefore, be concerned with what it is that makes something a reason for (or against) entering on a certain line of action. When we are deliberating about alternative courses of action before us, our deliberation progresses through two distinct stages, first, the surveying of the facts with a view to determining which of them are relevant considerations and, secondly, the determination of the relative "weight" of these considerations with a view to deciding which course of action has the full weight of reason behind it.

The Best Thing to Do

3 WHAT MAKES SOMETHING A REASON? THE RECEIVED ANSWERS

What, then, is it that makes something a reason for (or against) entering on a certain line of action? Let us look at the various received theories first. It is generally granted that reason tells us such things as whether a given course of action is in accordance with or contrary to reason, whether it has the weight of reason behind or against it. Another way of putting the same thing would be to ask whether the given course of action was supported or opposed by the best or strongest or most important reasons. Thus, the expression 'in accordance with (contrary to) *reason*' comes to the same as 'supported (opposed) by *the best reasons.*'

Moral philosophy, as previously stated, is required to answer these three fundamental questions: (i) How do we tell what is right and what wrong? (ii) Why do people do what is right and refrain from doing what is wrong? (iii) Why should people do what is right and refrain from doing what is wrong? A conceptual analysis of reason must deal with three analogous problems: (i) How do we tell what is in accordance with or contrary to reason? (ii) Why do people act in accordance with reason and refrain from doing what is contrary to it? (iii) Why should people do what is in accordance with and refrain from doing what is contrary to reason? I shall deal with (i) in this chapter, with (ii) in Chapter Six, and with (iii) in Chapter Twelve.

Before examining in detail our question (i), let us look at the main traditional answers. There are three major theories about how we tell what is in accordance with and what contrary to reason. The first, held for instance by Plato, maintains that reason is a mental organ or faculty or element, a sort of "eye of the soul," which enables us to "see" what is in accordance with and what contrary to reason. The second, held for instance by Hume, takes the view that reason is a sort of mental calculating machine which enables us to work out such things as causal connections between events and, therefore, also between our actions and their consequences. Reason thus enables us to work out what we must do in order to achieve certain ends. On this view we therefore determine what is according to reason and what contrary to it by determining what are suitable means to our ends. Our actions are in accordance with reason if we believe them (rightly or wrongly) to be suitable means to our ends, contrary to reason if we believe them not to be. As far as our ends themselves are concerned, reason can have nothing to say. For our ends are determined not by reason but by the passions. Hence the question whether our ends are in accordance with or contrary to reason simply cannot arise. The third theory, held very widely today,[2] takes the view that reason is neither a faculty nor a calculating machine. This theory accepts the equivalence of the expressions 'in accordance with (or contrary to) reason' and 'supported (or opposed by) the best reasons.' It takes the fundamental expression to be, not 'reason,' but 'reasons.' A reason for acting in a certain way, on this view, is something we have, but to have a reason is simply to know or to believe a certain fact. What sort of fact? Any fact which will, or will tend to, move us to act in a certain way. A fact is made a reason for us to move in a certain way if knowing or believing this fact will, or will tend to, move us in that way. That it will rain (as we truly or falsely believe) is our reason for taking an umbrella, for that belief (that it will rain) has the power to move us to take an umbrella.

The distinction between means and ends makes fairly plausi-

---

[2] I take C. L. Stevenson and his followers to hold a theory of this kind; see his *Ethics and Language* (New Haven: Yale University Press, 1944), ch. v, especially pp. 111–115.

ble the answers given by these theories to the question how we tell that certain sorts of action are in accordance with or contrary to reason, namely, those which are means to our ends. All three theories agree that our ends determine not only what are the best means to our ends, but also whether this line of action (which is a means to our ends) is in accordance with or contrary to reason. And, indeed, it is in accordance with reason to choose means which we believe suitable to our ends, and contrary to it to choose means which we believe unsuitable.

But these theories do not yield plausible answers to the question how we tell whether our ends are in accordance with reason or not. There are three obvious objections to the first theory. There is, after all, no such "eye of the soul." But even if there were, the theory would be untenable. For those things which would then have to be called its "perceptions" vary from person to person, as the perceptions of real eyes do not. Moreover, telling whether something is in accordance with reason or not is a matter of excogitating, working out, thinking through, weighing the pros and cons, not a matter of just "looking" and waiting for the "visions" to "flood in."

The second theory is less plausible still. It takes the heroic course of denying the obvious. Hume's dictum that it is no more contrary to reason to prefer the destruction of the whole world to the scratching of one's little finger than vice versa is plainly absurd. Hume's example might well be offered as a paradigm of what is meant by 'contrary to reason.' On Hume's view we would have to say, of a man who poured petrol over his hand and lit it with a match, that he acted in accordance with reason because he chose the appropriate means to his end, to burn his hand. But, clearly, aiming at that (for no reason whatever) is not in accordance with reason—it is mad.

The third view is a variant of, and a considerable improvement on, the second. It allows what the previous view denied:

the possibility of a conflict between our ends and reason. For our ends may conflict with what we really (that is, most) desire. If we do not face all the facts before us, if we dwell more on some, less on others, the moving power of some facts may be greater or less than it would be if we squarely faced these facts. We are then moved to do certain things which, had we squarely faced the facts, we would not have been moved to do and which, later on, of course, we come to regret, for we did not *really*, in the light of all the facts, desire that course. But reason can have nothing to say about what we really (that is, most) desire in the light of all the facts. For, on this view, to follow reason *is* to follow what we really desire, in the light of all the facts. To follow reason is to let oneself be moved by all the facts, and not to shirk any.

As it stands, this view is untenable, for it unjustifiably narrows the application of the word 'reason.' In particular, we would have to say of a good many moral reasons that they were not reasons at all. A person who is indifferent to his fellow men, who cares only about his own advancement, would never have a reason for refraining from cheating, hurting, or harming others when this promoted his own advancement and when he is reasonably sure that he would not be found out, or when he knows that, if found out, he could always bribe the police or the judge. In fact, however, we do say that such a person has a reason, to wit a moral reason, against doing these things and that he has it quite independently of his caring for others, quite irrespective of whether or not he *really* desires to pursue these courses of action, and even after he has taken everything fully into consideration.

4 WHAT MAKES SOMETHING A REASON?
THE TRUE VIEW

If all these theories are unsatisfactory, what is the true view of the nature of reasons? I have already said that we arrive at an answer to the question 'What shall I do?' or 'What is the best thing to do?' or 'What is the course that has the weight of reason behind it?' after we have engaged in the activity of deliberation. Deliberation is an activity that has two distinguishable stages. The first consists of a survey of the facts for the purpose of drawing up a list of those that are relevant considerations; the second, of the weighing of these considerations, of these pros and cons, with a view to determining their relative "weight" and so deciding the course of action supported by the weightiest reasons, the course that has the weight of reason behind it.

4.1 *The surveying of the facts*

What facts must I survey? How do I tell that a given fact is a relevant consideration? What makes a fact a pro or a con, a reason for or against?

Suppose I have been in the United States for some time and have just come back to Australia, bringing with me a brand-new Chevrolet which I am importing duty-free. My friend, Paddy Concannan, offers me £3,000 for it, although he knows quite well it cost me only £1,000 new. I am eager to accept the offer. Have I a good reason for doing so? One at least is quite obvious. In selling the car I would be making a profit of 200 per cent. That would normally be regarded as a consideration, a reason for selling. How can I show that it is? The proof might be set out in the following way.

(i) The fact that doing something would yield a high profit is a good reason for doing it.

(ii) It would yield a high profit to sell my car to Paddy now.

(iii) Therefore, the fact that it would yield a high profit to sell my car to Paddy now is a reason for selling it now.

Another way of putting the conclusion would be to say that *in the fact* that it would yield a high profit to sell it now *I* have a good reason for selling it now.

My wife, on the other hand, advises against selling. She says that, having brought the car into the country as my personal possession, I was exempted from paying duty on condition that I would not sell it for three years. Her argument could be put in this way.

(i) The fact that doing something is illegal is a reason against doing it.

(ii) It would be illegal to sell my car to Paddy now.

(iii) Hence the fact that selling it to Paddy now would be illegal is a reason against selling it now.

How did we make sure that certain facts were considerations? We examined the proposed line of action with a view to discovering whether it was of certain well-known sorts, for example, lawful or unlawful or yielding profit or loss. For we believe that these features provide us with reasons for or against entering on the proposed line of action. We begin with certain beliefs; let us call them "consideration-making beliefs" or "rules of reason." These are propositions to the effect that if a line of action is of a certain sort then the agent has a reason for or against entering on it. Consideration-making beliefs can function as major premises in our arguments or as inference-licenses in our inferences. The minor premises are the facts which, in accordance with the consideration-making beliefs, we conclude to be reasons.

It is, of course, possible to make mistakes in these deliberations. Our major premises may be wrong: we may believe wrongly that the fact that a proposed line of action is illegal is a reason against entering on it, that the fact that it would yield a high profit is a reason for entering on it. Or the major premise may not *apply to* the facts we have discovered about the proposed line of action: it may not be correct to say that a profit of 200 per cent is a high profit or that selling a car imported duty-free is illegal. Lastly, what we take to be a fact about the proposed line of action may not be a fact: it may not be true that selling to Paddy would yield 200 per cent, for Paddy, being a shrewd businessman and knowing the transaction to be illegal, may refuse to pay as much as £3,000 once he has got hold of the car.

There is no mystery about how to avoid or correct the second and third type of error, but it is not at all apparent how we guard against the first. We learn the consideration-making beliefs prevalent in our community as part of our education. They are taught us not as beliefs but as facts. Later we come to realize that they are only group convictions and that they may be wrong. But we are not at all clear about how to detect errors in this field. I shall deal with this problem in Chapter Twelve. For the time being, we shall simply accept our consideration-making beliefs as true.

To sum up. In reply to the question 'What are reasons?' or 'What are considerations?' or 'What are pros and cons?' we must answer, 'They are certain facts.' What *makes* these facts considerations? That certain (true) consideration-making beliefs apply to them. What follows from the fact that something is a consideration? That someone who is planning to do something of a certain sort has, in the fact that it is of this sort, a reason for or against doing it. That something is a reason, therefore, of necessity always involves some possible agent. That some fact is a consideration always implies the context of a course of action planned by someone.

Does this mean that what is a reason for me is not necessarily a reason for you? In the most obvious interpretation of this question, it certainly does mean that. The fact that Mrs. Smith has died is a good reason for Mr. Smith to wear mourning, but not for Mr. Jones to do so. There is another less natural interpretation of the above question. Mr. Jones may consider the illegality of some course of action a good reason against doing it, and Mr. Smith may believe that it is not a good reason. The view that what is a reason for me is not necessarily a reason for you may be interpreted to mean that neither Mr. Smith nor Mr. Jones need be wrong—that what Mr. Smith rightly thinks to be a good reason for doing something Mr. Jones may rightly believe not to be so. In other words, the popular view that the same facts are reasons for some people but not for others can be interpreted in two different ways. It may be taken to mean that the conclusions, or that the major premises, of the arguments set out above are 'speaker-relative,' 'true for some, false for others.' The latter view is false. Consideration-making beliefs, the major premises of the above arguments, are not relative to particular situations or particular persons. It is either true, or it is false, that the fact that some course of action is illegal is a good reason against entering on it. It cannot be true for me, false for you.

This may be readily admitted for consideration-making beliefs, such as that it would be illegal or bad manners to do something. But it might be denied for others, such as that it would not be in my interest or that I would not enjoy it. For it might be said that the fact that some course of action is in my interest is a reason *for me* to do it, but *not for you*.

This objection is based on a simple confusion connected with the use of the personal pronoun. 'That doing something is in *my* interest' can be read in two quite different ways: (a) that doing something is in *Baier's* interest; (b) that doing something is in *one's* interest. That something is in Baier's interest is indeed only a reason for Baier to do it. But then no one would hold that '(a) is a reason for doing it' is a consideration-making belief of our society. We are not, all of us, taught to regard as a reason for entering on it the fact that some line of action is in Baier's interest. What we are taught is that (b) is a reason for doing something. And against (b) we cannot raise the objec-

The Best Thing to Do

tion that it is person-relative. For it is simply true or simply false, not true for me and false for you, that the fact that doing something would be in *one's* interest is a reason for doing it.

Set out formally, the argument runs as follows.

(i) The fact that doing something is in *one's* interest is a reason for doing it.

(ii) Being polite to my boss is in *my* interest.

(iii) Therefore, that it is in my interest to be polite to my boss is a reason for my being polite to my boss: or, put differently,

Therefore, in the fact that it is in my interest to be polite to my boss I have a reason for being polite to my boss.

Some readers may still feel that there are some reasons which are person-relative. For instance, they might say, the fact that there is good fishing at Port Fairie is a good reason for one person to take a holiday there, but not for another. But here again, they would be confusing the conclusion of the argument with its major premise. The conclusion, like all such conclusions, is indeed person-relative, but the major premise is not.

(i) The fact that *one* enjoys a certain activity is a reason for taking a holiday in a place where there are good opportunities for engaging in it.

(ii) *I* enjoy fishing and there is good fishing at Port Fairie.

(iii) Hence in the fact that there is good fishing at Port Fairie *I* have a reason for taking my holiday there.

On the other hand, on the basis of the same major premise someone else may argue in this way.

(ii) I do not enjoy fishing.

(iii) Hence in the fact that there is good fishing at Port Fairie I do not have a reason for taking my holiday there.

There is admittedly an important difference between the last two types of reason and the others, but the difference does not lie in the fact that the consideration-making beliefs are not equally person-neutral. It lies rather in the place where one must look for the facts which are the considerations. In the case of illegality, bad manners, unconventionality, and so on, I have to look for features of my proposed line of action which would contravene *some kind of rule holding for everyone*. In the case of self-interest and enjoyment, it is not enough to find out that people generally are, or that this or that person is, benefited by or enjoys this sort of thing. I must find out whether the particular line of action is in *the agent's interest* or would be enjoyed *by him*. Only then has *he* a reason for entering on it, and no one else has.[3]

Although there are these differences, there is also the following identity. In both cases, *anyone* proposing to enter on an action of a certain sort has in the fact that it is of this sort a reason for or against entering on it. In the case of illegal and unconventional actions, the sort can be stated without reference to the agent; in the case of self-interest and enjoyment, the *sort* is agent-relative. We must say, 'in *one's* interest,' 'if *one* enjoys it.' But when put in this form, it is true for any and every agent, not true for some and false for others.

Our conclusion is this. All consideration-making beliefs are person-neutral. They are simply true or false, not true for me and false for you or vice versa. On the other hand, all considerations or reasons are considerations or reasons for someone in some particular context or situation and may not be reasons for someone else or for the same person in another context or situation. For a given fact is a reason only because it is a reason for a particular person when deliberating about a number of alternative lines of action open to him. Considerations or reasons are not propositions laid up in heaven or universal truths, but they are particular facts to which, in particular contexts, universally true (or false) consideration-making beliefs apply.

---

[3] For a modification of this, see below, Chapter Four, section 2.

4.2 *The weighing of the reasons*

Our first step in deliberation, the surveying of the facts, as we have seen, brings to light the pros and cons, those among the many facts which are relevant, those in which we have reasons for or against. Let us, then, turn to the second step, the *weighing* of the pros and cons. Our question now is 'Which consideration, or combination of considerations, is the weightiest?' Just as in the answer to our first series of questions we employed consideration-making beliefs, so here we employ *beliefs about the superiority of one type of reason over another*. These "rules of superiority" tell us which reasons *within a given type*, and *which types*, are superior to which. We all think, for instance, that the fact that we would enjoy fishing and that we would enjoy tennis are reasons of the same sort. They may conflict on a particular occasion for it may be impossible to do both. We then ask, 'Which would we enjoy most?' If we enjoy tennis more than fishing, then in the fact that we would enjoy tennis we have a better, weightier reason than in the fact that we would enjoy fishing.

Similarly, we employ principles of the superiority of one type of reason over another. We all believe that reasons of self-interest are superior to reasons of mere pleasure, that reasons of long-range interest outbalance reasons of short-range interest, and reasons of law, religion, and morality outweigh reasons of self-interest. On the other hand, there is considerable uncertainty about whether and when law is superior to morality, religion to law, and morality to religion.

As we have seen, it is most important to remember that the question 'Which type of consideration is superior to which?' is not identical with the question 'What sorts of fact tend to move most people or the agent most?' This is easily overlooked because, as shown previously, considerations are facts and in

99

being moved by considerations we are, therefore, moved by facts. But we can be said to be moved by considerations only if we are moved by these facts not merely in virtue of their intrinsic moving power but in virtue of the power we attribute to them *qua* considerations. The same fact may move different people in different ways. We can always ask whether people *ought* to be moved by a fact in the way in which they actually are moved by it.

We are, for instance, convinced that legal considerations are superior to considerations of self-interest, that the reason *against* selling my Chevrolet to Paddy (the reason which I have in the fact that doing so would be illegal) is better than the one *for* selling it (which I have in the fact that it would produce a very high profit). Yet we are quite ready to concede that many people would yield to the temptation to make such a high profit, for the fact that they would make it has perhaps a greater moving power than the fact that they would be doing something illegal. 'How great is the power of these facts to move various people?' is an empirical question. Answers to it will vary from person to person and from society to society, but these answers are logically independent of the answer to the question 'Which reason or type of reason is superior or better?' [4]

Suppose it is granted, then, that the main considerations involved in our problems are considerations of self-interest and illegality. The second step of my deliberation, leading to the final answer, can then be set out as follows.

  (i) (In the fact that selling now would be illegal) I have a reason *against* selling now.
 (ii) (In the fact that selling now would yield a high profit) I have a reason *for* selling now.
(iii) My reason against selling is a reason of law.
 (iv) My reason for selling is a reason of self-interest.
  (v) Reasons of law are superior to reasons of self-interest.

---

[4] For a further discussion of this, see Chapter Six, section 2.

(vi) Hence my reason against selling is superior to my reason for selling.

(vii) Therefore, in the fact that selling now would be illegal I have an overriding reason against selling now.

The correctness of the final outcome of my deliberation thus depends on the correctness and completeness of the first step, the finding of the considerations relevant, and on the correctness of the second step, the ascertaining of the relative weights of the considerations involved. It has already been explained how we guard against errors at the first stage. How can we guard against making mistakes at the second stage? The important steps here are (iii), (iv), and (v). Together (iii) and (iv) consist in the correct classification of the reasons we have. This step is important because our beliefs about the superiority of one reason over another may be formulated in terms of the types of reason there are. Moral reasons have a very high reputation. That is to say, we think that moral reasons are superior to most or all other types. Hence, many reasons are claimed to be moral which are not. For if they are believed to be moral, then in virtue of the high reputation they enjoy, these reasons will tend to be given a correspondingly great weight. All sorts of reasons, from self-interest to the wildest superstitions, are therefore passed off as moral reasons. Hence, too, moral reasons are beginning to lose their deservedly high reputation, for people accept many reasons as moral which are not and which they clearly see do not deserve to be evaluated highly. Moreover, we can evaluate correctly the popular beliefs about the superiority of one type of reason over another only if we are quite clear what are the criteria for saying that a reason is of a certain sort, for only then can we tell whether giving a certain weight to that sort of consideration is justified. In Chapter Twelve, I shall deal more fully with this particular problem.

Step (v) raises no special difficulties, for it consists merely in the correct application of the principles of superiority, and this involves merely the difficulties inherent in all cases of applying general rules to particular instances.

5 PRIMA-FACIE REASONS AND REASONS ON BALANCE

We can now review the whole procedure of deliberation. We are setting out to answer the question 'Which course of action has the weight of reason behind it?' or, what comes to the same thing, 'What ought I to do?' In answering this question, we are going through a preliminary stage of setting out those facts about the proposed line of action which are pros and those which are cons, respectively. Every fact which is a pro sets up a presumption that I ought, and every fact which is a con sets up a presumption that I ought not, to do the thing in question. Any one of these presumptions can be rebutted or confirmed later *by the weighing* of the various pros and cons. A given presumption is rebutted if some other reason or combination of reasons is found *weightier* than the one which has given rise to the original presumption. In other words, the fact that I have a reason for or against entering on the proposed line of action *does not entail* that I ought or ought not to enter on it —it merely "presumptively implies" it. That is to say, it must be taken to imply that I ought or ought not to enter on it un-less, later on, in the weighing of considerations, I find some that are weightier than this one. In that case, the original pre-sumptive implication has been rebutted.

The term 'presumption' is borrowed from legal language, and 'presumptive implication' is based on it. To give an ex-ample from legal reasoning: Concerning the life of any person, a court does not presume anything. However, one or the other of the interested parties can establish a presumption that the person in question is dead if it can be shown that his closest relative or any other person who, from the nature of the case, would be expected to hear from him has not in fact heard from him in seven years. In the absence of any further information, it must be accepted that this person is dead. But further evidence can be produced to rebut this presumption of death. Someone, for instance, may produce a witness who testifies that he has seen the person recently. In the absence of any further evidence, the original presumption has then been rebutted and replaced by the opposite, that he is now alive. But this presumption can again be rebutted, and indeed conclusively refuted, if a reliable witness testifies that he has seen the person die.

To say that a certain fact is a consideration, a pro or a con, is to say that this fact gives rise to a presumption, namely, that the agent ought or ought not to enter on the course of action in relation to which the fact is a pro or a con. Exactly the same point is made when it is claimed that some reasons are only *prima-facie* reasons, or reasons *other things being equal*. All that is meant is that the facts which are the reasons give rise merely to a presumption that the agent ought or ought not to enter on the line of action contemplated. Similarly, the claim that sometimes the word 'ought' is only a 'prima-facie ought' can be explained as follows. 'Because selling the car would be illegal, you ought not to sell it' means no more than that, other things being equal, the person addressed ought not to sell it, that unless he has some overriding reason to the contrary he ought not to sell it.

In contrast with this, someone might say to me that I ought not to sell the car now, meaning thereby that, *all things considered*, I ought not to sell it, that in his view no other contrary reason could be offered capable of overriding the reason or reasons on which he bases his judgment. We may call such a reason or such "an ought" a reason or "ought" *on balance* or, following Ross, a reason *sans phrase*.

6 PRESUMPTIVE REASONS

The distinction between reasons prima facie and reasons on balance must be kept apart from the distinction between presumptive and nonpresumptive reasons. Both distinctions are concerned with facts which give rise to a presumption. However, to say that some fact is a prima-facie reason is to say that it gives rise to the presumption that the agent on balance ought or ougth not to enter on a certain line of action. To say that something is a presumptive reason is merely to say that some fact gives rise to the presumption that it is a prima-facie reason. If the former presumption is rebutted, then it is still true that prima facie, though not on balance, the agent ought or ought not to enter on this course of action. If the latter presumption is rebutted, then it is not even true that the agent ought or ought not *prima facie* to enter on it.

Jones derives much pleasure from eating cucumber salad and cream. But he invariably gets a stomach-ache afterwards. We believe that the fact that one would derive pleasure from doing something is a good reason for doing it. Hence (if our belief is true) in this fact Jones has a reason for eating cucumber salad and cream. On the other hand, we also believe that in the fact that something gives us pain we have a reason against doing the thing in question. Hence (if our belief is true) Jones has a reason against eating cucumber salad and cream. If he wants to do what has the weight of reason behind it, he has to determine which of the two conflicting considerations is the weightier. If nothing else is involved, such as damage to his health, it will all hinge on whether the pleasure of eating outweighs the pain resulting from it, whether the enjoyment now is worth the ache later.

Contrast this with the case of James, who is a masochist. James derives pleasure from certain activities and experiences such as being whipped. Here it would seem that in the fact that he derives pleasure from these activities he has a reason for engaging in them, and in the fact that they cause him pain, a reason against. But on closer inspection, this turns out not to be so. For the fact that he derives pleasure from these activities is merely a presumptive reason, which can be and is rebutted by the fact that he derives pleasure from giving pain to himself. Note the difference. Jones in deriving pleasure from the cucumber salad and cream unavoidably causes himself pain later. But he derives the pleasure from the cucumber salad, not from the pain it causes. He would derive the same pleasure, or more, if he could avoid the pain connected with it. But James's pleasure is not derived just from whipping himself but from the pain which it causes him. If he were anesthetized so as not to feel the pain of the whipping, he would derive no, or less, pleasure from it. Jones's pleasure is *unavoidably linked with* his pain. James's pleasure is *taken in* his own pain. In eating cucumber salad and cream Jones may or may not have followed the better reason; at any rate he had a (prima-facie) reason for eating it. In whipping himself, James does not have a (prima-facie) reason at all. The fact—which he may mention in explanation or justification—that his pursuit gives him pleasure does indeed give rise to a presumption that he has a reason for his pursuit. But this presumption is rebutted when the nature of the pleasure is revealed. James cannot even claim that he acted in accordance with the admittedly weaker of two conflicting reasons. For he did not have *two* conflicting prima-facie reasons. He had only two conflicting *presumptive* reasons, one of which must be rebutted. One of James's "reasons" is only the semblance of a reason.

7 SUMMARY

Summing up, we can say that deliberating is a subsidiary calculative procedure. It is subsidiary because we engage in it for the sake of getting certain results which are intended to determine our conduct. Decision is deliberately postponed and made dependent on the outcome of deliberation. I might instead have spun a coin and determined to act in one way if heads, in another if tails, came top. But I have resolved to act in whichever way is supported by the outcome of my deliberation, that is, in that way which has the weight of reason behind it. Finding what is supported by the best reasons is a rule-guided and somewhat formalized activity consisting of two steps, surveying the facts and weighing the reasons. The facts are surveyed with a view to determining those which are relevant reasons. I do this by bearing in mind my convictions about what constitute good reasons, my consideration-making beliefs, for example, that doing something would be enjoyable to me, or in my interest, or harmful to someone else, or against the law, or immoral, and so on. This primary deliberation may at any moment become an examination of the question whether my consideration-making beliefs are true. This latter question will be discussed in Chapter Twelve.

The second step in my deliberation consists in weighing those facts which my first step has revealed as relevant. It is not enough to know which reasons speak for and which against entering on a certain course of action; I must also know which are the strongest or best reasons. Here, too, I am helped by certain beliefs, the rules of priority which I take over from my social environment. It is generally agreed in our society that moral reasons are superior to reasons of self-interest, reasons of long-range interest superior to reasons of short-range interest, and reasons of self-interest superior to mere pleasure or pain. I must postpone until Chapter Twelve the discussion of the question whether the beliefs prevalent in our society are correct or not.

Four

Individual Rules of Reason

IN this chapter and in Chapters Five and Seven I shall examine
the various rules of reason which are currently accepted in our
society. In a later chapter (Twelve), it will be our task to determine whether any or all of these beliefs are true or false.
If we cannot establish their truth or falsity, then clearly deliberation will be altogether useless. For our purposes, we shall
divide rules of reason into individual, social, and moral. In the
present chapter I shall deal with individual, in Chapter Five
with social, and in Chapter Seven with moral rules of reason.
Individual rules of reason are those which concern only single
persons, whether the agent himself (self-regarding) or someone
else (other-regarding). Again, they may be short-range or long-
range, depending on whether they concern themselves merely
with the present moment or a very short slice of the future
or whether they take in life as a whole or major portions
of it.

The Moral Point of View

1 SELF-REGARDING RULES OF REASON

1.1 *Short-range*

Enjoyment. There are two opposite ways in which we may feel about or react to what we are doing or what is being done to us, what we live through, experience, observe to happen, hear about, or know to be the case. These two ways of feeling about things can be formulated by means of several expressions: we may like or dislike something, we may find it enjoyable or painful, agreeable or disagreeable, pleasant or unpleasant.

Where these feelings are occasioned by something directly or indirectly under our control, there the fact that we feel in these ways is generally thought to constitute a reason for or against our doing it. That we find an activity (fishing), something being done to us (having our back scratched), a living through something (a bombardment), an experience (flying), a sensation (pins and needles) enjoyable, pleasant, or agreeable is thought a reason for doing it, having it done, living through it, experiencing it, feeling it, and, therefore, a reason for bringing it about or bringing it on where we cannot simply do it; on the other hand, if it is painful, unpleasant, unenjoyable, it is thought a reason against it.

How do we know that we are now finding something enjoyable or pleasant or agreeable or the opposite? To answer this, we must distinguish the case when we say sincerely and without being asked, 'I am enjoying this,' 'This is very pleasant,' or 'How enjoyable this is' from the case when we make these remarks in reply to a question. We are moved to say these things sincerely (that is, not from politeness or in order to curry favor) only if we *feel like* saying them, and feeling like this is part of enjoying ourselves. There are other features: we want to continue with our activity, we are absorbed by it, our eyes shine, we have a cheerful expression, we tend to smile and look happy, and so on. The opposite is the case when we find something unpleasant. When we say such things because we feel like saying them, we are not making any assertions or claims, we are simply releasing or expressing our enjoyment.[1]

Such utterances of mine constitute evidence for another person's claim that I am enjoying myself, unless I am being polite or trying to curry favor. If, in reply to a question whether I am enjoying myself, I cannot immediately give an answer, thereby releasing my joy or boredom, I might then look for the same signs by which others tell whether I am enjoying myself. However, the very fact that I cannot give an immediate reply is a strong indication that I am not enjoying myself very much, for if I did I would be bubbling over with enjoyment. If I can find no indication at all, then it is clear that I am neither enjoying myself nor not enjoying myself. I feel neutral.

That I am *now* enjoying a certain activity in which I am engaged cannot be a consideration for engaging or for continuing in it. It cannot have been a consideration before I started, for I was not then, of course, enjoying it; it cannot be a reason for continuing, for I may not continue to enjoy it. Only the fact that I *would* enjoy doing something *if* I did it can be a reason for doing it; that I would enjoy it if I continued, a reason for continuing to do it. It is more difficult to tell whether I *would* enjoy doing something if I did it now than it is to tell whether I am enjoying something I am already doing. It involves the judgment that what I am about to do is of a certain sort and that I normally enjoy doing that sort of thing, and also the judgment that there is no particular reason why I should not now enjoy it, as when I normally enjoy fishing but would not now because the weather is bad for it.

---

[1] Cf. Gilbert Ryle, *The Concept of Mind* (London: Hutchinson's University Library, 1949), pp. 187 ff.

How do I tell that I enjoy things of a certain sort? It is comparatively easy to be sure that I enjoyed last evening but not so easy to say *why*. Was it because I enjoy French films, or French films about certain delicate subjects which only the French know how to handle, or because I enjoy this sort of film music or because the color photography was superb or because of all of these things? 'Do I enjoy going to the pictures?' is therefore more difficult to answer than 'Did I enjoy the pictures last night?' And 'Would I enjoy doing this?' involves a judgment of what *sort* of thing doing *this* is, and whether I enjoy doing *this sort* of thing. Such judgments could be erroneous, but most people are able on most occasions to get them right. It is only comparatively seldom that we had looked forward to doing something which we expected to enjoy and which has proved disappointing in the end.

Desire. Another self-regarding rule of reason is this: actions which will satisfy a craving, longing, or desire of the agent are supported by reason. The fact that the agent now has a particular craving, longing, or desire which would be satisfied by entering on a particular line of action is a consideration (for that agent) in favor of doing so.

In order to be able to employ this particular type of reason, we must be able to tell when we have a craving, desire, or longing and what it is for. If we do not know the object of our desire, we call it a longing or yearning. If the object of our desire is the consumption of something, such as chocolates or cigarettes, we speak of a craving. If it is strong, arises regularly, and is satisfied habitually, we speak of an addiction. We can tell that we have one or the other of these by a feeling of restlessness, an inability to work, to concentrate, or to enjoy our current activity or rest. We recognize it as a craving or desire *for something in particular* if we know what would satisfy it, that is, would set it pleasurably at rest. It is an empirical question how we come to know what will set our restlessness at rest. We may have innate impulses to do the appropriate thing, or we may learn by trial and error.

The main difference between enjoyment and desire is that the latter involves a felt impulse toward doing something, the former does not. We may know that we would enjoy fishing or playing tennis or going to the pictures or listening to music, though we do not feel any impulse to do one of them. We say that we have such a desire only if we feel an impulse to do one of these things and feel restless and frustrated when we cannot do it. Eating strawberries and ice cream is enjoyable whether or not we have a craving or desire for them, whether we are hungry or not.

That we enjoy this and don't enjoy that, desire this and don't desire that, are "brute facts" about ourselves. Other people often have different desires and aversions from our own. As a matter of fact, most human beings are very much alike in what they find painful, but differ considerably in what they find enjoyable, pleasant, or agreeable. On the other hand, everybody must agree that the fact that he would enjoy doing something is a reason for him to do it; that he would not enjoy it, a reason for him not to do it. That there is good fishing in a certain holiday resort is a reason for some people, not for others, to spend their holiday there. What makes it a reason for some is that *they* enjoy fishing. It is a reason for *all* those who enjoy fishing.

That we enjoy doing something—a "brute fact" about ourselves—must be distinguished from the fact that we like to do something, which is not a "brute fact" but is dependent on reasons. It is of course true that sometimes we use 'like' to mean the same as 'enjoy.' I may say, 'I like fishing' when I mean the same as 'I enjoy fishing.' But sometimes they are used differently. We can, for instance, ask 'Why?' as in 'Why do you like to pay your debts?' whereas we cannot ask, in the same sense,

'Why do you enjoy fishing?' I like to pay my debts so that my credit should remain good or because I think it the decent thing to do. But I have and could have no reason for enjoying fishing. I just enjoy it.

This may be doubted. After all, we can ask, 'Why do you enjoy hot baths?' or 'Why do you enjoy fishing?' and we can answer it by saying, 'I enjoy a hot bath because I love that tingling warm feeling I get when it's really hot.' But this is a very different question from the previous one. It is never a request for my *reason for* enjoying it, since enjoying something is not an activity, not something I can be said to be doing. Hence the question is merely a request for an explanation [2] of my enjoyment, that is, for that particular feature of a hot bath which I enjoy and in the absence of which I would not enjoy it. I may enjoy everything about a hot bath, or perhaps just that tingling sensation it gives me. 'Why do you enjoy a hot bath?' is completely answered when I have enumerated the features I enjoy. There comes a point when I must say, 'For no particular reason at all. I just enjoy that tingling sensation.'

It might be objected that this is too simple an account. Sensitive ladies can no longer enjoy their steak after the story of the slaughterhouse has been told. This arouses their disgust and horror just as the sight of the slaughter would. That is their reason for not enjoying steak. Moreover, these ladies may have a bad conscience about it. They may feel that eating steak helps to perpetuate this method of slaughter, and that is a further reason for not enjoying steak.

But this objection is untenable. That these ladies would not enjoy witnessing the slaughter in the slaughterhouses is not *their reason (justification) for not enjoying steak*, it is *the reason (explanation) why* they can or do no longer enjoy it.[3] The pic-

---

[2] Cf. Chapter Six, section 2.

[3] For a detailed discussion of the difference between explanation and justification, see Chapter Six, section 2.

ture of cattle being slaughtered *interferes* with their enjoyment of eating steak. And their bad conscience is again not a reason for not enjoying steak, but a reason for not eating it. That they have such a reason may further spoil their enjoyment. It is notorious that some people cannot enjoy doing things which they would be able to do only with a bad conscience.

In the case of liking something, on the other hand, we can always ask 'Why?' in the sense of asking for someone's reason *for liking it* and not merely for an explanation of why he likes it. That I, as a matter of fact, enjoy doing something is a reason for me to like it. That I like to do it can never be a reason for enjoying it. That I have been given a certain injection or that I have been hypnotized or conditioned in a certain way cannot be a reason for liking or disliking it, though it may well be the reason (explanation) why I no longer like or dislike it, and equally why I no longer enjoy it or why I fail to enjoy it.

Thus enjoying and liking are comparatively independent of each other. There are plenty of things which I do not enjoy doing, but which nevertheless I like to do for some reason or other. I like to pay my debts on time, I like to visit my mother's grave at least once a year, I like to have my cold shower and my run before breakfast every morning, and so on. Conversely, there are lots of things I enjoy doing though I don't like to do them for one reason or another. Thus I do not like to pick a quarrel or to talk about myself, though I would enjoy doing these things if ever I did do them.

To sum up. Asking 'Why?' in the case of enjoying something is always asking precisely *what* it is that one enjoys and never asking for a reason for enjoying it; in the case of liking, on the other hand, it is often asking for a *reason for* liking it. That someone likes to do something is not always a "brute fact" about how he feels. That someone enjoys doing something always is such a brute fact.

That we like or do not like to do something is not, therefore, another brute fact about ourselves, as is the fact that we enjoy doing it or that we don't. That we like to do something may or may not be a good reason for doing it, depending on whether we have good or bad reasons for liking it. If my reason for 'I like to take my Vitagen B tablets every morning' is that I think it will make me strong, then, if the latter is false, that I like to have my Vitagen B tablets every morning is a bad reason for 'I must go and buy another bottle of Vitagen B.'

Want. Is the fact *that one wants to do something* a reason for doing it? We must distinguish two different senses of 'want.' If I say in a restaurant or at home to my wife, 'I want a cup of tea,' then this is rightly interpreted as a request. In these cases I am entitled to make this sort of request and I can expect to have it complied with. In these cases it would be true to say that I wanted a cup of tea. In such a context, that I want a cup of tea means only that I have made or am about to make or would make if I had the chance a request for a cup of tea. It does not assert or imply anything about my state of mind.

But now my wife might be difficult. She might ask, 'Do you really want another cup? You have had five already.' She knows, of course, that in one sense I want one, but she doubts whether in another I do. What is this other sense? Roughly it is the same as 'Do you really desire another cup? Would you really enjoy another cup? Are you really still thirsty or dissatisfied because you have not had enough tea? Do you not perhaps want something else?'

The fact that one wants something, in the first sense, is not a reason for having it. It is only if I have a reason for requesting a cup of tea that I have reason on my side when making the request. My wife is quite entitled to ask, 'Why do you want (ask for) another cup? You can't be thirsty any more.' But if I want something in the second sense, that is, have a craving, desire, longing, or "feel like" it, then I do indeed have a reason. I have already discussed this type of reason under 'Desire.'

Even at this low level of deliberation, we shall often need some ingenuity in order to avoid mistakes. Satisfying our desires will often require a series of complicated steps to bring about the situation, state of affairs, or arrangement which is necessary to satisfy them. Doing the things which we would enjoy doing will involve similar difficulties. Desires will conflict, that is, the satisfaction of one will mean the frustration of others and we shall have to weigh against each other the various reasons we have in order to see which course of action has the weightiest on its side.

1.2 Long-range

Self-interest. In an orderly society, people's lives follow certain patterns. We do not live from day to day, having no idea what the morrow will bring. Most of us, through our occupations, membership in a family, class, church, trade union, or club, have mapped out for us certain routines and careers, a line of progress from youth to old age. The important decisions or accidents determining the patterns of the rest of our life occur early in our youth. We decide to become doctors, businessmen, or soldiers, or our parents make the decisions for us, or the economic or political conditions of our society relieve us of the burden or deprive us of the opportunity to decide for ourselves. Once our career and perhaps our social status is determined, we set ourselves almost automatically certain aims or goals. We naturally adopt certain points of view, because our position in society determines for us what is in our interest. There are certain factors which would be generally recognized to promote or retard our interests, and different positions in society determine different developments, conditions, and states of affairs as being to our advantage or disadvantage.

The Moral Point of View

There is, for instance, general agreement that it is in our interest to have a bigger rather than a smaller income, to belong to an upper rather than a lower class, to have a higher rather than an inferior position in our profession, trade union, or church, and so on. In all branches of life, there are recognized upward and downward moves on the ladder of success. Whatever lifts us a step up that ladder is believed to be in our interest.

How do we know that this is really so? Ordinarily, we check claims to the effect that some development is in our interest by the use of certain criteria, that it is good for our health, our career, our professional group, our class, our country. If a given development, say the election of a certain party, a trade crisis in some other country, or a war somewhere, answers to any of these criteria, then that development is thought to be in our interest. There will not normally be any difficulty in principle about how to ascertain whether a particular occurrence satisfied one of the criteria. But it is possible that sometimes we may not have enough factual knowledge to tell, as when we don't know whether exercise after the age of fifty is good for our health or whether the nationalization of coal mines is in the interest of the coal-consuming public. Or we may not be able to say whether something is in a friend's interest because it satisfies both a positive and a negative criterion, as when Jones is promoted to be manager of a provincial branch of a big bank, which is a move up since he is now a manager, but also a move down since he is now away from the main office where the really good positions are offered.

How do we tell that something really is a criterion of being in our interest and not merely generally believed to be? The criteria we learn to use—I have in mind criteria such as earning a bigger salary, promotion, marrying a wealthy or titled person, improving our health—are, in most cases and other things being equal, real criteria of our interest. But how do we know this and how do we tell in which cases they are and in which they are not?

The answer is simple. People have certain life plans leading to certain goals and allowing for certain aims, ambitions, aspirations, and perhaps ideals. For most people the patterns and goals are roughly the same: to have a satisfying occupation, a loving husband or wife and a few children, to be free from poverty, anxiety, and ill-health, to live to a ripe old age and be decently buried, and the like. Most people, moreover, have ambitions, perhaps to become heads of their departments, to travel round the world, or to "consume conspicuously." Some people have aspirations such as to lead decent and useful lives, to make lasting contributions to their special field of interest or skill, or to be fearless and faithful missionaries. Some have ideals such as to be just to everyone, to love their neighbors as much as themselves, or to serve their country unselfishly.

We say that something is not really in someone's interest when it would not satisfy or help in the realization of his life plan or the satisfaction of his ambitions, aspirations, and ideals, even though it would do so for most ordinary people. A man who wants to make a lasting contribution to his subject might be better off as a badly paid research assistant in a comparatively small university than as a well-paid but administratively overburdened professor in a large one. Promotion to such a post would not be in his *real* interest, for he would be prevented from making the contribution he wants and is perhaps capable of making, and this will frustrate his greatest ambition and aspiration, though satisfying his minor ones.

This contrast between what is in someone's *real* interest and what might falsely be thought to be comes out in such expressions as 'getting on,' 'doing well,' 'being successful.' These expressions mark the sort of things which are generally thought to be in a person's interest and, indeed, usually are. Most people simply want to get on. They are not in any way frustrated by doing well or getting on—only a very few people are. But if someone is, say, a poet or a priest, then getting on is *not really in his interest*.

The ramifications of what is and what is not in my interest are very wide. A publisher writes to me saying that he is willing to publish a book of mine on a certain subject, as well as the work of some of my colleagues. Is it in my interest to tell them? One of them has a book ready on the same subject as I. If he heard about it, he might submit his draft before I can finish mine. He will be my competitor for an important chair. Is it in my real interest that he should have one *more* book to his credit? Is it in my real interest to get that chair? I certainly think it is; hence (if I am right) it is not in my interest to have strong competitors, hence not in my interest to tell him about the possibilities of publication.

There may be stronger reasons still for saying that it is not in my interest to tell him. It may be my life's ambition to become a professor in just that university. The present offer may be my only chance. It may be one of my highest aspirations to be able to teach there in a certain way, to promote there certain religious, moral, and political ideals. My colleague does not share my views and would pursue very different aims. All these things are good reasons for saying that it is not in my interest to tell him.

2 OTHER-REGARDING RULES OF REASON

Enjoyment. We must now ask ourselves whether the way other people feel about something is regarded as a reason for us to act in certain ways. Is the fact that Jones is pleased by what we are doing or enjoys what we are doing to him, or that Jones would enjoy a state of affairs or situation or item of information which we could bring about or let him have, regarded as a good reason why we should do these things?

Precisely what are we asking? Consider the case of Aunt Elizabeth who would enjoy a visit from her nephew Charles. Suppose that Charles does not care for his aunt, but that he cares for his mother and that his mother would be pleased if he visited her sister. Let us say that Charles enjoys pleasing his mother, or at any rate likes to please her from a sense of duty or a feeling of filial piety although he does not actually enjoy doing so. In that case, he has a reason for visiting his aunt, because doing so is also *eo ipso* pleasing his mother and he enjoys doing, or likes to do, that. If he hesitates, his mother might appeal to him in this way: 'If you don't do it for your aunt's sake, do it for mine.' This is not the exact case we want, because here the agent has at any rate a self-regarding reason, that he enjoys or likes pleasing his mother.

Suppose now that his mother does not care any more than Charles about her sister. Has he then a reason to visit her? We would not urge him on by saying, 'Do it for your aunt's sake,' since we know that he does not care about his aunt. He cannot therefore be expected to do anything *for her sake*. But there is still the fact that she would be pleased if he visited her, grieved if he did not. Does this constitute a reason even if the thought of his aunt's being pleased or grieved, respectively, *has no appeal of any sort?* If, all other things being equal, Charles were to visit his aunt, we would have to say that he was acting in accordance with reason, not contrary to it. The fact that he is indifferent toward his aunt is irrelevant. If the woman were a complete stranger, he would still have the same reason, namely, that she would be pleased by such a visit and lonely if no one visited her.

Must we perhaps say that this reason merely justifies, but does not bind him, that is, that while visiting her would not be contrary to reason, not visiting her would be equally in accordance with it? But we have exactly the same grounds for saying that the fact that she would enjoy my visit is a binding reason for me to visit her, as for saying this about the fact that I would enjoy it. Since we mean only 'prima-facie reason,' 'reason all other things being equal,' there can be no difference between the two cases. For a prima-facie reason is as much a reason *for* doing something as a reason *against not* doing it. It is only reasons on balance which may be merely justifying without binding us. We feel that there is a difference between our two cases, because we do not carefully banish from our mind all counterbalancing reasons. If we are tired, have other things to do, or have other enjoyments open to us, then the fact that Aunt Elizabeth would be pleased may not be sufficiently weighty to bind us in the final outcome of our deliberations.

Consider a simpler case. Suppose I ask myself whether I have a reason for letting someone talk to me about her troubles. Suppose that she enjoys doing so and that it is all the same to me. In that case, I would surely be said to have a reason for letting her talk and a reason against stopping her. Suppose that she just prattles on without minding whether she continues or has to stop and that I don't mind what she does. Then I must be said to have no reason for stopping her but also no reason for not stopping her, beyond the general presumption that I need some reason for doing anything whatsoever, no reason for remaining inactive. Suppose now that I feel ever so slightly irritated by her talk and she does not care one way or the other; then I would be regarded as having a reason for stopping her and none for letting her continue. But if she enjoys chatting with me, then I must be said to have a reason against stopping her and a reason for letting her go on.

It is even clearer that I have a reason against doing a certain thing when another person would find my doing it unpleasant or painful and, *mutatis mutandis,* in those cases where someone else likes or dislikes, wants or does not want, desires or does not desire, a certain thing. These facts also are generally regarded as reasons for or against doing something. There is no relevant difference between short-range and long-range reasons, hence exactly the same considerations apply there also. The fact that something is (or is not) in someone else's interest is also regarded as a reason for (or against) doing the thing in question.

If we ask ourselves to which reasons, other things being equal, we attach the greater weight, to the self-regarding or other-regarding, the answer is that, if the two reasons are of exactly the same sort and importance, then we always (other things being equal) attach greater weight to the self-regarding reason. When there is a great difference between the two, then the question is sometimes open, as when by entering on a certain business transaction we would gain £10, whereas another firm would lose £10,000 or would be ruined by it. In such a case, either course of action would be in accordance with, neither of them contrary to, reason, though of course one would be the decent thing to do, the other would be selfish. (For a further discussion of these points, see also Chapter Twelve, sections 1 and 2.)

Five

Social Rules of Reason

SOME types of consideration imply the existence of social rules. We could never tell whether a given course of action was contrary to or in accordance with or required by custom, law, manners, etiquette, or good taste if there were no social rules to give a determinate content to these expressions. It is only because the law, manners, or customs of a given society forbid or prescribe certain types of behavior that we can tell whether some course of action is objectionable from the point of view of law, manners, or customs and that we can attach any weight to the consideration that some line of action would be illegal, rude, or unconventional.

Our first question must, therefore, be 'What are social rules and how do different types differ from one another?' There are many senses of the word 'rule' irrelevant to our inquiry which, however, have often been confused with one another and with those that are relevant. Discussions involving the notion of 'natural law' from Antiphon to the present day have been vitiated by the failure to distinguish between two senses of 'rule,' namely, 'regulation' and 'regularity.' It is quite impossible to clarify the complicated relationship between the individual's and the group's morality if the various senses of 'rule' are not kept apart. I shall begin, therefore, by setting out six different senses of the word 'rule': regulations, mores, maxims and principles, canons, regularities, and rules of procedure.

1 VARIOUS SENSES OF 'RULE'

We are all familiar with traffic regulations or with rules of a library, for example, "As from June 1st, cars must not be parked in such and such areas," "No fires must be kindled in the Library," etc. Regulations can be thought up, formulated, proposed, adopted or laid down, promulgated, altered, and finally abrogated. They are not valid or in force until they have been properly adopted or laid down. To speak of regulations makes sense only because they may or may not be in force. For them to be in force presupposes the whole social apparatus of rule-enforcement. There could be no regulations in a world of hermits or in the circle of the family. Regulations divide behavior into that which is in accordance with them and that which is contrary to them. When people know about regulations, they may observe or break them. Rules in the sense of regulations cannot be true or false, and they can be discovered only after they have been laid down. Their discovery consists in the discovery that they have been properly laid down. This sort of rule can be said to apply or not to apply to certain sorts of people and certain sorts of circumstances. The rules mentioned above, for example, apply to everybody planning to park cars in the area indicated and to everybody planning to kindle a fire in the library, respectively.

Regulations are simply a special and highly sophisticated case of another kind of rule exemplified by customs, rules of etiquette, or manners. These are sometimes called 'mores.' When a child is taught to say 'Please' and 'Thank you,' always to look people in the eye when speaking to them, to shake hands with them when he is introduced, he is taught what is proper or well mannered or well behaved. Rules of this sort have not been laid down by any one in particular nor are they modified or abrogated by specially authorized persons. Nevertheless, they "hold" in certain groups and usually vary from one group to another. Their "life" depends entirely on their being *taught* to the young and on social pressures. It is only because people generally adopt certain encouraging attitudes to conformers and discouraging attitudes to nonconformers that we can say that a group *has* these rules, that these rules are rules *of* that group. In most other respects, regulations and this sort of rule are alike.

A third sense of 'rule' is that in which this word is a near-synonym of 'maxim' or 'principle.' A rule in this sense differs from a regulation in that ruler and subject are not different. If something is to be a regulation, it must be supported by some sort of sanction. If something is to be someone's maxim, it cannot be supported. Of course, 'Don't drink beer in pubs after six' may be Smith's maxim and also supported by a sanction, but it is so supported not because it is Smith's maxim but because it is also a regulation. If a maxim or principle is adopted, it becomes the maxim or principle of the person adopting it. If a regulation is adopted, it becomes the regulation of the group. Hence regulations can be obeyed and disobeyed, maxims cannot. One can find out about other people's maxims or principles only after these persons have adopted them. One could not find, to his surprise, that he had certain principles which he had never adopted. If he finds out or is told that he has been behaving in certain ways, say, always giving alms to beggars, this may be explained as the result of habit, but it may not correctly be described as his having acted *on the principle* "Always give alms to beggars."

Maxims and principles also differ from mores in not being supported by social pressures. The fact that someone has made it a rule not to smoke after lunch does not mean that this is part of the mores or customs of his group. It does not become so even if everyone has made it his custom. It does not become part of the mores until it is true to say that to smoke after lunch violates a custom of that group. And this cannot be said until there is some sort of social pressure against smoking after lunch, even if it is only mild disapproval.

'Rule' may be used synonymously with 'canon,' as in 'rules of strategy' or 'simple rules for fishermen.' Such rules are formulations of practical wisdom. Their aim is to furnish learners with simple verbal aids in their efforts to acquire a skill. The skill involved in formulating such rules is not, of course, the same skill as that imparted by observing these canons. The best gamesman or lifeman is not necessarily the best teacher of or writer about these matters. But the latter can learn from careful observation of the former.

A fifth sense of 'rule' is that exemplified in 'As a rule, he comes in just before closing time' or 'Depressions usually begin in the building trade.' Both these sentences may be said to be the formulations of a rule or, as it is sometimes put, of a regularity or uniformity. There is a certain regularity in or uniformity about his coming, or about depressions, which can be formulated in these ways. Rules in this sense are statements (or misstatements) of what is regular in or uniform about something. They can be true or false; they can be discovered. But they cannot be obeyed or disobeyed. In this they fundamentally differ from regulations.

The last sense of 'rule' we must consider is that which we find in expressions such as 'rules of chess' or 'rule of bridge.'

Rules in this sense are what constitutes the nature of a certain rule-determined activity. Playing a game, prosecuting someone, celebrating mass, conducting the marriage ceremony, making a will, or supplicating for a university degree are instances of such rule-determined activities. Going for a walk, having breakfast, making a pair of boots, skiing, are not rule-determined in this sense. If I do not know the constitutive rules of such a rule-determined activity, I cannot even begin to engage in it. If I do not know the canons of cobbling or fishing, of skiing or rock-climbing, I shall probably be a bad cobbler, fisher, and so forth. I might have a try and I might be lucky. But if I do not know the constitutive rules of chess, it does not even make sense to say that I am having a try at playing.

We wish to examine the nature of social rules, hence only two senses of the six distinguished just now are relevant here —'mores' and 'regulations.' For only these two senses imply the existence of social pressures in support of the rules, thereby making them social in the required sense: 'wanted and supported by the society,' 'belonging to the way of life of the society.' Regularities are not social rules since they are not even capable of being followed or disregarded. Maxims and principles are not rules of a society but of an individual. Canons simply state ways of doing things well, but society does not require one to follow them.

In classifying social rules, we consider differences under the various "dimensions" or "determinables" of social rules. We take into consideration the way a rule comes into being, changes, and ceases to exist; the way it is supported or sanctioned in the group; the way it is applied; the criteria used in determining whether it is good or bad of its kind; and, lastly, the grounds for having such a rule at all.

Thus, 'mores' differ from 'regulations' in the first and second dimensions. Regulations come into existence by being laid down, mores simply by coming to be supported; regulations change by being deliberately altered by the person authorized to do so, mores change when new types of conduct come to be either backed or rejected; regulations come to an end by being abolished, mores by ceasing to be supported. They also differ in the second dimension, for while mores are supported by comparatively indeterminate and unorganized pressures, those which support regulations are highly organized and determinate.

A more detailed examination of law and custom will further clarify the nature of two types of consideration involving social rules, namely, 'it is against the law' and 'it is not customary.' It will also exhibit the various "dimensions" along which different types of social rule may differ from each other.

2 LAW AND CUSTOM

What, then, is a law? In order to answer this question, we must reverse the procedure normally adopted. Instead of beginning with the definition of 'a law' followed by the explanation of the legal system of a given society as a body of such units, we should start by explaining what it is for a group to have a legal system and then define 'a law' as a certain sort of part of that system.

A group has a legal system if and only if there is in that group: (i) a person, or group of persons, recognized to be entitled and required to ascertain whether anyone has acted in a way to which certain rules of the group (called laws or regulations) attach certain consequences, for example, penalties, fines, and payments of compensation, and then to administer (or have administered) to such an offender the consequences affixed by these rules; and (ii) an established procedure of determining whether a given rule-formula is part of the legal system, that is, whether it is what we call 'a valid law.' Anything less standardized or formalized than that cannot be called a legal system. Societies which have not reached this stage of development are prelegal. They do not have a system even of primitive law.

It is not difficult to imagine how a primitive system of law might have developed in a prelegal society. Suppose we find a tribe in which rules are supported by social pressures of an unformalized kind only, that is, by a penalization of the culprit by the tribe as a whole. In a very small group this type of social pressure will be very effective. The breach of a rule in such a group cannot be concealed from everybody, and once somebody knows about it, everybody knows. The "backward-looking aspect of the social pressure" then comes into universal operation at once. No one in particular is charged with dealing with the offender. The group as a whole exerts pressure on him. He is cut or ridiculed by everybody, or excluded from the common food-gathering expeditions and thereby from getting any food, and so on.

Suppose now that it is found by such a group that quarrels frequently break out among its members and that ostracism of a rigid sort interferes with the group's food supply. Too many members of the group tend to be excluded and too little food is gathered. The tribe as a whole suffers. Suppose then that the elders of the tribe, or the chief, take it upon themselves to deal with such rule breaches. If this becomes customary, if dealing with rule breakers by everybody comes to be frowned upon, if the chief guards this as his right, then the first step has been taken in the establishment of a legal system. The specialization in the job of "bringing the rule breaker to justice," the separation of the functions of public prosecutor, defense lawyer, police, judge, prison warder, and executioner, are only further steps made possible and useful by the growth of the group.

There is, however, one other step of great importance, the development of the job we call 'legislating.' We can speak of a political society only after this development has occurred. Up to now, the only distinction mentioned between custom and law was the entrusting to a group of specialists of the task of detecting, and dealing with, lawbreakers. A change of laws was still brought about in the same way as a change in customs, namely, by changes in group mores. But this is notoriously a slow and uncertain business. If societies are to change quickly, there must be a more efficient method of changing the rules in accordance with which the group is to live. To bring about such changes by a reasoned decision is the function of the legislator. Politics is the activity of some or all members of the group designed to bring about or prevent legislation of certain sorts, and thereby sudden and enforceable changes in some parts of the group's way of life.

We can now say more clearly how law and custom differ from each other. Take first the question how particular laws and customs come into being, change, and disappear. It is a defining characteristic of 'custom' that a particular custom emerges as it acquires the backing of, changes by modifications in, and disappears by losing the support of, the appropriate social sanction. It is a contradiction in terms to say that Jones laid down, modified, or abolished a certain particular custom. Of course, the Prince of Wales, by being a leader of fashion, may "set the fashion." But he can be said to have set the fashion only if and because people follow him. Wearing cuffs on men's trousers is not the fashion in England simply because the Prince of Wales is doing so. It is only when people generally support the wearing of cuffs on trousers that this has become the fashion.

In the case of laws, this is not necessarily, normally, or typically so, although it may sometimes be. Typically, laws are created, modified, and abolished by the legislator's fiat. A rule-formula has become a valid law when the legislator has formally declared it so. It ceases to be law when the legislator abolishes it. The legislator's fiat "binds" the judge, that is, the man whose function it is to declare whether or not an individual's behavior is in accordance with, or contrary to, the law. The judge must accept what the legislator declares law. It is well known, however, that the highest courts of appeal, in declaring certain cases contrary to or in accordance with a given law, exercise to some extent the function of legislators. For their decisions in turn bind those of lower courts, just as laws do.

While this way of making, changing, and terminating laws is typical, it is not logically necessary. We would not refuse to call something a legal system simply because it did not have this method of creating, modifying, and ending laws. The first legal systems consisted of the prevalent customs written up by "wise men."

Law and custom also significantly differ along the second dimension of the concept of social rule, the way in which a social rule is supported or sanctioned in the group. Customs are supported by social pressures which are comparatively indeterminate, unformalized, unorganized; laws by those which are comparatively determinate, formalized, and organized.

Take law first. In this case the social pressure is determinate, because the law itself says what shall be the consequences if one or the other law is broken by someone. Anyone contemplating a breach of the law can find out beforehand exactly what will be the consequences. It is, on the whole, easier to predict for our society the legal consequences, if any, of an illegal act than the psychological, physiological, economic, or political consequences.

The social pressure is formalized, because in order to set the legal machinery in motion and to bring about the legal consequences, highly formalized activities are necessary, such as getting the public prosecutor to launch proceedings, to arrest the suspect, to charge him with murder, to hold a judicial preliminary examination, to arrange a trial, to get a conviction, and finally, perhaps, to have him hanged. For each type of breach of law, there is a well-known procedure, leading from a charge that someone has acted contrary to some law, to a judge's judgment of whether this is so or not, and to the dismissal of the charge or the imposition of that which the law provides in that kind of breach of the law.

The social pressure is highly organized, for nothing or little is left to the public at large. Most of the performances necessary to set the legal machinery in motion are carried out by professionals, by organs of society, for example, the police, the public prosecutor, the judge, the executioner.

On the other hand, in the case of custom, the social pressure is comparatively indeterminate. It is not certain in what way different members of the society will respond. Some may cut the offender, some may merely discontinue to invite him for dinner, others may refuse to give their daughter permission to marry him, others may dismiss him, try to get him dismissed, or merely refuse to employ him, and so on. The seriousness of the response will depend on how strongly they feel about it, on what they are in a position to do about it, and on many other factors. Of course, in primitive societies, where law has not yet replaced any of the functions of custom and where the social fabric is more closely knit, the differences will not be so great. For there the whole group will respond in a much more uniform way. Both law and custom, as we now understand it, are the successors of a state of affairs in which the distinction between the two is not yet drawn. All the same, this prelegal state of affairs is properly described as a state in which custom alone prevails, even though custom has here a more uniform and more efficient sanction than in our society.

In contrast with law, social pressures supporting customs are not formalized; there are no special formalized procedures to set any machinery in motion. Every member of the society acts spontaneously.

Lastly, the social pressures supporting customs are not organized, that is to say, no special organs of society are entrusted with the job of exerting the social pressure. Anyone and everyone responds in certain ways to the breach of an established custom.

There are no important differences in the way laws and customs are applied. It is part of the content of a law or custom to specify the groups of persons to whom it is meant to apply. Ex-servicemen's preference, military draft regulations, aliens' registration regulations, the custom that men should take their hats off in lifts, that they walk on that side of a lady which is nearer the gutter, that young girls should not wear make-up or go out with boys without a chaperone, from their very nature apply to certain groups of persons only.

It would lead too far afield to enumerate the criteria of good and bad laws or customs. It must suffice here to say that by and large they are similar. In both cases, we are mainly concerned with the desirability from one point of view or another of having just this particular practice or that *made universal* in the group. There are, however, certain special considerations in the case of laws, due to the fact that these are made by legislators. Hence we can ask—what we cannot ask in the case of customs—how well made the laws are, how clearly and fairly they are drawn up, and how well they are achieving the legislator's purpose.

Again, roughly the same considerations are used to justify our having customs and laws at all. Living outside groups with a way of life would be living in a state quite accurately described by Hobbes under the title "State of Nature" in which life is "solitary, poor, nasty, brutish, and short," if it is possible at all. However, to remedy this it is not necessary, as Hobbes claimed, to impose laws on men. Customs are enough to meet the need pointed out by Hobbes. Law needs an additional justification which is not hard to find. The main advantage of laws over customs is that a group of well-informed persons can meet the problems and difficulties confronting the group in the conditions of rapid social changes by a deliberate and immediate change of certain harmful details in the way of life of the whole group.

3 RELIGION

For the sake of comparison, let me add a few words about one other type of consideration involving rules, namely, the consideration that something is against one's religion, that it is sinful or contrary to the will of God. It is impossible, in this book, to speak about religion in general. For that would involve speaking not only about the Christian religion but also about how far a social institution may differ from it and still be called a religion. Christianity, which must serve as our model of religion as such, is a system of supernatural beliefs and rules supported by supernatural sanctions modeled on an earthly legal system. The world picture conveyed is that of a cosmic society created and ruled by a divine and perfect ruler, legislator, judge, and controller of prisons, who governs the world in accordance with his own law or plan. Human beings, his creatures, children, and subjects, are capable of glimpsing parts of this divine law and plan because of a certain faculty of cognizing it, the faculty of reason or "the natural light," and also because God, in his wisdom, has revealed this law to Moses on Mt. Sinai. Our religion claims to put us in possession of a higher sort of law supported by a higher and more perfectly working sort of sanction. Christianity, therefore, implies a composite world picture: that of an omnipotent magician who, by his fiat, creates things, that of a loving and just father issuing orders, and that of an omniscient and just legislator, judge, and executioner. The full implications of our religion are, therefore, incomprehensible to people who are at a prelegal stage of development, for this religion of ours involves the notions of 'law,' 'judge,' 'damnation,' all of which make sense only within a legal framework. Hence religious considerations, as we understand them, are nothing but special sorts of legal consideration.

There is, however, one important difference which will occupy us when discussing moral considerations. Law is a social phenomenon in every sense. There can be no personal laws, no personal legal convictions. The ordinary individual cannot have his own laws, his own legal convictions, his own verdicts or sentences. The expressions 'my law,' 'my verdict,' 'my sentence' can mean only 'law which I made,' 'verdict which I gave,' 'sentence which I passed,' and these activities are properly performed by the social organs specially entrusted with these tasks. The individual has simply to learn what *are* the laws of his society, and he has to conform to them. He can, through his own political activity, exercise a certain amount of pressure on the legislative organs, but that is all. For the rest he is simply subject to the existing legal system.

This is not so in the case of religion. True, the individual first absorbs his religion from his environment. He is taught the faith of his parents or his schoolteachers. But later, he may become a convert, or even invent his own creed. It does not make sense to say that a man has become a convert to another legal system. He can, of course, favor another legal system and work for its adoption, but he cannot simply become a member of that legal system by deciding to do so. A man can become a member (the sole member) of a hitherto nonexisting religion. A man cannot become a member of a hitherto nonexisting legal system.

The word 'custom' is ambiguous. We may use it to mean individual or social custom. 'It is my custom to smoke after lunch' or 'to drink wine with my meals' or 'to shave every morning' is perfectly compatible with the fact that I am the only one whose custom this is. It is also compatible with the fact that in my country it is not customary to do these things. In this case, if my customs were known, I would probably be called unconventional and treated accordingly.

However, it is important to stress that there is a logical gap between these two uses. If everyone in a group is a Christian, then the religion of the group is Christianity. But if everyone smokes after meals, then it is not necessarily the custom of the group to smoke after meals. It is only if not smoking after meals is in some way *contrary to custom* that smoking after meals has become the custom, or customary. It may, indeed, be the case that if almost every member of the group were a Christian considerable pressure would be exerted on the few atheists and Mohammedans to become Christians also. But this is not by any means logically necessary or even desirable. An excellent case can be made for religious tolerance. However, it does not even make sense to attempt to make a case for legal tolerance. There is an obvious sense in which everyone is himself the final authority on religion. In the same sense, the legislator is the final authority on law, the group as a whole on custom.

One further point. It is obviously possible to ascertain whether a given course of action is or is not contrary to custom, good manners, etiquette, or the law. It makes sense to say, 'It is (not) true that belching after meals is rude, unconventional, contrary to custom, illegal.' But it would not occur to anyone to ask whether the custom, convention, rule, or law against belching was true or not true. The only question we can ask at this level is whether the custom, convention, rule, or law is good or bad, civilized or uncivilized, desirable or undesirable.

Social rules of reason, then, are those involving custom, law, manners, etiquette, conventions, traditions. It is a social rule of reason accepted in our society that actions which are required by custom, law, manners, etiquette, conventions, and traditions have the support of reason, those which are prohibited by them are rejected by reason. That a line of action is required by one or all of these is, therefore, accepted as a pro; that it is prohibited, as a con.

4 LAWS AND COMMANDS

There is a type of reason for doing something which may be either personal or social, because it arises out of the perfectly normal presocial relationship between children and parents, but is much expanded in the social setup: the fact that something has been commanded.

One may, of course, say that the question whether a father is *entitled* to give his children orders does not arise until there is a social setup in which this might be either true or false. I am not at present concerned with this question. All I wish to show just now is how the fully fledged and socially acknowledged relationship between commander and commanded develops out of a perfectly natural and possibly presocial relationship between parents and children.

Small children are completely dependent on their parents. They cannot do anything without first being shown how to do it. Later on, as they manage to perform certain small tasks for themselves, they still dare not enter upon them without the parents' permission. They feel, of course, that parents have the power to stop them and also the responsibility for the consequences of their, the childrens', acts. This relation of superordination and subordination is, therefore, perfectly natural. There is nothing conventional in the arrangement whereby parents give orders or commands to children, issue prohibitions or forbid them to do things, are asked for and give or refuse permission to do this or that.

This perfectly natural relationship of superordination and subordination which holds between parents and children *in all fields of activity* is repeated in *special fields* of activity elsewhere. It obtains between teacher and pupil, commanding officer and subaltern, employer and employee, policeman and driver or pedestrian. In these special relationships and with regard to the limited activities defined by them, one person is superordinated, the other subordinated; one person can command or prohibit, give or refuse permission, and the other must obey.

There is next a similar but in many important respects different relationship, that between the legislator and those subject to the law, which has often been confused with the relationship just mentioned. Hobbes, for instance, says that "Law, properly is the word of him, that by right hath command over others." [1] Hence he concludes that "The Sovereign of a Common-wealth, be it an Assembly, or one Man, is not Subject to the Civill Lawes." [2] But this is to confuse the relation of one who has the right to command with one who has the right to legislate. To legislate is not to command or to forbid or give permission to someone or other, but it is *to say*, to decree *what shall be forbidden* and what allowed and what enjoined, in what circumstances and for what sort of person. To have the right to legislation is to have the right to mold the whole group's way of life. It does not necessarily exempt the legislator. The right to legislate is like the lever in a certain machine which, when pulled in the right way, will do its job

---

[1] Thomas Hobbes (Everyman ser.; London: J. M. Dent & Sons, 1937), ch. xv, p. 83.

[2] *Ibid.*, p. 141.

whoever pulls it. The legislator is he who has rightfully (according to the practices of that society) got into the position of lever-puller. But the job which this machine performs may affect him as much as anyone else, for the legislator may also be a citizen. Of course, there have been or could be societies in which the legislator occupies the position described by Hobbes as "Sovereign." But if to legislate were to give commands, every legislator would *of logical necessity* be in that position. However, legislators may also be citizens, thus binding themselves qua citizens. If I am commander in chief and I give the order "All officers and men are to wear summer uniform, as from October 1st," I cannot be *addressed by* it. I can neither obey nor disobey my own order. It would be absurd to address a command to oneself. On the other hand, there is nothing absurd in laying down a law which will later *apply to* oneself because one happens to be the sort of person in the sort of circumstances to which that law applies.

It is clear how legislating has developed out of giving commands. Commands are *addressed to* others, laws *apply to people* of certain sorts in certain circumstances. It is when an order is addressed to many people, and addressed to them not directly but by a definition of the categories of men to whom it is supposed to be addressed, that the first step in the direction of law is taken. For in that case, a new question arises, a new task is created, whether the command, *as far as one can make out from its content alone,* has been addressed to a particular person. In the case of the law, this question always and necessarily arises, for laws are never directly addressed to people, as commands usually are. There is little room for a system of interpretation in the field of commands.

The second extension is a consequence of the first. Since a law applies to all persons in a certain category, it can also apply to those who have made the law, because they might be in that category.

Laws sometimes create positions of superordination and subordination. A law may, for instance, decree that anyone holding the position of ship's captain or army officer or policeman has certain commanding, prohibiting, permitting, or refusing powers. Again the law may lay down certain general rights for people of certain sorts. Sometimes the law may give a person powers certain uses of which may conflict with rights also guaranteed by the law, as when a policeman taps telephone wires or an employer refuses an employee permission to take leave.

Morality is sometimes construed on the model of either or both commands and laws. Moral rules are said to be the commands or commandments of God, or they are said to be individual members of the moral or natural law which has God or reason as its legislator. However, both commands and laws are inadequate models for morality, as we shall see in Chapter Seven, section 1.

Six

Reason and Motive

1 THE MOTIVE POWER OF REASON

WE can now answer the second of the three questions posed in Chapter Three, section 3: Why do people act in accordance with reason and refrain from acting contrary to it? Another way of putting the same thing is to ask what is the motive power of reason, its power to move us to act in certain ways.

All three traditional theories can give plausible answers to the question how it is that we are moved to act in accordance with reason where means to our ends are concerned. The answer is again that the end determines the means. Only now 'determines' means 'causes to be put into action' where previously it meant 'causes to be selected.' We know that a line of action is in accordance with reason when it is the necessary or best or most efficient means to our ends. But, it is argued, we *want* to achieve our ends or else they would not *be* our ends. Hence we must also *want* the necessary means to our ends.

Hence we must want to do what is in accordance with reason where means to our ends are concerned.

All three theories are in difficulties where the motive power of reason in relation to our ends is concerned. The first theory, which holds that we just "see" what is in accordance and what contrary to reason, takes the view not only that reason is a "cognitive" faculty or element of the mind, but also that it has a "dynamic" aspect, a moving force of its own. This force is so geared to the insights of reason that it drives us to do what reason "sees" to be "in accordance with reason" or "required by" it and to shun what is "contrary to" or "rejected by" it. This view is exposed to a well-known objection. There is no satisfactory way of accounting for the relation between the cognitive and the dynamic side of reason. It cannot be a causal connection, for that suggests that the relation could conceivably have been different, perhaps the opposite—causing a person to pursue what reason rejects and to shun what it requires— and that this might have been so for everybody. But that is absurd. And it is equally absurd to maintain that the connection is logical. For, of course, it is not logically impossible for people to act contrary to reason and to do so knowingly, even deliberately.

The second theory, as we have seen, deals with the problem in a cavalier manner, by simply denying that it can arise. For on that theory, reason has nothing at all to say about our ends. Hence the question about the origin of the power of reason to make us choose certain ends cannot arise. But this has already been shown to be absurd.[1]

The third theory has the most plausible answer to this question. It says that certain factual beliefs, true or false, have the power to move us to act in certain ways. This view is a variant of the first theory, for it makes the motive power of reason

---

[1] Chapter Three, section 3, p. 91.

causal. It is, therefore, unable to account for the cases in which someone, in the full knowledge of the facts and the full knowledge that his behavior would be contrary to reason, nevertheless acts in this way, as when a man, knowing it to be foolish and bad for his health, smokes yet another cigarette or when a husband, with his eyes open to the foolishness of his course of action, returns to his mistress after having taken "final" leave of her. The third theory, therefore, denies the occurrence of such cases. They must be interpreted as instances of not having "sufficiently" examined the facts. The theory can be upheld only by the dodge of not allowing any independent criteria for 'having fully examined the facts.'

How is it, then, that reason has the power to move us? It has already been pointed out that this is a metaphorical way of saying, how is it that we have the power to follow the best reasons even when this is contrary to our strongest desires? When raising the question 'What shall I do?' we are seeking the answer to 'What is the best course open to me, that is, the course supported by the best reasons?' When we deliberate, we are therefore attempting to accomplish two quite different tasks, a theoretical and a practical task. The theoretical is completed when we have answered the theoretical question 'Which course of action is the best?' The practical task is simply to act in accordance with the outcome of the theoretical. Our question about the motive power of reason is a question about how we are able to accomplish the practical task of deliberation, even when our strongest desires oppose it.

Normally, there is no difficulty in accomplishing it. We would not ask, 'What shall I do?' unless we were already prepared to act in accordance with the outcome of our deliberations, that is, in accordance with the results of the theoretical task. We do not ask for advice unless we want to follow it if we acknowledge it to be good. There is, then, no mystery about why we act

142

in accordance with the outcome of our deliberations, that is, in accordance with what we take to be the best reasons: it is because we *want* to follow the best reasons.

1.1 A short digression: The paradox of "subjectivity"

"But," it might now be objected, "are you not slurring over a problem here? Should you not say 'in accordance with what *are* the best reasons' rather than 'in accordance with what we *take to be* the best reasons'? For surely we could make a mistake, and then, if we act in accordance with what we *take* to be the best reasons, we may well be acting contrary to what *are* the best reasons. And that would never do, for we want to do what we should do and not what we think we should do." This is a variant of what, in ethics, is known as "the paradox of subjective duty." The paradox arises when we consider a case in which the agent has made a mistake in deliberation and we ask ourselves what the agent ought to do, that which he *thinks* he ought to do or that which he *really* ought to do. Neither answer seems tenable. If we say he ought to do what he thinks he ought to do, it follows that sometimes he *really* ought to do what he thinks *wrongly* he ought to do, that is, what he ought not to do. If we say he ought to do what he *really* ought to do, then it follows that he sometimes ought to do what he thinks (wrongly) he ought *not* to do, but he surely cannot be expected to do that.

Consider an example. Count O. believes his wife to have been unfaithful to him with Casanova. He believes he ought to kill both Casanova and the Countess. In fact, however, she has not been unfaithful to him and, therefore, he really ought not to kill either Casanova or the Countess. What, then, ought he to do? What he *thinks* he ought, "his subjective duty"? Or what he *really* ought, "his objective duty"?

The paradox disappears as soon as we remember that, in

deliberation, the agent has to accomplish a theoretical and a practical task and that, in evaluating the agent's performance, we can criticize him on two quite different grounds, the inadequate performance either of his theoretical task or of his practical task. When this distinction is drawn, the paradoxical question vanishes. For all that we can in reason demand of the *agent* is that he should first complete, to the best of his ability, his theoretical task *and then act in accordance with* whatever answer he has arrived at in completing that task. The agent, therefore, can never ask himself, 'Should I do what *I think* best or what *is* best?' For his theoretical task is to find out, to the best of his ability, what *is* best. The completion of his theoretical task will be what he thinks best. He cannot therefore *at the same time think another course of action to be the best.* Count O. can think either that killing Casanova and his wife is the best *or* that something else is the best. He cannot think that killing Casanova and his wife is what he *thinks* best and at the same time that not killing anybody *really* is the best. In the course of deliberation, only the question 'What is the best action?' can arise. Thus, for the agent the paradoxical question is impossible.

But can it not arise for a critic or judge? Surely, after he has acted, Count O. himself, or another critic or judge, can ask the paradoxical question: ought Count O. to have done what he thought he ought or what he really ought? But now the cramp is felt only because we do not take into account the many different grounds on which an agent can be criticized. The paradoxical question suggests that there are only two alternatives: either he must be criticized *whenever* he does not do what he ought, or he must be criticized *whenever* he does not do what he thinks he ought. But this is not so. He can be criticized for the inadequate performance of any part of his complex task.

Moreover, the criticism may have to be modified in the light of yet further facts. We must, for instance, criticize Count O. if he was negligent or careless in the performance of his theoretical task, if he has not taken sufficient care in finding out whether his wife really was unfaithful to him and with whom. In a matter as serious as the killing of two people, the utmost care about the facts is surely indicated. Count O. would have to be condemned for killing Casanova and his wife, not because he ought not to have killed them—that is, because he failed in his "objective duty"—but because he was careless in establishing what that "duty" was. He would have to be condemned for what he did because he culpably failed in his theoretical task.

The case would be different if, after careful investigations, Count O. had come to the conclusion that he had insufficient evidence and must wait for proof before killing either Casanova or his wife. But one day, on meeting Casanova and his wife in suspicious circumstances, he stabs Casanova in a fit of jealousy. In this case, we condemn Count O., not because he did not do what he really ought, but because he did not do what he thought he ought to do. We do not think him a whit more justified in killing Casanova and his wife even if it were true that they had committed adultery. Our condemnation of Count O. in this case is modified only by our knowledge that neither Casanova nor the lady had any right to complain or to feel aggrieved. They got their deserts, but Count O. is to be condemned for unjustifiably administering them.

The following is an even more complicated case. Suppose Count O., having concluded that both ought to die, relents after killing Casanova. He is then guilty of a double failure: he has culpably failed in his theoretical and in his practical task. Nevertheless, we do not condemn him for sparing his wife. A great variety of considerations enters into this verdict: the fact that great harm was avoided, that his motive was good (he may have loved or felt pity for her or thought she was seduced by a great master of the art), and so on.

To sum up, the paradox vanishes when we realize that the question cannot arise for the agent at all and that, though it can arise for a critic, it does not then force on him condemnation on only one of two grounds, failure either in his 'objective' or in his 'subjective' duty. The reason why only these two alternatives are thought to be available is, of course, that the question is always construed as arising for the agent, who is imagined as wavering between doing what he thinks he ought and doing what he really ought. For between what other alternatives could the agent be wavering? But, of course, the agent cannot waver between these two alternatives at all, and the critic has other alternatives to consider. Hence no paradox.

The whole problem could never have arisen if moral philosophers had not so blatantly misused the words 'right,' 'duty,' and 'ought.'[2] For then they could never have telescoped so many different questions into one, namely, 'Ought he to do the subjectively or the objectively right act?' This question can perplex us only because we have no more than a confused understanding of its sense. As soon as we make clear to ourselves the various different things it can mean, the problem vanishes. If we mean 'Does thinking that something is one's duty make it so?' the answer is obviously 'No.' If we mean 'Does the moral man do what after careful consideration he has worked out to be what he ought to do?' the answer is, of course, 'Yes.' If it means 'Should a person who has worked out what he ought to do as carefully and conscientiously as can be expected be rebuked for acting on his results?' the answer is plainly 'No.' If

---

[2] H. A. Prichard, "Duty and Ignorance of Fact," in his *Moral Obligation* (Oxford: Clarendon Press, 1949), pp. 18–38; W. D. Ross, *Foundations of Ethics* (Oxford: Clarendon Press, 1939), pp. 148–156.

it means 'Is a man ever to be rebuked for doing what he thought he ought to do?' the answer is, of course, 'Yes, sometimes, for he may culpably have failed in his theoretical task.'

Having shown that the so-called paradox of subjective duty is merely a muddle, we can ignore the above objection.[3] Admittedly, when we ask, 'What shall I do?' we want to know what we really ought to do. Hence we should make as careful and determined an effort as we can to complete our theoretical task. For then the chances are that what, as a result, we shall *think* the best course of action *really* will be so. But whatever in the light of later critical examination our success may be pronounced to have been, at the time we can of course follow nothing but the outcome of our careful deliberations. We can never be condemned for doing that, except when we have been careless in our theoretical task, and then we are not really condemned for following the outcome of our theoretical endeavors, but for not being careful in them.

1.2   *The motive power of reason (continued)*

We can return, then, to our question of how we are able to act in accordance with reason. We said there was no mystery about why we act in accordance with the outcome of our deliberation, that is, in accordance with what we take to be the best reasons, because when we ask, 'What shall I do?' we already *want* to act in accordance with the outcome of our deliberations, or else we could not begin to deliberate.

The puzzle is, therefore, not why a man follows the best reasons, once he knows them. For when he starts working this out, he is already set on acting in whatever way is required by reason. The puzzle is rather why people should bother to stop and think, to deliberate, to complete their theoretical tasks. The answer to this question is simply that they have been

---

[3] See p. 143.

trained to do so. And if they have not, then they will not stop to think.

From early in our lives we have all been taught to think before we act, not to follow impulse or instinct or inclination, but to think first. We have been told that to neglect this will frequently give us cause to regret our action. We are taught that what distinguishes man from the beast is that he possesses reason, and we normally understand very well that this is connected with thinking before we leap, rather than following instinct or mere impulse. Moreover, we are constantly encouraged or bullied to do what we ought rather than what we would like to do and to refrain from doing what we ought not to do even when we would like to do it. In our deliberations we are trying to work out what we should or ought to do, that is, what is supported by the best reasons. It is not surprising, then, that we are able to do this, for we have been trained to do it even in the face of strong contrary impulses.

The question 'How is it that we *do* follow reason?' is no substitute for the question '*Should we* follow reason?' I shall deal with the latter in Chapter Twelve. Here I have merely explained why it is that most people do follow it. My answer is: upbringing.

2 DELIBERATION, JUSTIFICATION, AND EXPLANATION

This point, that the power of reason lies in people's *acquired respect* for reasons, is of some significance, but it is not widely recognized. Many confusions and false theories have obscured this truth. Among them is the common failure to distinguish between three similar, yet importantly different activities: deliberation, justification, and explanation. In all three, the word 'reason' occurs, but is employed for rather different purposes. Hence although the same sentences occur in these three different activities, they do not make the same claims. The attention of philosophers has been riveted on only one of them, explanation. In explanation, the word 'reason' occurs in expressions such as 'my (his, etc.) reason for doing this . . .' or 'the reason why I (he, etc.) did this . . .' and is there used to claim that some fact (which is declared to be *the* reason) has actually moved the agent to act as he did. From this it is erroneously inferred that 'moving the agent' is part of the meaning of 'being a reason.' In explanation, it is indeed true that no factor can be *the reason why* the agent did something, or can be *the agent's reason for* doing something, unless the agent actually was moved to act in this way by that factor. But though all explanatory claims containing the word 'reason' must indeed refer to the decisive factor, to that which actually moved the agent, 'actually moving the agent' is not part of the meaning of 'reason' nor is it a necessary element of all claims containing that word. In deliberation and in justification, a fact may be said to be a reason for doing something although the agent was not moved by it to do that thing, or although he knows that he will not be moved by it.

Let me now illustrate this point in detail. I want, for the moment, to confine myself to deliberate human behavior. For I wish to contrast the use of 'reason' in deliberation, in justification, and in explanation. And it is only in deliberate behavior that all three occur. For all behavior which follows deliberation is of necessity deliberate. The converse is not, of course, true. As long as behavior is not unintentional, absentminded, engaged in by mistake; as long as it is not a yielding to temptation, a being carried away by passion, a not doing something because one has forgotten all about it, or a doing something under hypnosis or the influence of drugs or because one has a complex—as long as it is not one of these, behavior may well be deliberate even though it is not preceded by deliberation, as when the judge refers to the plaintiff as "the accused" (deliberately, not by a slip of the tongue, but on the spur of the moment and because he dislikes the man).

Deliberation and justification use 'reason' in similar ways. In deliberation I try, before acting, to determine which is the best course open to me with a view to entering on it. In justification I try, after someone has acted, to determine whether he has taken the best course open to him, with a view to determining whether he is to be condemned or praised. In justification, I try to show, after the event, that the agent has taken the best course or that, at any rate, he is not to be condemned for not taking it. In both cases, I am looking for what *are* the best reasons for and against the courses open to the agent. In deliberation and in justification I am primarily interested in working out what is the best course of action. In deliberation, I cannot be at all interested in why I have not got it right, for I am still trying to get it right. In justification, I may be interested in why the agent did not get it right, but only secondarily.

In explanation, on the other hand, I am not interested in the rights and wrongs, but merely in what actually did move the agent. There always is an explanation of why the agent did something, though of course investigation need not always bring it to light. There always is a result in justification, but it can be of two sorts, that the agent was justified or that he was not. 'Tout comprendre, c'est tout pardonner' cannot, therefore, be true. Sometimes understanding the agent's behavior involves condemning him. Judges finding the accused guilty are not necessarily wrong or lacking in understanding. The better one understands a certain sort of deed, the more one may have to condemn it, and the doer.

To repeat. In justification, we are primarily interested in the rights and wrongs of the case. In explanation, we are primarily interested in what moved the agent. This is obscured by the fact that the same form of words can be used in either inquiry. We may ask someone whether he had a reason for his conduct, and what it was. This may be interpreted as a request for a justification or for an explanation. These are very different sorts of request and very different matters are relevant to them.

Consider the case of a posthypnotic suggestion. A man has been told, under hypnosis, to open the window five minutes after coming out of his hypnotic sleep. He acts accordingly. When asked (i) whether he had a reason for opening the window, he says 'Yes.' When asked (ii) what his reason was, he says, 'It is awfully hot in here.' Note that question (ii) cannot arise if the answer to (i) is in the negative.

Interpreted as a request for a justification, question (i) depends on two things and two things alone: (a) Is it hot in the room? (b) Is the fact that it is hot in the room a reason for opening the window? If (a) and (b) can be truly answered in the affirmative, then he had a reason, justificatorily speaking, for opening the window. Interpreted as a request for an explanation, on the other hand, question (i) depends on three quite different things: (c) Was his behavior deliberate or not? (d) Did he know what the decisive factor was? (e) Did he believe that in this decisive factor he had a reason for opening the window? If these three questions are answered in the affirmative, then he did have a reason in the explanatory sense, otherwise not.

Note that there is no overlap of the relevant conditions. Justificatorily speaking, he had a reason only if it *was* hot in the room and if this really *is* a reason for opening the window. Explanatorily speaking, all that matters is that he *thought* it was hot and that he *thought* this was a reason for opening the window. It would not matter if he thought so wrongly. When a man says that *his* reason for refusing to play tennis is that it is wrong to play games on Sundays, he may speak truly even though it is Saturday and though there is nothing wrong with playing on Sundays. He has a reason for refusing and that is *his* reason (explanatorily speaking) though he has no reason and, therefore, this cannot be *the* reason (justificatorily speaking).

On the other hand, our man has a reason for opening the window (justificatorily speaking) even if his behavior was not deliberate but followed irresistible impulse (caused by the hypnotic suggestion), even if he does not know what the decisive factor was (he thinks he opened the window because it was hot, whereas in fact the decisive factor was the hypnotic suggestion), and even if he does not believe that the heat in the room is a reason for opening the window.

To recapitulate. When we say that someone had a reason for doing something, justificatorily speaking, we may make two mistakes: (a) that the supposed fact adduced as a reason is not a fact (it was not hot in the room); (b) that the adduced fact is not a reason for behaving in this way (there is nothing wrong with playing games on Sundays). On the other hand, when we say that someone had a reason for doing something, explanatorily speaking, we may make three quite different mistakes: (c) that the person's behavior was not deliberate (he acted under a hypnotic spell); (d) that he did not know what the decisive factor was (he thought that the heat in the room was, but in fact the hypnotic suggestion was; for he would have opened the window even if it had been cold in the room, but he would not have opened it if he had not been told to do so under hypnosis); (e) that he did not think that the decisive factor was a reason for acting in this way. (*My* reason for refusing to play tennis cannot be that playing tennis on Sundays is wrong if I do not think that there is anything wrong with playing on Sundays, if I do not think that its being Sunday *is* a reason for refusing to play.)

Reason and Motive

The first point to remember is that when we deliberate we are looking for reasons in the same way as in justification. We are looking for facts which *are* reasons, or which, at any rate, are reasons in our view. *We are not looking for things which we know will move us.* We are not looking for incentives or motives. When we ask other people to give us advice, to survey and weigh the reasons for us, we are not asking them to look for incentives, to provide us with motives, to mention facts which will move us. We are asking for facts of a certain sort, namely, facts which are properly called reasons, that is, facts such that (as we believe) if anyone were to follow them, he would be entering on the *best* course of action. If we are fully rational, if we are prepared to follow reason (and we are not likely to look for reasons unless we intend to follow them, or else we are wasting our time), then we shall be moved by these facts, and not because they are intrinsically capable of moving us but only because, in the circumstances in which we find ourselves, they constitute *reasons for us* to do certain things.

If, on the other hand, we are looking for reasons in an explanatory context, we are looking not just for reasons: we are looking for *that person's reasons, his* reasons for doing what he did. We are not, then, trying to survey the facts and trying to make out whether they are pros and cons. We are trying to find out what facts *he* surveyed and what facts *he* regarded as reasons. We are interested in *his* answers, whether true or false, not in getting true answers.

The difference between the two cases is analogous to that between a man who is trying to work out a sum and a man who is trying to tell us how another man has arrived at the figures he reached.

Now, if we do not keep the deliberative (and justificatory) use of 'reason' apart from the explanatory and if we use as our model the explanatory use, then we are likely to think of a reason as a fact which of necessity moves the agent. For in explanation, we are not looking for reasons, but for *a person's reasons*, that is, those facts which actually *have* moved him, whether they are reasons or not. As employed in explanatory contexts, 'reason' seems to imply 'moving to action.' In fact, of course, this is not part of the meaning of 'reason,' but part of the claim made by means of the word 'reason' in an explanatory context, where we always speak of '*someone's* reason.'

The second point is even more important, though a little more complex. It has to do with condition (e): that a man cannot be said to have had a reason for doing something (explanatorily speaking) unless he *believes* (rightly or wrongly) that what moved him to act was a reason for acting in that way. This point lays bare the link between the use of reason in deliberative and in explanatory contexts. It shows how explaining a person's (deliberate) behavior is connected with his deliberation. We can explain a person's behavior simply by reporting his deliberation and its outcome. Such a report is a complete explanation if the person deliberated correctly and acted in accordance with the outcome of his deliberation. If his deliberation yields incorrect results, then we must explain where he slipped up and how this came about. If he acts contrary to the outcome of his deliberation, we must explain why he did so, for example, whether he yielded to temptation or to threats or whether he was prevented by circumstances from carrying out his decision.

Condition (e) is of some importance to our inquiry, for it shows that the fact adduced as a reason must be *believed* by the agent to be a reason. If it were not, then an agent could be moved by a reason without his believing it to be one. The force of the reason that moved him could not then *lie in his belief* that the fact in question is a reason for acting in this way. But condition (e) is a genuine condition of anything being someone's reason for doing something. If I do not believe that the fact of its being Sunday is *a* reason against playing tennis, then I cannot say that this fact is *my* reason for refusing to play. It is absurd to say, 'I shall tell you my reason for not playing: it's Sunday today; though of course I do not believe that its being Sunday is a reason against playing.'

It will perhaps be objected that this proves nothing. In saying, 'James is my father,' I may speak the truth even though I believe that James is not my father. Similarly, in saying, 'My reason for refusing to play is that it's Sunday today,' I may speak the truth even though I believe that its being Sunday is not a reason for refusing to play. Of course, I cannot claim both that 'it is Sunday' is my reason for refusing to play and that I do not believe this to be a reason for refusing, any more than I can claim both that James is my father and that I do not believe he is. But from the fact that I cannot, without absurdity, claim both these things in one breath, it does not follow that both these things cannot be true.

Speaking more technically, " 'It is Sunday' is my reason for refusing to play" implies (in Moore's sense [4]) but does not entail "I believe that 'it is Sunday' is a reason for refusing to play." The absurdity of 'I shall tell you my reason for not playing: it's Sunday today; though of course I do not believe that its being Sunday is a reason against playing' does not prove that 'it's Sunday' cannot *be* your reason for refusing to play when you do not believe it to be a reason against playing, any more than the absurdity of 'James is my father but I don't believe he is' proves that James cannot *be* your father when you do not believe he is.

But the cases are not parallel. For what makes the claim 'James is my father' true is the fact that James is my father.

---

[4] G. E. Moore, "A Reply to My Critics," in *The Philosophy of G. E. Moore*, ed. by P. A. Schilpp (Evanston: Northwestern University, 1942), pp. 540–543.

Hence my claim 'James is my father' can be true even if I do not believe it. But what makes my claim " 'It is Sunday' is *my* reason for refusing to play" true is not the fact that 'it is Sunday' *is* a reason for refusing to play. We have already seen that the truth or falsity of that is quite irrelevant to the question whether something or other was *my* reason for doing something. When explaining behavior, we are not concerned with the rights or wrongs of the case. If I believe that selling my car to Paddy is illegal, then that may be my reason for refusing to sell, even if it is not really illegal. If I believe that its illegality is *a* reason for refusing to sell, then this may be *my* reason for refusing to sell, even if its illegality is *not* really a reason for refusing to sell. Conversely, the fact that something *is* a reason for doing something cannot make that fact *my* reason for doing it, if I do not believe it to be a fact or a reason for doing it. Where explanation of my deliberate behavior is concerned, it is not the facts that count, but my beliefs; not the rights and wrongs of the situation, but my beliefs of the rights and wrongs of the situation. Proving the facts and rights of a case only shows that a person had a reason for doing it, *justificatorily speaking*, not that he had a reason, *explanatorily speaking*. When speaking explanatorily, what counts is what the person believed. For only that could "have weighed with him." Only that could have exerted any force on him. Only that could have had motive power. This is part of the meaning of 'believe.' If it does not weigh with me at all, I cannot be said to believe that it is a fact or a reason.

3 REASONS AND MOTIVES

Another important confusion that has prevented philosophers from seeing the truth about the motive power of reasons is their indiscriminate interchange of 'reason' and 'motive.' They do not draw any distinction between these two, or where distinctions are drawn, they are quite arbitrary and add further confusion to the already hopelessly distorted picture. Words like 'motives,' 'motivation,' 'being motivated by' all suggest something dynamic, something containing a force or power that is acting on an agent. If reasons are not distinguished from motives, it is obvious that reasons must also be something of this sort, and if they are facts, then the moving power must somehow be lodged in these facts, even if this means no more than that these facts are the stimuli which arouse certain responses in the agent or that they are the conditions which must be satisfied if an agent's tendency to act in a certain way is to be realized. But all this is wide of the mark.

In the first place, let us remember that the word 'reason' occurs in deliberation, justification, and explanation. 'Motive,' on the other hand, is at home only in explanation. When we distinguish 'reason' from 'motive,' we are therefore merely distinguishing 'reason' as used in explanation from 'motive.' But even that is not sufficient warning. We must add that there are two main uses of the word 'reason' in explanation, as in 'my reason for . . .' and as in 'the reason why . . . .' The former expression implies a certain sort of behavior, namely, deliberate behavior, and a corresponding type of explanation, namely, explanation by way of the *agent's own reasons*. The latter expression is synonymous with 'the explanation why . . . .' The first expression implies a particular type of explanation applicable only to certain highly sophisticated levels of behavior; the second expression does not imply any specific type of explanation.

Next, we must remember that when we speak of someone's motives we imply a certain type of explanation applicable only to behavior above a certain degree of complexity, albeit not as high as that implied in the expression 'his reasons for . . . .' Hence, when we ask, 'Did he have a motive?' we sometimes simply inquire whether the person's behavior was of the required level of complexity. If, after having a meal, Othello is suddenly seized by a terrible fury in the course of which he slays Rodrigo, Cassio, Iago, Emilia, and finally Desdemona, we might suspect that his food was poisoned, that the poison had destroyed his reason, and that he had run amuck. If this is the explanation of his behavior, then it was not of the required level of complexity or sophistication. The explanation of his behavior is in causal terms. In reply to the question 'Did he have a motive?' the answer must be, 'No, he did not have a motive. The food he ate was poisoned and he went mad.'

But now suppose that Iago reports to Othello that Cassio has just left Desdemona after making love to her. On hearing this, Othello flies into a rage and kills Desdemona, or he carefully plans to humiliate her by making her "guilt" publicly known and after so doing stabs her. In both these cases, we would have to say that Othello had a motive and that it was jealousy. In other words, to have a motive is to have certain complex tendencies, in our case the tendency to become angry or sad when one suspects or knows that one's beloved is unfaithful to one and to have certain desires such as to destroy one's rival and/or one's love.

To say, in this sort of context, that someone had a motive is to say that his deed required a certain sort of explanation, one in terms of motives, and not another sort, for example, in terms of causes. To say what the motive was, for example, 'He acted from (or out of) jealousy,' is to give the required explanation.

What, precisely, does the explanation consist in? Two points emerge. First, the agent must have beliefs about the situation he is in. If what he believes about his situation does not make any difference to his behavior, then his behavior must be explained in causal terms. Secondly, it makes no difference whether these beliefs are right or wrong. Othello killed Desdemona from jealousy even though he wrongly believed himself a cuckold.

This, too, distinguishes causal explanations from explanations in terms of the agent's motives.

Let us summarize. Explanations in terms of the agent's motives consist (a) of the agent's beliefs about the situation in which he finds himself and (b) of the behavioral tendencies to which these beliefs give rise. Usually, there is a name for the whole complex. Thus, when we say, 'He killed her out of jealousy,' we are giving an explanation in terms of a motive, but we are not explicitly mentioning the agent's beliefs and the tendencies to which they give rise. The word 'jealousy' implies that the agent thought he was in a situation in which there was at least a danger of his beloved being unfaithful and that this belief aroused in him certain standard tendencies, for example, to be angry with his rival or his love.

How, then, does explanation in terms of the agent's motives differ from explanation in terms of his reasons? Note first a similarity which distinguishes both from causal explanations: both are based on the agent's belief, not on the facts themselves. Othello can be said to have *acted from* jealousy even though he was wrong in thinking that Desdemona was unfaithful to him. Similarly, it can be said that Othello's *reason for* killing Desdemona was her believed unfaithfulness to him, even though she was not unfaithful and he merely wrongly believed her so.

Here the similarity ends. We have already said that the two types of explanation apply to different levels of sophistication. We can speak of the agent's reasons for doing something only if he believes that the supposed facts which make him act in this way are reasons for so acting, while this is not required in motive explanations. Othello's *reason for* killing Desdemona cannot be that he thinks her unfaithful to him unless he believes that a wife's unfaithfulness is a reason for killing her. Othello might, however, kill her *from jealousy* even if he does not think that a wife's unfaithfulness is a reason for killing her.

There is a further important difference between the two types of explanation. The words 'reason' and 'motive' single out different features of the two respective explanations. The agent's reason for doing something is a supposed fact, the agent's motive is a mental state or disposition. When we say that Othello's reason for killing Desdemona was that she was unfaithful to him, we are referring to a supposed fact, her having been unfaithful. In order to complete this explanation we have to remember (a) that Othello must be presumed to want to do what is in accordance with reason and (b) that he thought that a wife's unfaithfulness was a reason for killing her. Assuming that he has carried out, however swiftly, some sort of deliberation and that he has found "the fact" of her unfaithfulness the strongest reason, we see how it is that this supposed fact could be the explanation of his behavior: it has become the decisive factor in the situation.

But when we say that Othello killed Desdemona from jealousy, we are not referring to any supposed facts. We are referring to a certain mental condition, characterized by a great many strong dispositions and tendencies and emotions, among them the tendency to kill the beloved, brought about by certain beliefs about the situation. 'Jealousy' is the name not of a certain supposed fact, but of a number of beliefs-cum-dispositions.

Thus, when we speak of the agent's reasons, we speak of certain supposed facts, but when we speak of the agent's motives we speak of certain dispositions. When we speak of his reasons, we merely hint at his disposition to follow reason. When we speak of motives, we merely hint at his beliefs which have brought about his behavioral tendencies. Roughly speaking we can say, therefore, that the difference between reasons and motives is twofold. Firstly, it is a difference between the types of behavior to which the explanations are properly applicable; explanations in terms of the agent's reasons refer to behavior involving deliberation, explanations in terms of motives do not. Secondly, the parts of the explanation referred to by 'reason' and 'motive' are not the same; 'reason' refers to supposed facts, 'motive' to the agent's behavioral dispositions or tendencies.

One last point. It is well known that certain deeds such as murder are not readily committed by ordinary people. Unless they are mad, we can assume that murderers are acting under great emotional pressure. Now, we know what sorts of situation cause this sort of emotional pressure, for example, jealousy. Sleuths are known to use this knowledge for the detection of the culprit. When they do not know who did it, but know the situations in which the murdered person lived, they can work out which of the persons in his life "had a motive." The question 'Who had a motive?' or 'Did he have a motive?' as the sleuths use it is slightly different from the question asked with the same words and discussed above. It is worth pointing out the difference.

Suppose I have come into the room as Othello is stabbing Desdemona. A few minutes later, a detective comes in. I know that Othello killed her, but I do not know why. The detective does not know whether Othello or I killed Desdemona. When I ask, 'Did Othello have a motive?' I want to know whether the killing was that of a madman or of a sane person. When the detective asks the question, he wants to know whether Othello was related in such a way to Desdemona as would constitute a motive for killing her. He wants to know whether Othello's relation to Desdemona is one of the standard relations constituting a motive from which people commit murder. We are both looking for the same thing with different purposes in mind. I wish to determine the logical type of his deed: mad or sane, caused or motivated. The detective, in order to ascertain the culprit, wishes to determine which of the persons who were in a position to kill her were so related to her as to have been likely *to want* to kill her.

There are important logical differences which are frequently misunderstood. The differences have nothing to do with the meaning of 'motive,' but solely with the different claims that are made by means of this word in two entirely different contexts. The detective's claim 'Othello had a motive, jealousy' does not imply that Othello killed her. It merely implies that there would be a perfectly good explanation of the deed if we assume that he did. This is a reason for thinking that he was the culprit. My claim 'Othello had a motive, jealousy' implies that he was the culprit. The detective's claim, furthermore, does not imply that Othello acted from a motive. Othello might have been mad. His deed might require a causal explanation. My claim, on the other hand, does imply that Othello acted from a motive, namely, jealousy. This shows that we are not required to postulate different senses of the word 'motive,' an occurrent and a dispositional sense. All we need to understand is that in different contexts entirely different claims can be made by the same word, with the same meaning.

4 RATIONALIZATION

One reason for the persistence of the view that reasons are facts which are intrinsically moving is the conviction that the only alternative to it is to say that reasons have no power of their own to move us, thus turning reason either into a mere calculating machine in the service of our desires or into a device to cover up by elaborate rationalizations the working of our basic instincts and unconscious motives. It has already been demonstrated that such fears are groundless. Another account of the motive power of reason is at hand. The view that all reasoning is merely a cover-up of our instinctual drives amounts to the obliteration of the difference between reasoning and rationalizing. As this view is popular among people who have read Freud, including professional phychologists and social scientists, a few words on this topic may be in order here.

Rationalization consists in so explaining one's behavior that it will not be open to any sort of criticism, when in fact it is. It is a form of unconscious hypocrisy. We all know cases of behavior which do not stand up to criticism, whether from the point of view of morality or etiquette or law. We then sometimes choose to explain it in such a way as to make it look respectable, well mannered, in accordance with the law. Now sometimes we do this sort of thing without being aware of departing from the truth. We are then rationalizing.

Consider again the case of a person who has been ordered, under hypnosis, to open a window after coming out of his hypnotic sleep. Five minutes after he wakes up, he rushes to the window to open it. When people block his way and try to hold him back, he pushes them aside, using considerable force. Asked why he wants to open the window, he says that it's hot, that he feels as if he were suffocating. In other words, he gives a perfectly good explanation of why he behaves in the way he does, but it happens not to be *the* explanation of his behavior, though he does not know that. It is tempting to argue that we can never know what are the true reasons for our behavior, that we always only believe we know our reasons, that the real machinery moving us to act in this or that way is hidden from us, that the reasons we actually give are mere rationalizations, mere embellishments of the forces actually at work.

Let us examine exactly what the person under hypnosis says and wherein his mistake consists. Note, in the first place, that he behaves in a strange manner, one calling for explanation of a certain sort. And note that he himself must be aware of the strangeness of his behavior. He finds himself suddenly impelled to open the window. To admit honestly that he suddenly had an irresistible impulse to open the window would be to admit something quite odd and irrational, something like the cravings of pregnant women or of drug addicts. Only in his case there is no known causal explanation of this impulse. Moreover, while there is no obvious explanation in terms of reasons why a person should crave an orange or a cigarette, there is available a possible explanation, in terms of reasons, of one's desire to open the window. Since the person in question is not aware that an irresistible impulse has been set up in him by the hypnotic suggestion and since he is embarrassed by his own behavior and does not like to think of himself as a person given to irresistible impulses (what might he not be impelled to do next?), he hits on some plausible fact as the explanation. His procedure is to look for *an* explanation and to declare it *the* explanation.

What are his mistakes? In the first place, he misconstrues the nature of his behavior, taking it to be based on reasons for behaving in this way, whereas in fact it is simply following irresistible impulse. It is understandable that he should make this mistake, for behavior such as his, opening a window in a crowded room, is *normally* based on reasons.

In the second place, and partly as a result of his first error, he is of course unable to identify the decisive factor. He is prevented from doing this because he cannot know that he was given an order under hypnosis. As soon as he hears that an order given under hypnosis causes the person ordered to experience irresistible impulses to do as ordered and is told that he has been ordered to open the window, he understands his behavior. He now knows why he opened the window. He may of course still deny that this was the reason why he opened it. But then he is no longer rationalizing, but simply not telling the truth.

Summing up, we can say this. One type of rationalization arises because the agent's behavior seems to him to call for a certain sort of explanation, explanation in terms of his own reasons for behaving in this way, whereas in fact it is not behavior of this sort and does not call for this sort of explanation. In such cases, 'Why did you do this?' does not mean 'For what reasons did you do this?' or 'From what motive did you do this?' but 'What was the cause of your doing this?' Beginning with this misapprehension, the agent naturally looks for a fact which he would regard as a reason for doing what he finds himself doing and readily assumes that he must have acted because of this fact. His mistake can be rectified as soon as he is told the nature of his behavior.

It is quite obvious that not all our reason-guided behavior is of this sort. Not all our behavior is strange, as was that of the window opener. Frequently we can make sure whether or not we have been hypnotized by anyone. We can, moreover, prove to the man in question that, though his reasons would be good reasons if they were based on fact, they are bad reasons because they are not so based. It is not hot in the room, it's hotter outside, and so on.

Not all rationalization is of this sort. There are cases in which a man is mistaken about what was *his* reason for doing something. These are cases in which the rationalization does not involve a misunderstanding of the type of behavior involved, but merely about what is the decisive factor. I may, for instance, explain my refusal to sell my Chevrolet to Paddy on the grounds that it would be illegal. Someone else, however, might claim that *that was not my real reason.* My real reason, he might say, was that I did not think Paddy would pay the promised £3,000.

It might be objected that it simply does not make sense to say that I was mistaken about my real reason. My reason for doing something is what, after deliberation, I regard as the weightiest matter, in accordance with which I finally act. How could I be wrong about that, except in the trivial way of having forgotten? Must not my reason for doing something be totally transparent, wholly on the surface?

The answer is No. I can be mistaken about what was my real reason for doing something, because I can be mistaken about what was the decisive factor, that is, about how I *would* act if the circumstances were slightly different. Would I refuse to sell the car if Paddy offered cash in bank notes? If I am wrong in thinking that I would not sell even then, then I am wrong about the relative strength of two of my propensities, the propensity to sell when I expect large profits and the propensity not to do what is illegal. I may think the second propensity stronger than it is. I may think that I refuse to clinch a deal yielding high profits because doing so would be illegal, that is, I think my propensity not to do what is illegal is stronger than my propensity to do what yields high profits. The proof that I am mistaken in this lies in the fact that I would clinch the deal if my fear of not getting payment is eliminated (by the offer of ready cash) and only the illegality remains. This shows that it was not the illegality that held me back but only the fear of not getting the money.

Thus, a person may be mistaken about his real reasons for doing something, because he may underestimate or over-estimate the *power* which a given reason actually has over him. One is particularly likely to make that mistake where many propensities are involved and it is difficult or impossible to vary them independently in order to test the strength of each. In such a case, one is likely to rationalize, that is, to attribute to each propensity that degree of strength which one thinks (justificatorily speaking) it *ought* to have. In this way, one appears to oneself as a person who acts in accordance with reason, moral or otherwise.

Lastly, there are the cases of rationalization in which a system of justification is invented in order to make one's indefensible behavior appear justified. Thus, the greed and selfishness of the entrepreneurs and the government's unconcern for the misery of the working class were justified by the theory of the Hidden Hand, which was supposed to harmonize in the long run the conflicting interests involved, or by the theory that it was for the common good that everyone should promote his own interest as much as possible since thereby, automatically, the good of everyone was promoted.

Quite often it will be difficult or impossible to tell whether the explanation one is giving of someone's behavior (including one's own) is not really a rationalization. Many honest people, therefore, have a tendency to give "safe," that is, unfavorable, explanations in order to avoid the accusation of putting too favorable a construction on someone's behavior. Attributing noble reasons to others and, most of all, to oneself is regarded as naïve. No doubt, there is a lot of justification for this. But it does not seem to me in the least plausible to say that we are always rationalizing, for frequently the explanations we give are unfavorable. Nor is it plausible to say that we can never tell whether we are rationalizing or giving a correct explanation.

One further point must be made. Supposing for the moment that it is not possible ever to be sure that one is not rationalizing. It does not follow from this that one is never justified in doing what one has done. For if there are good reasons for a course of action, then one is justified in following them, even if it later turns out or could turn out that these good reasons were not the decisive factors in making one act the way one did. It does not follow that one was not right in giving a large donation to charity even though one's real reason for giving the money was not one's desire to help the poor, but to gain tax exemption or publicity. If a certain line of action is supported by the best reasons there are, then it is quite unimportant, justificatorily speaking, by what devious unconscious drives we are propelled to follow it.

Seven

Moral Considerations

WE can now resume our discussion, interrupted in Chapter Six, of various types of consideration. What exactly are moral reasons or considerations, as opposed to those other kinds which we have already examined? They are obviously those which occur in moral deliberation and the occurrence of which makes deliberation moral. We say of someone that he is a person of good will if he is always prepared (should it be necessary) to enter, before acting, into moral deliberation, that is to say, to work out what is, morally speaking, the best course open to him, that is, the course supported by the best moral reasons, and also prepared to act in accordance with the outcome of such deliberations.

Like all other types, moral deliberation has to pass through two stages, that of surveying the facts with a view to ascertaining which of them are relevant to the problem in hand, that is, which of them are pros and which are cons, and that of weighing the various considerations against one another, with a view to determining the weightiest. Again, in surveying the facts, we must bear in mind the moral consideration-making beliefs or moral rules of reason, such as 'That stealing is wrong is a reason against stealing' or 'That giving alms is meritorious is a reason for giving alms,' for we determine whether this or that fact is relevant to our question by determining whether it falls under one or the other of these moral rules of reason. If it is a fact that a certain contemplated line of action is a case of stealing, then in that fact I have a moral reason against entering on that line. If it is a fact that a certain proposed line of action is a case of giving alms, then in that fact I have a moral reason for entering on it.

Having ascertained all the relevant facts, all the moral pros and cons, I must proceed to weigh them in order to determine which course of action is supported by the weightiest moral reasons, which course has the weight of moral reason behind it. We do this by applying the rules of superiority, such as 'Lying to someone is preferable to doing him serious harm' or 'It is better to inflict a small amount of harm on one, than a great amount on another, innocent person,' and so on.

What I have called 'moral rules of reason' or 'moral consideration-making beliefs' are what are usually called 'moral convictions.' Ordinarily, of course, our moral convictions are formulated simply as 'Stealing is wrong,' 'Lying is wrong,' and so on. They are not normally stated in the form I have given them, namely, 'The fact that stealing is wrong is a reason against stealing.' Nevertheless, although they are not formulated in this way, they are *used as* moral rules of reason.

A brief comparison with reasons of self-interest will show this. One of our consideration-making beliefs, we have seen, is the fact that doing something is in one's interest is a reason for doing it. Hence the fact that a certain line of action is a case of flattering the boss together with the fact that flattering the boss is in one's interest provides one with a reason for entering on that line of action. The fact that a certain line of action is a case of flattering the boss is a *self-interested reason* for entering on that line. Why? Because the fact that doing something is *in one's interest* is a reason for doing it, and this is such a fact.

Similarly it is a rule of reason that the fact that something is contrary to morality is a reason against doing it; and the fact that something is required by morality, a reason for doing it. Just as we call those things dictated by self-interest reasons of self-interest, so we call those things dictated by morality moral reasons. To say that something is morally wrong is merely another way of saying that it is prohibited by, that it is against or contrary to, morality. Hence in the fact that something is wrong one has a reason (a moral one) against doing it. If something is a case of stealing and if stealing is wrong, that is, contrary to morality, then one has a moral reason against doing that thing.

It should now be obvious that what we normally call our moral convictions function as moral rules of reason, as moral consideration-making beliefs.

Some readers may have noticed the similarity between what I call "moral rules of reason" and what Ross calls "prima-facie duties." My view differs from that of Ross only in the following respects. In the first place, I do not think that we know these moral rules of reason "by intuition." Secondly, I do not think that in cases of conflict between such rules which, as Ross agrees,[1] is extremely frequent we have to rely on flair. Just as, at the first level of deliberation, we rely on moral rules of reason, so, at the second level, when weighing the conflicting considerations, we rely on moral rules of

---

[1] W. D. Ross, *The Right and the Good* (Oxford: Clarendon Press, 1930), pp. 33–34.

superiority. Again, I do not agree that we know these, even the most general ones, "by intuition." However, it must for the moment suffice to say that we learn these rules in the course of our moral and linguistic upbringing. This is not the whole story, for we can always ask whether we have been taught the right rules. A full discussion of this problem will have to wait until Chapter Twelve.

Note further that it is unimportant which of the so-called ethical terms we use in formulating these moral rules, or moral convictions. There is no significant difference between 'It is wrong to kill,' 'Killing is wrong,' 'One ought not to kill,' 'Thou shalt not kill,' 'It is morally objectionable to kill,' and so on. The same claims can be made in a great many different expressions. What counts is not the expression used, but the point made. We tell what point exactly is made by the way the speaker would defend or disprove it. Of course, it needs to be stressed that in this field many speakers are confused. This is no accident, for the nature of morality is not at all clear to most people.

Moral deliberation, like all kinds of deliberation, is a sort of calculus, a method of reckoning, of working out something— which course of action is supported by the best moral reasons. All that can be expected of moral philosophers is the clarification of the calculus, the statement of the general rules, and the methods of using them in particular calculations. It cannot be expected that philosophers should answer all moral questions or problems beforehand, or that, after the elucidation of this calculus, its users will find solving their problems much easier, or even that all problems will now be capable of solution. The procedure is very much like weighing. One can only explain the weighing machine and check the weights: the weighing itself has still to be done on each particular occasion. There is, moreover, the danger that the considerations will be evenly balanced, in which case no decisive answer can be given.

1 MORAL CONVICTIONS CAN BE TRUE OR FALSE

It is often argued that our moral convictions are merely expressions of our feelings, emotions, or attitudes, or that they are commands or pseudo commands, and that, therefore, they cannot be true or false. It might be added that they must have some kind of imperatival force, for it must be possible to act in accordance with or contrary to them. But one cannot act in accordance with or contrary to truths or facts. Truths or facts are compatible with any sort of behavior. Truths are, therefore, useless in morality. There we need something in the nature of precepts.

This argument is unsound. Moral convictions can be true or false and also imperatival. To say 'Killing is wrong' is to say that killing constitutes the contravention of a certain sort of rule or commandment, 'Don't kill,' 'Thou shalt not kill.' Hence, 'Killing is wrong' may be true or false, for it may or may not be the contravention of such a rule. On the other hand, it also makes this remark imperatival, for killing is thereby declared to be the contravention of a rule or commandment. If, in a train, I say to my neighbor, 'No smoking in here,' I say something which can be true or false (for it may or may not be a nonsmokers') and also imperatival (for if it is a nonsmokers', then there is a rule forbidding smoking in the compartment). Thus, what makes 'No smoking in here' and 'Killing is wrong' capable of being true or false is the fact that the rules alluded to by these remarks are capable of passing a certain test. 'No smoking in here' can be true (or false), because the rule 'No smoking in this compartment' is (or is not) properly laid down by the Railway Company which is (or is not) entitled to do so. Our main task will, of course, be to show what are the appropriate tests which a moral rule must pass in order that remarks alluding to it should be said to be true. We have to answer questions such as what are the tests which the rule 'Thou shalt not kill' must pass if it is to be true that killing is wrong.

The proof that moral convictions could be true or false and also imperatival seems to me to constitute quite a strong argument in favor of saying that they actually are true or false, for this is what we all naturally think. The only reason why we have doubts is that philosophers have various reasons for saying that propositions cannot be both imperatival and true or false. However, in view of the great popularity of the emotive and imperativalist theories, it is perhaps not out of place to devote some additional space to establishing this conclusion.

My main contention is that we could not properly speak of *a morality*, as opposed to a system of conventions, customs, or laws, until the question of the correctness or incorrectness, truth or falsity, of the rules prevalent in a community is asked, until, in other words, the prevalent rules are subjected to certain tests. It is only when the current rules are no longer regarded as sacrosanct, as incapable of alteration or improvement, only when the current rules are contrasted with other possible, improved, ideal rules, that a group can be said to have a morality as opposed to a mere set of taboos.

We distinguish a great many different moralities—Greek, Roman, Arapesh, Christian, Mohammedan, Communist, feudal, bourgeois, proletarian, and so on. Moralities are always someone's, whether an individual's or a group's. In these respects, moralities are like customs and legal systems.[2] But in another respect, moralities on the one hand and legal systems and

---

[2] For a slight modification, see above, Chapter Five, section 3, p. 134.

customs on the other differ radically. When we have settled whether a line of action is in accordance with or contrary to the law or the customs of the group in question, we have settled conclusively whether this line of action is lawful or unlawful, customary or not customary. We cannot go on to ask, 'Well, perhaps it is legal here or customary there, but is it *really* legal, is it *really* customary?' Nor does it make sense to say, 'There is no law or custom against this sort of thing anywhere, but perhaps this sort of thing is *really* illegal or *really* contrary to custom.' By contrast, this kind of distinction can be and is drawn in moral matters. When we hear that in certain countries virginity above a certain age is regarded as selfish and immoral, or that not having scalped anyone by a certain age is regarded as effeminate or lazy, or that it is "wrong" for women to pass a certain stone without veiling their faces, we do not think that the question whether these sorts of conduct are *really* wrong has been decisively settled. Even whether these things are *wrong in that country* has not been answered. It has only been established that these types of conduct are *believed wrong in that country*.

When we have settled that something is against the customs or laws of a certain group, we cannot go on to ask whether it is merely believed or actually known to be illegal or contrary to custom. A person who goes on to ask that question must be said not to know what he is talking about. On the other hand, a person likewise does not know what he is talking about if he believes that finding out whether some course of action is contrary to the morality of a certain group settles the question whether this course of action is morally wrong. For he ignores the crucial question 'Is what the morality of that group forbids *really* wrong?' or, put differently, 'Are the moral convictions of that group true?' I take it for granted, then, that ordinary usage draws just that distinction between morality on the one hand and custom and law on the other.

But, it might be asked, what does that prove? Our language might be confused. Perhaps we allow that question without having provided a method of answering it. Our moral locutions may be the embodiment of wishful thinking. It is not enough to point out that we *ask*, 'But are the moral convictions of this group really true?' If that question is to make sense, a procedure for answering it has to exist and it must be a sensible one.

I agree with the principle behind this objection. It is not enough to show, for instance, that we frequently do ask the question 'But is this religion true?' If it were enough, certain modern analyses of religious language would be obviously false. Certain philosophers who say that religious language is purely evocative could then be refuted simply by the reminder "But we do ask the question 'Is his religion true?' and your analysis does not permit it to be asked." Or when other philosophers say that the claim 'God exists' is a complex empirical assertion implying that things will not go from bad to worse in the future, but will in the end be all right, they could be refuted simply by saying that this is not implied in the religious assertion that God exists. I do not think that such philosophers can be so easily refuted. A refutation would have to show not only that we all *think* that this is not implied in such remarks or that we all wish to ask whether such remarks are true, but also that what we imply or what we wish to ask is sensible, that there is room for this question, that we can sensibly imply what we intend to, that we can ask this question and imply what we intend without making nonsense of our religious assertions. It is just because this is so difficult that some philosophers have been driven into these alternative analyses of religious assertions.

176

This is true of moral claims also. It is not enough to say, 'But we *do* ask whether our moral convictions are true.' We must also show what exactly is the sense of this question and how exactly it can be answered. When this is shown, as I shall do presently (in Chapters Seven, Eight, and Twelve), our original claim has been made good. Since we want to ask whether our moral convictions are true and since it can be explained what this question means and how it is answered and since it can be shown that it is an eminently sensible question, there can no longer be any objection to allowing it.

It follows from this that one of the most popular models of the nature of morality, the conception of it as divine or natural law, is inappropriate. For since we cannot ask the question whether, given that it is contrary to a certain law, a line of conduct is *really* illegal, morality cannot be any sort of law, however exalted. In view of the immense popularity of that conception of morality, it is worth showing its untenability in some detail.

At first sight, the notion of law looks promising. Like its moral analogue, the question whether something is in accordance with or contrary to law is completely objective: everybody within or outside a given society could be wrong about the legality or illegality of a given line of conduct. An enterprising lawyer may unearth an old law that is relevant. Before his find everyone including himself might well have considered that line of action lawful. His discovery shows that this universal belief was false. In this respect law is much closer to morality than custom. For if everyone in a certain society *believes* that something is contrary to custom, then it *necessarily* is. We all think it customary for gentlemen to take off their hats when the national anthem is played, hence it *is* customary. Not so with law, or with morality.

Nevertheless, the concept of law does not fit the case of

morality. The very feature that makes it so attractive to religious persons renders it unsuitable as a model of morality.
Religious people like to think of morality as a sort of law,
because law implies or at any rate strongly suggests a legislator.
If morality is a perfect law, then there must be a perfect
legislator: God. But this is precisely the objection to law as
a model of morality. For a legislator authoritatively settles
the question whether a type of conduct is lawful or otherwise:
he makes it so. The legality or illegality of a type of action is
the logical consequence of the legislator's decision. It is the very
function of the legislator to bring into being or abolish the
illegality of something, as he thinks fit. However, the rightness
or wrongness of a type of action cannot be the logical consequence of anyone's decision. An omniscient person would
indeed *know* the difference between right and wrong and
could reliably inform us of it, but he can only show us where
the line runs—he cannot draw it. It is nonsense to say, 'Yesterday God decreed that killing shall no longer be morally
wrong' or 'The moral law against lying was promulgated on
May 1st.' Morality, therefore, cannot be any sort of law.

It must not be inferred from this that legal systems cannot
be criticized on moral grounds. Even though the legislator is
entitled to make whatever laws he thinks fit and even though
whatever he enacts is really law, and even though it is true
that there is no superlaw with which the legislator must
attempt to make his own enactments agree, nevertheless the
legal enactments are open to criticism *from the moral point of
view.*

The same point can also be made in the following way.
Law and morality have this in common: everyone in this
country can be wrong about this or that type of action being
legal or illegal, right or wrong. This distinguishes both law
and morality from mere custom. It is therefore more plausible

to say that morality is a sort of law than to say that it is just convention. All the same, it is misleading. For when it has been established that adultery, say, is permitted by our law, then no further mistake is logically possible, in the field of law. It is then certain that in our country adultery is not unlawful. Incorporation of a rule in the legal system of a country is a final guarantee of the legality or illegality of the type of conduct in question. The law of the group cannot be illegal. It might perhaps be said against this that the law can be illegal when there is a constitution. But then my point can be made by saying that the constitution can't be unconstitutional. On the other hand, embodiment in the morality of the group is no final guarantee of the morality or immorality of the type of conduct in question. The morality of the group may be wrong. The moral convictions of the group may be mistaken.

Law is not, therefore, an adequate model of the nature of morality. It cannot explain the most important logical feature of morality, the fact that we can speak of moral convictions and of their being true or false. It cannot even account for the peculiar imperatival nature of our moral convictions, for the sake of which it is usually adopted. If morality were a sort of law, it would indeed seem as if the imperatival nature of morality were explained. For laws command or, at any rate, request obedience. But such a view of the nature of morality can offer only two reasons for obedience: love of the legislator or fear of his penalties. But these are at best *explanations why people obey*, not *reasons for obeying*. They are explanatory, not justificatory reasons. If morality were simply some sort of law, then no justificatory reasons for obeying it could be given at all.

I take it as established, then, that it is the very meaning of 'a morality' that it should contain a body of moral convictions which can be true or false, that is, a body of rules or precepts for which there are certain tests. If this is true, then morality is a comparatively sophisticated system of rules, and we have to admit the possibility of nonmoral or premoral societies, just as there are nonpolitical or prepolitical societies, such as the Australian aborigines. I believe that, as a matter of fact, moralities have appeared for the first time at roughly the stage when religion superseded magic (or whatever else may have preceded it) and law began to be added to custom. At that time, I believe, morality developed out of taboo. The main step in that direction is the dim realization, expressed in the powers given to a legislator, that the group's way of life is not altogether sacrosanct. The slow, unthought-out, uncontrolled way of social change is superseded by the method of deliberate, thought-out, sudden changes introduced by the legislator. At the same time, it is understood that the legislator is capable of making mistakes, that his legislation is not arbitrary, but is supposed to aim at certain things. In the absence of a clear understanding of what he is supposed to be aiming at, it seems a plausible thing to say that he is aiming at The Perfect Law which is laid up in heaven. But, as we have seen, on closer inspection, this is not satisfactory. As long as we are dealing with a legislator and his law, the same question necessarily arises: what are the grounds on which the legislator, however perfect he may be, is drawing up his legislation? Until these grounds are found, we cannot tell of any piece of legislation or its author whether it or he is perfect. And when we know the grounds, we no longer need, as a sitter for our legislative portrait, the perfect legislator and his law.

2   TRUE MORALITIES AND ABSOLUTE MORALITY

Our discussion has brought to light an essential characteristic of a morality: that it should make sense to ask, 'But are these moral convictions true?' or 'Is this moral code correct?' or words to that effect. The question implies that the moral rules and convictions of any group can and should be subjected to certain tests. It implies a distinction between this and that morality on the one hand and true morality on the other.

Let us be quite clear, however, what this distinction amounts to. It is not, in the first place, that between 'a morality' and 'morality as such,' which is analogous to the distinction between a legal system and law as such or between a disease and disease as such. Talking about a morality, say Greek or Tikopia or *fin de siècle* morality, is like talking about Roman, canonic, or Napoleonic law, or about Bright's disease, cancer, or leprosy. But talking about morality as such or the nature of morality is like talking about law as such or the nature of law, disease as such or the nature of disease. When talking in this way, we are drawing attention to the essentials of the concept. We are thinking of the conditions which something must satisfy in order to be properly called 'a morality,' 'a legal system, 'a disease.' We are asked to neglect all those additional features in virtue of which a given morality, legal system, or disease is always more than just that, is always a particular one, Christian morality, or Napoleonic law, or hepatitis. Morality as such is not a supermorality, any more than law as such is a superlaw, or disease as such a superdisease. Morality as such is not even a morality, but a set of conditions. Morality as such cannot, therefore, be either true or false.

And this brings out an important point. There is no a priori reason to assume that there is only one true morality. There are many moralities, and of these a large number may happen to pass the test which moralities must pass in order to be called true. It would, therefore, be better to speak of 'a true morality' or of 'true moralities' than of 'true morality.'

However, there is one point that makes it desirable to speak of 'true morality' in addition to speaking of 'true moralities.' It is this. True moralities are particular moralities which pass certain tests. We may abstract from all the particular existential conditions of given moralities and think of true morality as a system of true moral convictions not embodied in, but completely independent of, the particular conditions of this or that way of life. There may therefore be true moral convictions which, though possibly no one actually holds them, are true in and for all possible social conditions. But there could be such true moral convictions only if their content had nothing to do with social conditions. It may, of course, be argued that there are no such convictions, but I think there are.

'True morality' in this sense cannot, of course, be just *one* moral code, the same for any morality which can be said to be true. For there will be many different moralities all of which are true, although each may contain moral convictions which would be out of place in one of the others. Thus, 'Lending money for interest is wrong,' 'A man ought not to marry his brother's widow,' 'It is wrong to take more than one wife,' and so on may be true moral convictions in one set of social conditions, but false in another. However, moral convictions, such as 'Killing is wrong,' 'Harming others is wrong,' 'Lying is wrong,' 'Misusing the institutions of one's society is wrong,' are true quite irrespective of the particular setup of given societies. If these are true moral convictions at all, then they must be absolutely true, for they are based solely on human nature. They are, from their very nature, independent of particular variations of the social pattern. However, they are not true for "all rational beings," as Kant thought, but only for human beings, and they would not necessarily remain true for human beings if there were radical changes in human nature. Thus, if being killed became generally desired and were a pleasurable experience and if one were reborn soon afterwards with a new body but with all memories intact, it would no longer be true that killing was wrong.

I shall, then, distinguish between true moralities and absolute morality. True moralities are actually embodied moralities, those forming part of a given way of life of a society or an individual, which would pass a certain test, if they were subjected to it. Absolute morality, on the other hand, is that set of moral convictions, whether held by anyone or not, which is true quite irrespective of any particular social conditions in which they might be embodied. Every true morality must contain as its core the convictions belonging to absolute morality, but it may also contain a lot more that could not be contained in every other true morality.

It is clear, furthemore, that true moralities are the applications of the most general true moral convictions to the specific conditions of a particular social order. 'It is wrong to misuse social institutions' is part of absolute morality, for it is neutral to the particular form the social institutions take. But even very general precepts, such as 'Stealing is wrong,' 'Adultery is wrong,' 'Promise breaking is wrong,' 'Neglecting your duties is wrong,' 'Failing to discharge your obligations is wrong,' cannot be part of absolute morality, for these refer to specific ways of misusing specific social institutions, which a given society may not have. It is conceivable that in a given society there might be no institution of property or marriage, no such thing as promising or having duties or obligations, and still the group might have a morality, for it might believe that killing is wrong or that hurting others is wrong.

3 POINTS OF VIEW

What, then, is the test (if any) which a moral conviction must pass in order to be called true? Many philosophers have held that there is not and cannot be such a test. They would perhaps admit that we may reduce our moral convictions to a few basic moral principles, or perhaps even only one, from which all others can be derived, but they would hold that at least one such principle must simply be selected as we please. Such basic principles are matters for deciding, not for finding out.

I shall argue, on the contrary, that our moral convictions are true if they can be seen to be required or acceptable *from the moral point of view*. It is indeed true that a person must adopt the moral point of view if he is to be moral. But it is not true that this is an arbitrary decision. On the contrary, I shall show, in Chapter Twelve, that there are the very best reasons for adopting this point of view.

Answers to practical questions can be arrived at by reference to a point of view, which may be defined by a principle. When we adopt a certain point of view, we adopt its defining principle. To look at practical problems from that point of view is to be prepared to answer practical questions of the form 'What shall I do?' 'What should be done?' by reference to its defining principle.

Suppose the problem under discussion is whether or not a certain traffic roundabout should be erected at a certain intersection. I can look at this from various points of view, that of a pedestrian or a motorist, a local politician or a manufacturer of roundabouts, and so on. In cases such as these, we have in mind the point of view of self-interest as applied to certain special positions or jobs or functions in a society. To look at our problem from the point of view of a motorist is to ask whether the erection of a roundabout at this intersection is in the interest of a motorist. For different points of view there may, of course, be different, even opposing, answers to the same practical questions. The roundabout may be in the interest of a motorist but not of a pedestrian, in the interest of a manufacturer of roundabouts but not of a local politician who depends for his votes on the poorer section (the pedestrians) of the population.

However, a point of view is not necessarily defined by the principle of self-interest or its more specific application to a particular position in society. We can, for instance, look at this problem from the point of view of town planners or traffic experts, who may favor the roundabout because their special task is to solve traffic problems. Their point of view is defined by the principle 'Favor anything that keeps the traffic flowing; oppose anything that is likely to cause traffic holdups.' But the erection of the roundabout can hardly be said to be *in their interest.* They do not derive any personal advantage or benefit from the scheme. There are many such disinterested points of view, for example, the point of view of a social worker, a social reformer, an advocate of public health schemes, a missionary.

A person is of good will if he adopts the moral point of view as supreme, that is, as overriding all other points of view. When asking the question 'What shall I do?' or 'What is to be done?' such a person will always engage in moral deliberation, survey and weigh the moral considerations, and give them greater weight than any others. A person has adopted the moral point of view when he reviews the facts in the light of *his* moral convictions. We do not require him to test his moral convictions every time, but only because we presume that he already has true moral convictions. This presumption may be false. He may simply have accepted without much questioning the moral convictions of his group, or he may have departed from them without getting any nearer the truth. In such a case, he merely *means* to adopt the moral point of view, but has not succeeded. He has adopted something which he wrongly believes to be the moral point of view. He must still be called a person of good will because of his intentions, but he cannot arrive at true answers to his question.

Clearly, our central problem is to define the moral point of view.

Eight

The Moral Point of View

THROUGHOUT the history of philosophy, by far the most popular candidate for the position of the moral point of view has been self-interest. There are obvious parallels between these two standpoints. Both aim at the good. Both are rational. Both involve deliberation, the surveying and weighing of reasons. The adoption of either yields statements containing the word 'ought.' Both involve the notion of self-mastery and control over the desires. It is, moreover, plausible to hold that a person could not have a reason for doing anything whatsoever unless his behavior was designed to promote his own good. Hence, if morality is to have the support of reason, moral reasons must be self-interested, hence the point of view of morality and self-interest must be the same. On the other hand, it seems equally obvious that morality and self-interest are very frequently opposed. Morality often requires us to refrain from doing what self-interest recommends or to do what self-interest forbids. Hence morality and self-interest cannot be the same points of view.

1 SELF-INTEREST AND MORALITY

Can we save the doctrine that the moral point of view is that of self-interest? One way of circumventing the difficulty just mentioned is to draw a distinction between two senses of 'self-interest,' shortsighted and enlightened. The shortsighted egoist always follows his short-range interest without taking into consideration how this will affect others and how their reactions will affect him. The enlightened egoist, on the other hand, knows that he cannot get the most out of life unless he pays attention to the needs of others on whose good will he depends. On this view, the standpoint of (immoral) egoism differs from that of morality in that it fails to consider the interests of others even when this costs little or nothing or when the long-range benefits to oneself are likely to be greater than the short-range sacrifices.

This view can be made more plausible still if we distinguish between those egoists who consider each course of action on its own merits and those who, for convenience, adopt certain rules of thumb which they have found will promote their long-range interest. Slogans such as 'Honesty is the best policy,' 'Give to charity rather than to the Department of Internal Revenue,' 'Always give a penny to a beggar when you are likely to be watched by your acquaintances,' 'Treat your servants kindly and they will work for you like slaves,' 'Never be arrogant to anyone—you may need his services one day,' are maxims of this sort. They embody the "wisdom" of a given society. The enlightened long-range egoist may adopt these as rules of thumb, that is, as *prima-facie* maxims, as rules which he will observe unless he has good evidence that departing from them will pay him better than abiding by them.

The Moral Point of View

It is obvious that the rules of behavior adopted by the enlightened egoist will be very similar to those of a man who rigidly follows our own moral code.

Sidgwick appears to believe that egoism is one of the legitimate "methods of ethics," although he himself rejects it on the basis of an "intuition" that it is false. He supports the legitimacy of egoism by the argument that everyone could consistently adopt the egoistic point of view. "I quite admit that when the painful necessity comes for another man to choose between his own happiness and the general happiness, he must as a reasonable being prefer his own, i.e. it is right for him to do this on my principle." [1] The consistent enlightened egoist satisfies the categorical imperative, or at least one version of it, 'Act only on that maxim whereby thou canst at the same time will that it should become a universal law.'

However, no "intuition" is required to see that this is not the point of view of morality, even though it can be universally adopted without self-contradiction. In the first place, a consistent egoist adopts for all occasions the principle 'everyone for himself' which we allow (at most) only in conditions of chaos, when the normal moral order breaks down. Its adoption marks the return to the law of the jungle, the state of nature, in which the "softer," "more chivalrous" ways of morality have no place.[2]

This point can be made more strictly. It can be shown that those who adopt consistent egoism cannot make moral judgments. Moral talk is impossible for consistent egoists. But this amounts to a *reductio ad absurdum* of consistent egoism.

Let B and K be candidates for the presidency of a certain country and let it be granted that it is in the interest of either

---

[1] Henry Sidgwick, *The Methods of Ethics*, 7th ed. (London: Macmillan and Co., 1907), pref. to the 6th ed., p. xvii.

[2] See below, Chapter Twelve, section 3.

to be elected, but that only one can succeed. It would then be in the interest of B but against the interest of K if B were elected, and vice versa, and therefore in the interest of B but against the interest of K if K were liquidated, and vice versa. But from this it would follow that B ought to liquidate K, that it is wrong for B not to do so, that B has not "done his duty" until he has liquidated K; and vice versa. Similarly K, knowing that his own liquidation is in the interest of B and therefore anticipating B's attempts to secure it, ought to take steps to foil B's endeavors. It would be wrong for him not to do so. He would "not have done his duty" until he had made sure of stopping B. It follows that if K prevents B from liquidating him, his act must be said to be both wrong and not wrong—wrong because it is the prevention of what B ought to do, his duty, and wrong for B not to do it; not wrong because it is what K ought to do, his duty, and wrong for K not to do it. But one and the same act (logically) cannot be both morally wrong and not morally wrong. Hence in cases like these morality does not apply.

This is obviously absurd. For morality is designed to apply in just such cases, namely, those where interests conflict. But if the point of view of morality were that of self-interest, then there could *never* be moral solutions of conflicts of interest. However, when there are conflicts of interest, we always look for a "higher" point of view, one from which such conflicts can be settled. Consistent egoism makes everyone's private interest the "highest court of appeal." But by 'the moral point of view' we *mean* a point of view which is a court of appeal for conflicts of interest. Hence it cannot (logically) be identical with the point of view of self-interest. Sidgwick is, therefore, wrong in thinking that consistent egoism is one of the "legiti-mate methods of ethics." He is wrong in thinking that an "intuition" is required to see that it is not the correct moral point of view. That it is not can be seen in the same way in which we can "see" that the Court of Petty Sessions is not the Supreme Court.

2 MORALITY INVOLVES DOING THINGS ON PRINCIPLE

Another feature of consistent egoism is that the rules by which a consistent egoist abides are merely rules of thumb. A consistent egoist has only one supreme principle, to do whatever is necessary for the realization of his one aim, the promotion of his interest. He does not have *principles,* he has only an aim. If one has adopted the moral point of view, then one acts on principle and not merely on rules of thumb designed to promote one's aim. This involves conforming to the rules whether or not doing so favors one's own or anyone else's aim.

Kant grasped this point even if only obscurely. He saw that adopting the moral point of view involves acting on principle. It involves conforming to rules even when doing so is unpleasant, painful, costly, or ruinous to oneself. Kant, furthermore, argued rightly that, since moral action is action on principle (and not merely in accordance with rules of thumb), a moral agent ought not to make exceptions in his own favor, and he interpreted this to mean that moral rules are absolutely inflexible and without exceptions. Accordingly he concluded that if 'Thou shalt not kill' states a moral rule, then any and every act correctly describable as an act of killing someone must be said to be morally wrong.

Kant also saw that this view required him to reject some of our deepest moral convictions; we certainly think that the killing of a man in self-defense or by the hangman is not morally wrong. Kant was prepared to say that our moral convictions are wrong on this point. Can we salvage these moral convictions? The only alternative, to say that acting on principle does not require us not to make exceptions in our own favor, seems to be equally untenable.

It is therefore not surprising that many philosophers have abandoned Kant's (and the commonsense) view that the moral rightness of an act is its property of being in accordance with a moral rule or principle. Thus, the deontologists claim that rightness is a simple property which we can "see" or "intuit" in an act, and the utilitarians, that rightness is a complex property, namely, the tendency of an act to promote the greatest happiness of the greatest number. But, as is well known, these accounts are not plausible and lead to considerable difficulties.

However, this whole problem arises only because of a confusion, the confusion of the expression 'making an exception to a rule' with the expression 'a rule has an exception.' As soon as this muddle is cleared away, it can be seen that Kant is right in saying that acting on principle implies making no exception in anyone's favor, but wrong in thinking that therefore all moral rules must be absolutely without exception.

'No parking in the city' has a number of recognized exceptions which are part of the rule itself, for example, 'except in the official parking areas,' 'except in front of a parking meter,' 'except on Saturday mornings and after 8 p.m. every day.' A person who does not know the recognized exceptions does not completely know the rule, for these exceptions more precisely define its range of application. A policeman who is not booking a motorist parking in front of a parking meter is not granting exemption to (making an exception in favor of) this motorist. On the contrary, he is administering the rule correctly. If he did apply the no-parking rule to the motorist, *he* would be applying it where *it* does not apply, because this is one of the recognized exceptions which are *part of* the rule. On the other hand, a policeman who does not book a motorist parking his vehicle in a prohibited area at peak hour on a busy day is making an exception in the motorist's favor. If he does so because the man is his friend, he illegitimately grants an exemption. If he does so because the motorist is a doctor who has been called to attend to a man lying unconscious on the pavement, this is a "deserving case" and he grants the exemption legitimately.

Apply this distinction to the rules of a given morality. Notice first that moral rules differ from laws and regulations in that they are not administered by special administrative organs such as policemen and magistrates. Everyone "administers" them himself. Nevertheless, it makes sense to speak of making exceptions in one's own favor. For one may refuse to apply the rule to oneself when one knows that it does apply, that is to say, one may refuse to observe it even when one knows one should. And what is true of making exceptions in one's own favor is true also of making them in favor of someone else. It is almost as immoral to make exceptions in favor of one's wife, son, or nephew as in favor of oneself.

When we say, therefore, that a person who has killed a burglar in self-defense has not done anything wrong, we are not making an exception in the houseowner's favor. It is much nearer the truth to say that, in our morality, the rule 'Thou shalt not kill' *has several recognized exceptions*, among them 'in self-defense.' We can say that a man does not know fully our moral rule 'Thou shalt not kill' if he does not know that it has, among others, this exception.

Like other rules of reason, our moral convictions are so only *presumptively*.[3] Killing is wrong *unless* it is killing in self-defense, killing by the hangman, killing of an enemy in wartime, accidental killing, and possibly mercy killing. If it is one of these types of killing, then it is *not* wrong.

---

[3] See above, Chapter Two, sections 5 and 6.

Even if it is one of the wrongful acts of killing, it is so only *prima facie*, other things being equal. For there may have been an overriding moral reason in favor of killing the man, for example, that he is about to blow up a train and that this is the only way of stopping him.

One further point should be made to avoid misunderstanding. Unlike laws and regulations, moral rules have not been laid down by anyone. Knowing moral rules cannot, therefore, involve knowing exactly what a certain person has enjoined and forbidden and what exceptions he has allowed, because there is no such person. In the case of regulations and laws, it was precisely this knowledge which enabled us to draw the distinction between saying that someone was granting an exception and saying that he was merely applying the rule which, for cases of this sort, provided for an exception. Our distinction seems to collapse for moral rules.

However, the answer to this is simple. When a magistrate is empowered to make exceptions or grant exemptions in "deserving cases," the question of what is a "deserving case" is not of course answered in the regulation itself. If it were, the magistrate would not be exercising his power to grant exemption, but would simply apply the regulation as provided in it. How, then, does the magistrate or policeman know what is a deserving case? The doctor who parks his car in a prohibited spot in order to attend to an injured man is such a case, namely, a *morally deserving* case. The principles in accordance with which policemen or magistrates grant exemptions to existing regulations are moral principles. In the case of moral rules, there cannot be any distinction between exceptions which are part of the rule and deserving cases. *Only* deserving cases can be part of the moral rule, and *every* deserving case is properly part of it. Hence while in the case of laws and regulations there is a reason for going beyond the exceptions allowed in the regulation itself (when there is a morally deserving instance), in the case of moral rules there is no such reason. For all deserving cases are, from the nature of the case, part of the moral rule itself. Hence it is never right to make an exception to a moral rule in anyone's favor. Kant is therefore quite right in saying that it is always wrong to make exceptions to moral rules in one's own favor (and for that matter in anyone else's), but he is wrong in thinking that this makes moral rules inflexible.

All this follows from the very nature of moral principles. They are binding on everyone alike quite irrespective of what are the goals or purposes of the person in question. Hence self-interest cannot be the moral point of view, for it sets every individual one supreme goal, his own interest, which overrules all his other maxims.

3 MORAL RULES ARE MEANT FOR EVERYBODY

The point of view of morality is inadequately characterized by saying that I have adopted it if I act on principles, that is, on rules to which I do not make exceptions whenever acting on them would frustrate one or the other of my purposes or desires. It is characterized by greater universality than that. It must be thought of as a standpoint from which principles are considered as being acted on *by everyone*. Moral principles are not merely principles on which a person must always act without making exceptions, but they are principles *meant for everybody*.

It follows from this that the teaching of morality must be completely universal and open. Morality is meant to be taught to all members of the group in such a way that everyone can and ought always to act in accordance with these rules. It is not the preserve of an oppressed or privileged class or individual. People are neglecting their duties if they do not teach the moral rules to their children. Children are removed from the homes of criminals because they are not likely to be taught the moral rules there. Furthermore, moral rules must be taught quite openly and to everybody without discrimination. An esoteric code, a set of precepts known only to the initiated and perhaps jealously concealed from outsiders, can at best be a religion, not a morality. 'Thou shalt not eat beans and this is a secret' or 'Always leave the third button of your waistcoat undone, but don't tell anyone except the initiated members' may be part of an esoteric religion, but not of a morality. 'Thou shalt not kill, but it is a strict secret' is absurd. 'Esoteric morality' is a contradiction in terms. It is no accident that the so-called higher religions were imbued with the missionary spirit, for they combine the beliefs of daemons and gods and spirits characteristic of primitive religions with *a system of morality*. Primitive religions are not usually concerned to proselytize. On the contrary, they are imbued with the spirit of the exclusive trade secret. If one thinks of one's religion as concentrated wisdom of life revealed solely to the *chosen* people, one will regard it as the exclusive property of the club, to be confined to the elect. If, on the other hand, the rules are thought to be for everyone, one must in consistency want to spread the message.

The condition of universal teachability yields three other criteria of moral rules. They must not, in the first place, be "self-frustrating." They are so if their purpose is frustrated as soon as everybody acts on them, if they have a point only when a good many people act on the opposite principle. Someone might, for instance, act on the maxim 'When you are in need, ask for help, but never help another man when he is in need.' If everybody adopted this principle, then their adoption of the second half would frustrate what obviously is the point of the adoption of the first half, namely, to get help when one is in need. Although such a principle is not self-contradictory—for anybody could consistently adopt it—it is nevertheless objectionable from the moral point of view, for it could not be taught openly to everyone. It would then lose its point. It is a parasitic principle, useful to anyone only if many people act on its opposite.

The same is true of "self-defeating" and "morally impossible" rules. A principle is self-defeating if its point is defeated as soon as a person lets it be known that he has adopted it, for example, the principle 'Give a promise even when you know or think that you can never keep it, or when you don't intend to keep it.' The very point of giving promises is to reassure and furnish a guarantee to the promisee. Hence any remark that throws doubt on the sincerity of the promiser will defeat the purpose of making a promise. And clearly to *let it be known* that one gives promises even when one knows or thinks one cannot, or when one does not intend to keep them, is to raise such doubts. And to say that one acts on the above principle is to imply that one may well give promises in these cases. Hence to reveal that one acts on this principle will tend to defeat one's own purpose.

It has already been said that moral rules must be capable of being taught openly, but this rule is self-defeating when taught openly, for then everyone would be known to act on it. Hence it cannot belong to the morality of any group.

Lastly, there are some rules which it is literally impossible to teach in the way the moral rules of a group must be capable of being taught, for example, the rule 'Always assert what you think not to be the case.' Such *morally impossible* rules differ from self-frustrating and self-defeating rules in that the latter could have been taught in this way, although it would have been quite senseless to do so, whereas the former literally cannot be so taught. The reason why the above rule cannot be taught in this way is that the only possible case of acting on it, doing so secretly, is ruled out by the conditions of *moral teaching*.

(1) Consider first someone secretly adopting this rule. His remarks will almost always mislead people, for *he will be taken to be saying what he thinks true*, whereas he *is* saying the opposite. Moreover, in most cases what he thinks (and not what he says) will be true. Thus, it will usually be the case that p is true when he says 'not-p,' and not-p when he says 'p,' whereas people will take it that p is true when he says 'p,' and not-p when he says 'not-p.' Thus communication between him and other people breaks down, since they will almost always be misled by him whether he wishes to mislead them or not. The possibility of communication depends on a speaker's ability *at will* to say either what he thinks to be the case or what he thinks not to be the case. Our speaker cannot communicate because by his principle he is forced to mislead his hearers.

Thus, anyone secretly adopting the principle 'Always assert what you think not to be the case' cannot communicate with others since he is bound to mislead them whether he wants to or not. Hence he cannot possibly teach the principle to anybody. And if he were to teach the principle without having adopted it himself, then, although he would be understood, those who adopted it would not. At any rate, since moral teaching involves teaching rules such as the taught may openly avow to be observing, this case is ruled out. A principle which is taught for secret acceptance only cannot be embodied in a *moral* rule of the group.

(2) Of course, people might soon come to realize what is the matter with our man. They may discover that in order not to be misled by what he says they have only to substitute 'p' for 'not-p' and vice versa. But if they do this, then they have interpreted his way of speaking, not as a reversal of the general

presumption that one says what one thinks is the case (and not the opposite), but as a change of the use of 'not.' In his language, it will be said, 'not' has become an affirmation sign, negation being effected by omitting it. Thus, if communication is to be possible, we must interpret as a change in usage what is intended as the reversal of the presumption that every assertion conveys what the assertor believes to be the case.

If everyone were, by accident, to adopt simultaneously and secretly our principle 'Always assert what you think is not the case,' then, for some time at least, communication would be impossible. If, on the other hand, it were adopted openly, then communication would be possible, but only if the adoption of this principle were to be accompanied by a change in the use of "not" which would completely cancel the effect of the adoption of the principle. In that case, however, it can hardly be said that the principle has been adopted.

(3) The case we are considering is neither (1) nor (2). We are considering the open teaching of the principle 'Always assert what you think is not the case,' for open acceptance by everybody, an acceptance which is not to be interpreted as a change in the use of 'not.' But this is nonsense. We cannot all *openly* tell one another that we are always going to mislead one another in a certain way and insist that we must continue to be misled, though we know how we could avoid being misled. I conclude that this principle could not be embodied in a rule belonging to the morality of any group.

These points are of general interest in that they clarify some valuable remarks contained in Kant's doctrine of the categorical imperative. In particular they clarify the expression "can will" contained in the formulation 'Act so that thou *canst will* thy maxim to become a universal law of nature.' "Canst will" in one sense means what I have called "morally possible." Your maxim must be a formula which is morally possible, that is, which is logically capable of being a rule belonging to the morality of some group, as the maxim "Always lie" is not. No one *can* wish that maxim to be a rule *of some morality*. To say that one is wishing it is to contradict oneself. One cannot wish it any more than one can wish that time should move backwards.

The second sense of "can will" is that in which no rational person can will certain things. Self-frustrating and self-defeating moral rules are not morally impossible, they are merely senseless. No rational person could wish such rules to become part of any morality. That is to say, anyone wishing that they should, would thereby expose himself to the charge of irrationality, like the person who wishes that he should never attain his ends or that he should (for no reason at all) be plagued by rheumatic pains throughout his life.

The points just made also show the weakness of Kant's doctrine. For while it is true that someone who acts on the maxim 'Always lie' acts on a morally impossible one, it is not true that every liar necessarily acts on that maxim. If he acts on a principle at all, it may, for instance, be 'Lie when it is the only way to avoid harming someone,' or 'Lie when it is helpful to you and harmful to no one else,' or 'Lie when it is entertaining and harmless.' Maxims such as these can, of course, be willed in either of the senses explained.

4 MORAL RULES MUST BE FOR THE GOOD OF EVERYONE ALIKE

The conditions so far mentioned are merely formal. They exclude certain sorts of rule as not coming up to the formal requirements. But moral rules should also have a certain sort of content. Observation of these rules should be *for the good of everyone alike*. Thrasymachus' view that justice is the advantage of the stronger, if true of the societies of his day, is an indictment of their legal systems from the moral point of view. It shows that what goes by the name of morality in these societies is no more than a set of rules and laws which enrich the ruling class at the expense of the masses. But this is wrong because unjust, however much the rules satisfy the formal criteria. For given certain initial social conditions, formal equality before the law may favor certain groups and exploit others.

There is one obvious way in which a rule may be for the good of everyone alike, namely, if it furthers the common good. When I am promoted and my salary is raised, this is to my advantage. It will also be to the advantage of my wife and my family and possibly of a few other people—it will not be to the advantage of my colleague who had hoped for promotion but is now excluded. It may even be to his detriment if his reputation suffers as a result. If the coal miners obtain an increase in their wages, then this is to the advantage of coal miners. It is for their common good. But it may not be to the advantage of anyone else. On the other hand, if production is raised and with it everyone's living standard, that is literally to everyone's advantage. The rule 'Work harder,' if it has these consequences, is for the common good of all.

Very few rules, if any, will be for the common good of everyone. But a rule may be in the interest of everyone alike, even though the results of the observation of the rule are not for the common good in the sense explained. Rules such as 'Thou shalt not kill,' 'Thou shalt not be cruel,' 'Thou shalt not lie' are obviously, in some other sense, for the good of everyone alike. What is this sense? It becomes clear if we look at these rules from the moral point of view, that is, that of an independent, unbiased, impartial, objective, dispassionate, disinterested observer. Taking such a God's-eye point of view, we can see that it is in the interest of everyone alike that everyone should abide by the rule 'Thou shalt not kill.' From the moral point of view, it is clear that it is in the interest of everyone alike if everyone alike should be allowed to pursue his own interest provided this does not adversely affect someone else's interests. Killing someone in the pursuit of my interests would interfere with his.

There can be no doubt that such a God's-eye point of view is involved in the moral standpoint. The most elementary teaching is based on it. The negative version of the so-called Golden Rule sums it up: 'Don't do unto others as you would not have them do unto you.' When we teach children the moral point of view, we try to explain it to them by getting them to put themselves in another person's place: 'How would you like to have that done to you!' 'Don't do evil,' the most readily accepted moral rule of all, is simply the most general form of stating this prohibition. For doing evil is the opposite of doing good. Doing good is doing for another person what, if he were following (self-interested) reason, he would do for himself. Doing evil is doing to another person what it would be contrary to reason for him to do to himself. Harming another, hurting another, doing to another what he dislikes having done to him are the specific forms this takes. Killing, cruelty, inflicting pain, maiming, torturing, deceiving, cheating, rape, adultery are instances of this sort of behavior. They all violate the condition of "reversibility," that is, that the behavior in question must be acceptable to a person whether he is at the "giving" or "receiving" end of it.

It is important to see just what is established by this condition of being for the good of everyone alike. In the first place, anyone is doing wrong who engages in nonreversible behavior. It is irrelevant whether he knows that it is wrong or not, whether the morality of his group recognizes it or not. Such behavior is "wrong in itself," irrespective of individual or social recognition, irrespective of the consequences it has. Moreover, every single act of such behavior is wrong. We need not consider the whole group or the whole of humanity engaging in this sort of behavior, but only a single case. Hence we can say that all nonreversible behavior is morally wrong; hence that anyone engaging in it is doing what, prima facie, he ought not to do. We need not consider whether this sort of behavior has harmful consequences, whether it is forbidden by the morality of the man's group, or whether he himself thinks it wrong.

The principle of reversibility does not merely impose certain prohibitions on a moral agent, but also certain positive injunctions. It is, for instance, wrong—an omission—not to help another person when he is in need and when we are in a position to help him. The story of the Good Samaritan makes this point. The positive version of the Golden Rule makes the same point more generally: 'Do unto others as you would have them do unto you.' Note that it is wrong—not merely not meritorious—to omit to help others when they are in need and when you are in a position to help them. It does not follow from this, however, that it is wrong not to promote the greatest good of the greatest number, or not to promote the greatest amount of good in the world. Deontologists and utilitarians alike make the mistake of thinking that it is one, or the only one, of our moral duties to "do the optimific act." Nothing could be further from the truth. We do not have a duty to do good to others or to ourselves, or to others and/or to ourselves in a judicious mixture such that it produces the greatest possible amount of good in the world. We are morally required to do good only to those who are actually in need of our assistance. The view that we always ought to do the optimific act, or whenever we have no more stringent duty to perform, would have the absurd result that we are doing wrong whenever we are relaxing, since on those occasions there will always be opportunities to produce greater good than we can by relaxing. For the relief of suffering is always a greater good than mere enjoyment. Yet it is quite plain that the worker who, after a tiring day, puts on his slippers and listens to the wireless is not doing anything he ought not to, is not neglecting any of his duties, even though it may be perfectly true that there are things he might do which produce more good in the world, even for himself, than merely relaxing by the fireside.

5 UPSETTING AND RESTORING THE MORAL EQUILIBRIUM

So far, we have considered only primary moral rules, that is, those which prohibit or enjoin certain types of behavior, such as 'Thou shalt not kill,' 'Thou shalt not steal,' 'Thou shalt help thy neighbour when he is in need of your help,' and so on. Secondary rules of morality are those which prohibit or enjoin certain types of behavior *in response to* some "upset of the moral balance," for example, 'An eye for an eye, a tooth for a tooth,' 'Let him who is free from guilt throw the first stone,' 'One good turn deserves another.'

What is it to "upset the moral balance"? The moral balance is preserved when everyone is "strictly minding his own business." Plato was right in connecting morality with minding one's own business; he was wrong only in his explanation of the connection. Minding one's own business and not interfering with anyone else are not all there is to morality, though it is true that when everyone minds his own business the moral equilibrium is maintained. This equilibrium can be upset in two quite different ways. I may behave in a manner which upsets the moral balance against me or in my favor. I may accumulate a moral debit or credit account; the first when I do what I ought not to do, the second when I do "more than my duty"; the first when I violate a "rule of duty," the second when I observe a "rule of supererogation." When, for example, I kill someone, steal something, am cruel to someone, or commit adultery, I am accumulating a moral debit balance. If, on the other hand, at great risk to myself I save someone's life or make great financial sacrifices for the sake of a good cause, I am acquiring a moral credit balance. It is for cases of this sort that the secondary moral rules are devised. Primary moral rules define what it is, morally speaking, to mind one's own business, to preserve the moral equilibrium. Secondary moral rules indicate what is to be done by whom when the balance has been upset.

Secondary moral rules are determined by the concept of desert, of positive or negative moral merit. They state what a person deserves, that is, ought to get or have done to him, as a result of the upset of the moral balance. A person who has not upset the moral balance deserves nothing. He has neither positive nor negative moral merit.

The aim of a morality is to prevent the upsetting of the moral equilibrium by violation of "rules of duty" and to encourage it by the observation of "rules of supererogation." At the same time, the methods of deterring and encouraging potential rule breakers must not themselves interfere with the primary rules. The secondary rules are therefore seen as designed to "restore the moral balance." They have the object of deterring or encouraging rule breakers, but also of bringing the process to an end. When the balance is "restored," the secondary rules no longer apply.

Take first the case of preventing violations of rules of duty. An obvious, if crude, way of "restoring the moral equilibrium" is provided by the institution of revenge. The person injured returns the harm. The supreme principle governing such secondary rules is 'One bad turn deserves another.' This has the serious disadvantage that it is difficult to "restore" the moral equilibrium. Since revenge is itself the infliction of harm on an individual, the secondary rule applies again. In the institution of the vendetta or the blood feud, what is designed to discourage violations of primary moral rules in fact leads to endless mutual harming.

The substitution of punishment for revenge remedies this drawback. The infliction of hardship on the wrongdoer is taken out of the hands of the injured person or his aggrieved relations and handed over to a disinterested official. By making a ceremony of it, it is clearly indicated that this is not intended as merely the infliction of harm on an individual, but as the application of a secondary moral rule designed to "restore" the moral balance. The object of the practice is to deter future wrongdoers. The infliction of hardship on a given individual is justified by his prior violation of a primary moral rule. There is now no aggrieved person left. Punishment has restored the moral equilibrium. The wrongdoer has expiated, atoned for, his wrong. Everyone has a clean slate again. It is wrong for the aggrieved to continue to harbor a grudge, to refuse to forgive the wrongdoer.

The situation is somewhat different in the case of an upset of the moral balance by observing (not breaking) a rule of supererogation. Obviously, the point of these rules is that they should be observed rather than broken, although observing them (not breaking them) constitutes an upset of the moral equilibrium. Such breaches of the moral equilibrium are desirable. In order to encourage them, we have secondary rules of morality, guided by the general principle 'One good turn deserves another.' We say that a person who engages in works of supererogation thereby acquires moral desert or merit.

However, in the case of the personal requital of a good turn, there is nothing undesirable about the unending reciprocation of such good turns. It is desirable that the person who received the returns of gratitude should in turn feel grateful. There is, therefore, no reason why the state should take personal reciprocations out of the hands of the recipients and put communal rewards in their place. 'Mine is the vengeance' has a point; 'Mine is the gratitude' has not.

There are two conceptions which belong in this secondary field of morality, but which have usually been assigned to the primary field, obligation and justice. When we say that we are under an obligation to someone, we mean that we ought to restore the moral equilibrium by "discharging our obligation." To discharge one's obligations *is* to restore the moral equilibrium. Doing so terminates the special moral relationship created between two people by the upset of the moral balance which gave rise to the obligation. To say that killing is wrong or that one ought not to kill is to say something that does not involve the secondary field of morality. To say that one ought to discharge one's obligations is to say something that does. Many confusions and paradoxes could have been avoided if this distinction had been clearly grasped.

Justice is a moral concept involving the secondary field of morality. For 'doing justice' means 'giving to everyone what he deserves,' that is, restoring the moral equilibrium by the appropriate action—giving a reward, repaying a debt, passing sentence, administering punishment, and the like. Plato's examination of morality in the Republic is vitiated by his failure to distinguish between the primary notions of rightness and wrongness and the secondary notion of justice.

6 SOCIAL MORALITY

We have so far considered absolute morality only. As we have noted, the moral point of view is characterized by a formal and a material condition. The formal condition is this: a man cannot be said to have adopted the moral point of view unless he is prepared to treat the moral rules as principles rather than mere rules of thumb, that is, to do things *on principle* rather than merely to act purposively, merely to aim at a certain end. And, furthermore, he must act on rules which are meant for everybody, and not merely for himself or some favored group. The material condition is this: the rules must be for the good of everyone alike. This does not mean that they must be for the common good of all human beings, past, present, and future, for such a condition would be impossible to satisfy. Its meaning can be elucidated by setting forth the criteria of saying that a rule is for the good of everyone alike. As far as absolute morality is concerned, only one condition must be satisfied, namely, that these rules should be "reversible," that is, not merely for the good of the agent, but at least not detrimental to the persons who are affected by the agent's behavior.

An examination of social conditions will yield some further criteria of 'being for the good of everyone alike.' A society is more than just a number of individuals living in a certain area and behaving in ways directly affecting others, such as killing, maiming, and robbing. Life in society involves a social framework which multiplies the points of contact between individuals and which can transform the effects of a man's behavior on his fellow men. Within a given social framework, behavior may be harmful which is not, from its nature, the infliction of harm on another. It may be harmful only if and because a great many people in that society engage in it. No harm is done if one person walks across the lawn. But the lawn is ruined if everyone does. No harm is done if one person uses the gas. But if everyone uses it during peak hours, then the gas supply may break down, and everyone will be adversely affected.

The Moral Point of View

That such behavior is morally objectionable is widely recognized. We acknowledge that it is, by the well-known formula 'You can't do that; what if everyone did the same!' Kant thought of it as the core of his categorical imperative, 'Act only on that maxim whereby thou canst at the same time will that it should become a universal law.' This is precisely what we "cannot will" in the cases in question. Although it is not true that, as Kant put it, a will willing such a maxim to become a universal law would, literally, contradict itself, nevertheless, in making such a maxim *a universal law*, one would enjoin people to do evil, and such a law would obviously be wrong.

It is, however, important to distinguish behavior which is "nonuniversalizable" from behavior that is "nonreversible." The latter can be seen to be *wrong in itself*, irrespective of the consequences and of how many people engage in it. This is not so in the case of nonuniversalizable behavior. There we have to consider the consequences, and not merely of a single act but of a great many of them. There is nothing wrong in itself with putting one straw on the camel's back, but one of them will be the last.

What exactly does this prove? That no one is allowed to lay even one straw on the camel's back? That every act of this kind is wrong? Surely not. Before we can say that any act of this sort is wrong, a number of conditions must be satisfied.

In the first place, all concerned must be *equally entitled* to behave in the nonuniversalizable way. It would, for instance, be most undesirable if everyone had dinner at 6:30 P.M., for all the nation's service would then come to a standstill at that time. But it cannot follow from this that eating at 6:30 P.M. is wrong for everyone. It cannot follow because the argument applies equally for any time, and it must be all right to eat at *some* time. Of course, there is no serious problem here. Not everyone is equally entitled to have his dinner at

6:30 P.M. Those who are on duty at that time must have it before or after or while they are attending to their duties.

There are further conditions. If everyone were celibate all his life, mankind would die out, or, at any rate, the number would soon be so seriously reduced as to make life unbearable. Those who do not find the prospect of the end of the human race upsetting will have to admit that the return to primitive conditions is undesirable. Again, if everyone suddenly stopped smoking, drinking, gambling, and going to the pictures, some states might go bankrupt and this would be undesirable. All the same, it can hardly be true that abstinence in matters of sex, smoking, drinking, gambling, and visits to the cinema can be wrong in any and every case, even though we are surely all equally entitled to refrain from these ways of spending our time.

There must, therefore, be a further condition. Everyone must not only be equally entitled to engage in these forms of activity, but people must also be inclined to do so. There would have to be a real danger that, unless they are stopped somehow, many will engage in this sort of behavior. People are lazy, so they will not go to the polling booth or make the detour round the newly planted lawn. People like picking flowers, so they will destroy the rare wild flowers. People want to heat their rooms, so they will want to use their radiators during peak hours. But there is no great danger that they will all go celibate, or give up smoking and drinking.

This point, by the way, shows that nonuniversalizability cannot be adduced to show that suicide is wrong. Suicide is no more wrong than celibacy and for the same reason. People are less keen on suicide even than on celibacy. There is no danger of the race dying out. In fact, all over the world people are so keen on procreation that the suicide rate could go up a long way before anyone need be alarmed. Of course if, one day, life and sex were to become burdens to all of us and if, nevertheless, it really is desirable that the race should go on, then reckless suicide or slothful celibacy might become morally wrongful types of conduct. Until then, those weary of life and sex need not have a bad conscience about their un-common indulgences.

There is one further point in this. To say that it is wrong to walk across the lawn or switch on the gas during peak hours, provided (a) it would have undesirable consequences *if* every-one did it, (b) we are all equally entitled to do it, and (c) doing it is an indulgence, not a sacrifice, amounts to saying that since refraining from doing these things is a sacrifice such a sacrifice for the common good should not be demanded of one or a few only, but equally of all, even if a universal sacrifice is not needed. Since no one is more entitled than anyone else to indulge himself and since *all* cannot do so without the undesirable consequences which no one wants, *no one* should be allowed to indulge himself.

Now the conditions are complete. If the behavior in question is such that (i) the consequences would be undesirable if everyone did it, (ii) all are equally entitled to engage in it, and (iii) engaging in this sort of behavior is an indulgence, not a sacrifice, then such behavior *should be prohibited by the morality of the group*.

But now suppose that it is not prohibited. Is it wrong all the same? Kant certainly thought so. I think he is mistaken. For since, by indulging in the behavior in question, I am not actually doing any harm, my behavior is not wrong in itself, but only when taken in conjunction with that of others. I cannot prevent the evil by refraining. Others must refrain too. In the case of nonreversible behavior, *my action alone* is the cause of the evil. I can avoid the evil if I refrain. In the case under discussion, however, if I have reason to suppose that

the others will not refrain, I surely have reason not to refrain either, as my only reason for refraining is my desire to
avoid causing the evil consequences. If these cannot be avoided,
I have no reason not to indulge myself. If the grass is not
going to grow anyway, why should I make the detour?

It is no good arguing that I am not entitled to do wrong
just because other people might or probably would. For I am
not doing wrong. I have no moral reason for the sacrifice. I
need no justification or excuse, for my behavior is wrong only
if I have no reason to think that others will refuse to make
the sacrifice. If I have reason to think they will refuse to make
it, then I have reason to think that my own sacrifice will be in
vain; hence I have reason against making it.

Of course, if the results are *very* undesirable and my sacrifice
is *very* small and I am not very certain what the others will do,
I should take the risk of making the sacrifice even if it turns
out to have been in vain. But, otherwise, reason will support
the opposite course.

The situation is different if the morality or the custom or
the law of the group does already contain a rule forbidding such
behavior. If there is such a rule, then the behavior is wrong,
for such a rule has the backing of morality. As we have said,
a group ought to have rules forbidding nonuniversalizable
behavior. And when there is such a rule, then the community
has regulated behavior of this sort and I ought to do my share
toward the success of the regulation.

I should like to add one word about the morality of individual initiative in these matters. Some people think that
individuals should go ahead with a good example and not
wait until the rule-making powers of the group are used.
Others argue that this is putting too great a burden on the
public-spirited. Thus, compulsory military service with exemptions granted to those engaged in important national

industries is said by some to be fairer, volunteering for national service is said by others to be morally preferable. I can see no reason for the latter view. It may indeed seem preferable from the military point of view, for it may be argued that volunteers are better soldiers. But there is no reason why if keenness is wanted volunteers should not have preferential rights to serve in the army rather than in industry. On the other hand, there is no reason why the sacrifices involved in the defense of their country should be borne only by those who are taking their moral responsibilities seriously, and no reason why those who are not should benefit gratuitously. In the absence of argument showing that the method of individual initiative yields a more efficient army, the other seems to me preferable and, in any case, obviously fairer. Hesitation to use the lawmaking force of the community is understandable, for such use may endanger individual freedom, but often this hesitation is supported on the grounds of the moral preferability of individual sacrifice and initiative. Such arguments seem to me unsound.

Nine

Duties to Oneself

THE question is often raised whether morality arises out of the relations between people or whether moral precepts could apply to one single solitary person living on a desert island. Can such a person stand in any moral relations to himself? Can he have duties or obligations to himself? Is he morally at fault if he neglects his talents, commits suicide, ruins his health? Or is that entirely his own affair and, therefore, not a moral matter?

What exactly are we asking? The problem to be discussed is not what contribution society makes to morality, but what contribution is made by *oneself* and by *others*. The point at issue is whether someone's behavior, his feelings or thoughts, which could never affect anyone else, can be morally right or wrong, moral or immoral, or whether these attributes can apply only where there is interaction between persons. It should be noted that the question we are discussing has nothing to do with the level of education or sophistication reached by an individual. Our problem arises as much for Robinson Crusoe as for the father of a large family in a modern society insofar as he is engaged in activities that do not involve anyone else, such as when he strolls aimlessly around in his deserted orchard on a Sunday afternoon all by himself and when he has no duties or obligations to attend to.

It will be obvious from the position I have taken elsewhere that in my view morality arises out of the relations between individuals, that there would be no need for and no point in having a morality if people had no sort of contact with others, that the solitary individual could employ his reason in practical matters only from the point of view of self-interest, never from the moral point of view. If individuals live by themselves and cannot affect one another, then, morally speaking, there is nothing they may not do or refrain from doing. A world of Robinson Crusoes has no need for a morality and no use for one. Moral distinctions do not apply to it.

1   OBLIGATIONS TO ONESELF

The main objection to the view just stated rests on the conviction that we have obligations or duties to ourselves. Some moral philosophers have indeed claimed that we have obligations or duties only to ourselves and none to others. Broad [1] distinguishes three types of ethical theory, ethical egoism, ethical altruism, and ethical neutralism, according to the person to whom it is believed "each man has a predominant obligation." Ethical egoism is the view that each man has a predominant obligation to himself as such, ethical altruism the view that each man has a predominant obligation toward others as such, and ethical neutralism the view that "the

---

[1] C. D. Broad, "Certain Features in Moore's Ethical Doctrines," in *The Philosophy of G. E. Moore*, ed. by P. A. Schilpp (Evanston: Northwestern University, 1942), pp. 43 ff.

fundamental duty of each of us is simply to maximise, so far as he can, the balance of good over bad experiences throughout the whole aggregate of contemporary and future conscious beings."

I think Broad would allow mixed views, such as those of Ross and Carritt, who claim that everyone sometimes has obligations or duties to "others as such," as when it is someone's duty to keep a promise, or to "himself as such," as when it is someone's duty to promote his talents or his knowledge, and then again to no one in particular, as when someone simply has the duty to do "the optimific act." Is it true that anyone ever has an obligation to himself? (I do not think Broad meant anything very significant when he added the words "as such.")

The word 'obligation' occurs naturally in remarks such as 'I am under an obligation to the Bairds.' In this use, 'obligation' has three logical dimensions, 'the partner,' 'the ground,' and 'the content' of the obligation. We mention the partner of an obligation when we answer the question '*To whom* is A under an obligation?'; the ground when we answer the question '*On account of what* is A under an obligation to B?'; and the content when we answer the question '*What* does A's obligation to B *consist in?*' It is obvious from this that moral obligations are moral relationships between at least two people. They arise only when the normal moral relationship between two or more people, that of moral noninvolvement, is disturbed, and they end only when the state of moral noninvolvement is restored. Restoring this state is called 'discharging the obligation.' Not restoring it is failing to discharge it. When one does not discharge it, one's partner of the obligation is morally entitled to complain. He is entitled to do so until the obligation is discharged and, furthermore, any harm or damage done by the delay is compensated for.

216

Duties to Oneself

Clearly, one cannot be literally under an obligation *to* oneself. There could be no such thing as upsetting the moral relation between oneself and oneself, no such thing as restoring it. It would be absurd for oneself to complain because one had failed to discharge one's obligation to oneself or to have a clear conscience because one had discharged it.

There is a slightly different use of 'obligation,' as in 'You are under an obligation to return the sleeping bag by Friday; they want it before the weekend' or 'You have an obligation to look after that dog for the Bairds—you promised, remember?' Sometimes we ought to do a certain specific thing, because we promised *someone* to do it; we have an obligation *to him* to do it. There are still the three dimensions of an obligation. The partner is the one to whom we have given a promise; the ground is the fact that we promised; the content is what we have promised. However, there are slight differences. The ground is not a benefit we have *received*, but a specific undertaking we have *given*. The content is not something indefinite, *some* good turn in return, but a definite performance specified in the undertaking. Promises are simply socially recognized ways of bringing into being at will highly specific moral ties between at least two people. Again, an obligation may arise when someone has done some damage to someone else. Then the person who has caused the damage has an obligation to repair it, whether he has inflicted it deliberately or accidentally.

It is obvious that in these uses also it does not make sense to say that one has an obligation to oneself. If I "promise myself" a holiday, I cannot complain if I do not finally take one, nor can I boast of a clear conscience if I do. And if I deliberately or accidentally damage my car, I cannot argue that I ought to use my money to repair the damage since otherwise I would be failing to discharge one of my obligations, to wit one to myself.

What makes it appear that the expression 'obligation to oneself' is meaningful is the confusion between the three logical dimensions of the obligation. When I promise my wife to look after my health or to give myself a holiday at Christmas or to buy myself a new overcoat, I have an obligation to my wife to do these things. But since *what* I have an obligation (*to her*) to do is something "for myself," that is, to my advantage, it is not unnatural to say in such a case that this is an obligation *to myself*. If one furthermore forgets that the ground of my obligation was my promise to my wife, one might think that the fact that something is for my advantage is what gives rise to this obligation. From this it is only a short step to the view that *only* the fact that something is for my advantage can give rise to an obligation, that is, that all obligations are obligations to myself.

It should be obvious now that ethical egoism, the view "that one has a predominant obligation to oneself as such," is false. Since it does not make sense to say that one has an obligation to oneself, it cannot make sense to say that one has a predominant obligation to oneself as such. Nor can it be true that one, let alone the only, ground of an obligation (to someone, or to do something) is the fact that doing it would be advantageous to oneself. For obligations between people can arise only on account of what has already happened or been done. The future is indeed morally relevant, but it does not create obligations. The fact that if I were to put prussic acid into someone's tea he would die after drinking it does indeed imply that I *ought not* to put prussic acid into his tea, but it does not give rise to an obligation. It is not the case that I am under an obligation *to him* not to do so. Everyone else is in broadly the same position as he. What is more, I can, at no time, discharge this obligation. No sooner have I "discharged it" (by not putting any prussic acid into his tea) than I am under the same obligation again. Moreover, there is an indefinite number of such obligations on me all the time. But obligations which, from the nature of the case, cannot be discharged are not obligations at all.

It will, perhaps, be objected that I have completely misunderstood what philosophers have said. After all, they were not talking about obligations in the sense of social, but of moral obligations. 'We are under an obligation to the Bairds, we must invite them to our next party' is not a remark involving a moral obligation. It merely says that we have a social obligation.

This contrast between social and moral obligation is a muddle. My obligation may well be both social *and* moral. To say that an obligation is social is to say something about the content, that is, about how it can be discharged; to say that it is moral is to say what is involved in discharging or failing to discharge it. To say that an obligation is social is to say that its discharge involves a "social performance," that is, something like an invitation to a party, a dinner, a theater performance, the sending of flowers, or the arrangement of a picnic. To say that an obligation is moral is to say that it is morally wrong not to discharge it. When I am under an obligation to the Bairds because I have been invited to their place many times, then in order to discharge this obligation I must invite them back or take them to the pictures or send them flowers, that is, do something "in the realm of the social." Just what is the appropriate thing will be regulated by custom. In Malaya, if you have been invited to a wedding, "the guest of a dinner party after a wedding hands over a pound note to his host, who calls out the amount of the contribution loudly so that all the guests may hear, while a clerk sits by and writes it down." [2] In Europe, this would not be the proper way of discharging an obligation incurred by being invited to a wedding. To say that I have many social obligations is simply to say that I have many dates, appointments, dinner parties, that I have little free time because my diary is full of such appointments. Among these may be my dinner party for the Bairds, a social obligation into which I have entered in order thereby to discharge my obligation to the Bairds.

The question whether my social obligations are also moral obligations is open. When I have accepted an invitation, then I have given a promise to go there. This is both a social and a moral obligation; social because it consists in going to a party, moral because failure to discharge it would be a breach of a promise, a breach which is morally wrong. If I refuse an invitation, then I have no obligation, social or moral, to go there. Of course, if the Bairds want to give a party to a number of single or grasswidowed women and they are short of single or grasswidowed men, and I satisfy the condition, then *accepting* their invitation may be doing them a favor, and if I am under an obligation to them, I can and should discharge it by accepting the invitation.

That my obligation is social is perfectly compatible with its being moral, but of course it is also compatible with its being nonmoral. When a gentleman offers a lady a seat in the tram, he puts her under an obligation. It is so slight that a 'Thank you' or 'Much obliged' from her not merely acknowledges but discharges it at the same time. If she does not bother to say even this, she has failed to discharge her obligation, but that is not immoral—it is merely rude. Whether my obligation is moral or nonmoral depends on the seriousness of what is involved. The dividing line is obviously not sharp.

---

[2] Raymond Firth, *Elements of Social Organization* (London: Watts & Co., 1951), p. 194.

Duties to Oneself

Some philosophers might still object. They might say that they are not concerned with the word 'obligation' in this sense. They mean to use it as the noun of 'ought.' Moreover, while quite prepared to admit that obligations, in their sense, had all sorts of *immediate* grounds, they would say that, ultimately, there is only one ground, or at most there are a few grounds, of our moral obligations.

It is, of course, true that moral philosophers really wished to use the word 'obligation' (and for that matter also the word 'duty') as simply the noun of 'ought.' Some of them would be quite prepared to speak of "an ought" instead of 'an obligation' or 'a duty' if the latter expressions were thought confusing. When asked what they meant by 'obligation,' they would be quite prepared to say that 'A has an obligation to do *x*' meant the same as 'A ought to do *x*.'

We have already seen that, literally, this is a mistake. Admittedly, whenever A has an obligation to do *x*, it is also true that he ought to do *x*. But the converse is not true. I have never killed anyone or stolen anything. These are things which it would have been *wrong* for me to do and which, if I had done them, I ought not to have done, but they are not things which I had, or was under, *an obligation not* to do. In refraining from doing them, I refrained from doing what is wrong or what I ought not to do, but I did not discharge an obligation to anyone or everyone. It is certainly not true that I ever discharged any obligations to Stalin or Chiang Kai-shek, for the simple reason that I never had any obligations to these gentlemen. Nevertheless, if I had killed either of them, I would (or at any rate, I might) have done something wrong, something I ought not to have done.

It might be thought that this was merely a verbal victory. I have proved that these philosophers have used the word 'obligation' in an unorthodox way. If the word 'obligation' is replaced by the word 'ought,' and the necessary grammatical adjustment made, their point is restored in accordance with ordinary usage. This is not merely a verbal point. These philosophers wish to defend the view that we have obligations to ourselves. Though at first plausible, it rests on the confusion of partner, ground, and content of an obligation. If the word 'obligation' were not substituted for 'ought,' even its initial plausibility would vanish. The question 'To whom have you an ought?' would not be found perplexing or urgently in need of an answer by anyone.

Consider next the distinction between "the immediate" and "the ultimate" ground of an obligation. The traditional view is that we can trace the grounds of our obligations back and back till we finally reach the ultimate ground, or one of the several ultimate grounds, of obligations. The three theories mentioned by Broad are alternative views on what is the ultimate ground of obligations.

Let us first make the necessary verbal alterations. When we say that someone *ought* to do something, we lay ourselves open to the question 'Why?' A person who says, 'A ought to do *x*,' and when asked 'Why?' replies that there is no reason must be said not to know the use of the word 'ought.' 'A ought to do *x*' is another way of saying, 'There is a reason for A to do *x*' or 'There is a reason why A should do *x*.' Among the reasons given may be nonmoral or moral ones. The moral reason may be that it would be *wrong not* to do it (for example, not to help a man in distress) or that he *has an obligation* to do it (for example, when he has promised to or when he is under an obligation to someone and that person asks him to) or that *it is his duty* to do it (for example, to put stamps on the envelopes and to post them on his way home). These are very different grounds for saying that someone ought to do something. We have already seen how we tell that a certain sort of act is morally wrong: it has to be of a certain general type. We have just discussed the conditions under which we say that someone has an obligation to someone. We have seen how such obligations arise. This is a very different matter from saying that something is wrong. We shall discuss in the next section what conditions must be fulfilled for saying correctly that it is someone's duty to do something. All these different facts, that something is wrong, that someone has an obligation to someone to do something, that it is someone's duty to do something, are moral *reasons for saying* that he ought (or ought not) to do it.

There is no natural chain of reasons here, beginning with a first link, an immediate or preliminary reason, and ending with a last link, the ultimate reason. When we have given these reasons, we have given reasons for saying that someone ought (or ought not), prima facie, to do something. We have given all the reasons we need to give. It is not true that our chain of reasons has only just begun and must be completed. Our reasons do not, as it were, hang in the air. We do not have to anchor or secure them to something such as a self-evident ultimate reason, a First Cause, an Unmoved Mover, or a Tortoise on which it all rests.

Of course, when we have given these reasons, we may still be assailed by doubts, but these are not set at rest by further installments of the same story. They arise not because part of our story is as yet untold, but because we may not believe, or be certain about, what has already been said. We claimed that someone ought, prima facie, to do something, because it would be wrong for him not to do it or because he had an obligation or a duty to do it. We may, therefore, have two quite different doubts: (a) whether the adduced "facts" really are facts; (b) whether the adduced facts really constitute moral reasons.

There is no special difficulty about doubt (a). We simply

have to investigate empirically whether the factual claims made are true or false. Again, concerning (b), it is not difficult to see that, in the fact that a certain line of conduct is morally wrong or is the failure to discharge an obligation or the neglect of a duty, one has a good reason for saying that the person concerned ought not to engage in this sort of conduct. It is a good thing for everyone alike that people should be discouraged from engaging in what we call wrong conduct, a good thing that people should be encouraged to enter into the sort of personal relationships which are said to give rise to obligations and a good thing that they should be encouraged to reciprocate. Similarly, it is a good thing that people should have specific tasks, that is, duties, assigned to them and that they should be encouraged to execute them to the best of their ability. It is equally obvious that the practice of giving promises is extremely useful. In a complex society it is impossible for the relationships between people to be completely uniform and standardized. There must be special undertakings between individuals. It is therefore of great advantage that such relationships should be entered into and completed, that people can tie one another morally by a socially acknowledged device, such as the handshake, the signature, the expression 'I promise,' and the like.

The use of the words 'ought,' 'duty,' and 'obligation' as synonyms helps to perpetuate the myth that moral reasoning consists in something like tying a moral judgment by a chain of reasons made up of links of the same kind to something that is not in need of reasons. And this myth inevitably leads to skepticism. As soon as this picture gains a hold on us, it drives us to look for something ultimate, indubitable, self-evident, not in need of further support, while at the same time it leaves no room for the existence of any such thing. For if there is a chain of reasons consisting of links of the same kind, then the doubt which arises about the first link can and must equally arise about all others. Removing the doubt about the first link by mentioning a second link is only putting off the evil day. We cannot stop at any link. The doubt that arose about the first must arise about the second. There can be no ultimate ground of our moral obligations any more than there can be a First Cause or an answer to the question what the earth rests on. The ultimate ground is no more satisfactory than the immediate, just as the Very First Cause is no more satisfactory than the immediate cause, and the Tortoise no more satisfactory than the Elephant.

The distinction between the different uses of 'ought,' 'duty,' and 'obligation' shows us clearly where reasons are called for and what sorts of reasons. We know that one sort is required when we ask, 'Why ought he to do this?' namely, reasons such as 'It would be wrong not to do it' or 'It would discharge his obligations' or 'It is his duty.' We know that another kind is required when we ask, 'Why has he an obligation?' namely, reasons such as 'Because he promised to do it' or 'Because they were very nice to him.' And an entirely different thing is called for when we ask, 'How is it that this is his duty?' namely, reasons such as 'Well, he took on the job, didn't he?' or 'He is the father, isn't he?'

All this helps us to see that there is no hopeless, endless chain of reasons, but only a few possibilities of error, each of which can be eliminated by taking the necessary care. And when once the hold of the model of an endless chain of reasons is broken, we can also see that the original question, 'What is the ultimate ground of moral obligation?' is a muddle. It breaks up into a number of separate questions each of which has a perfectly simple and straightforward answer.[3]

---

[3] See my article "Proving a Moral Judgment," *Philosophical Studies*, IV (no. 3, 1953), 33–43.

2 DUTIES TO ONESELF

But perhaps we have *duties* to ourselves? Consider how we ordinarily use this word. When we take on a job, we are told what our duties are. They consist of a certain number of tasks. A university teacher is required to give lectures and tutorials at certain times fixed by the university. He is supposed to set examination questions and mark them. He must do a certain amount of research, and so on. As far as his job is concerned, he has a certain number of duties. Every day, every week, every year in his life, he can look back and ask himself whether, during that time, he has attended to or neglected his duties. At any given moment, he may ask himself whether he is, there and then, attending to his duty or neglecting it or whether he is "free" or "off-duty," that is, neither attending to nor neglecting any one of his duties.

The important points about this use of 'duty' are the following. Duties are the sort of thing a man has in virtue of his job or station in society. Knowledge of his job and the ways of society include knowledge of his duties. Duties are tasks requiring attention to them. They determine certain times of one's life at which one is required to attend to them and other times when one is free.

As previously stated, the fact that a man has certain duties is a reason for saying that he ought to do certain things. What his duties are is determined by his job or position in society. We can, therefore, say at any given time what a given person's duties are, what it is his duty to do at that time. And if it is A's duty to do x here and now, then A ought (therefore) to do x here and now.

However, the word 'duty' is also used for other purposes. Since neglecting one's duty is a moral lapse, whereas attending to one's duty does not in itself yield any moral kudos, the expression 'I am (merely) doing my duty' has come to be used to rebut the suggestion that one is deserving moral praise or commendation. A lifeguard might say, 'I was only doing my duty,' when declining the thanks of the lady he has rescued. A holidaymaker might, modestly, say the same. But while both are using the expression to rebut the lady's thanks, the lifeguard is speaking the truth, for it was merely his duty, and the holidaymaker is not, for it was not his duty. Of course, if there were no lifeguards and no other swimmers about, then the holidaymaker *ought* certainly to have tried to rescue her if he could swim. He deserves moral censure if he does nothing. All the same, 'It was his duty to rescue her' would here be used in an extended way. The moral urgency of the claims of duties on us and the moral seriousness of the failure to attend to them have here been borrowed to make the point. Failing to jump in and rescue her is as bad, or almost as bad, as failing to attend to one's duties. However, strictly speaking, it is merely wrong not to jump in and help her, for reasons given above [4]; it is not really a neglect of one's duty unless one is a lifeguard.

The very question 'To whom do you have this duty?' is obscure. It may mean 'Who is entitled to complain if you fail to attend to your duty?', as in 'The soldier has a duty to his country' or 'The employee has a duty to his firm.' Obviously, no one can have a duty to himself, in this sense. No one can feel aggrieved by and complain about his own neglect of duty.

Another interpretation of the above question is, 'Who benefits from your attention to your duty?' as in 'The father has a duty to his children' or 'The rider has a duty to his horse.' Now, obviously, a person can have a duty to himself, in this sense, as when he has signed a contract to play professional tennis and there is a clause in the contract that he must spend half an hour under a hot shower every morning, run for an hour after breakfast, and so on. In that case, he has a duty to

---

[4] See p. 221.

do these things which are in his interest; though not because they are in his interest, but because he has signed the contract. No one ever has a duty to do something simply because it would be beneficial to someone if he did it. One comes to acquire duties by concluding contracts in which they are mentioned or by acquiring a certain status, such as citizen, husband, or father, of which they are a recognized part.

3 THE DUTY TO LIVE

But surely there are duties to oneself, it will be said. Surely we have a duty to ourselves to develop our talents, to study and work to make the best of our lives, to look after our health, and in any case to keep alive. We would be neglecting our duty to ourselves if we committed suicide. Surely, suicide is wrong.

As I explained in the previous section, it may indeed be true that we ought not to engage in some of the types of conduct mentioned. It may be that we ought not to do these things because it would be foolish to do them. It may even be that there are moral reasons against it. But certainly if there is a moral reason, it cannot be that engaging in these things would be neglecting duties to ourselves. The reason could only be that these types of conduct are morally wrong. Put in this way, the claim is now free from absurdity and open to investigation. It is now claimed, not that we have obligations or duties to ourselves—a contention which would be absurd—but that certain types of activity which are to our own detriment and no one else's are morally wrong, presumably *because* they are to our own detriment.

But even if this is true, these things are not *wrong in themselves*. Moral philosophers have not distinguished sharply enough between types of conduct which are wrong in themselves, because of what they are by their nature, and types of conduct which are wrong because of their consequences or wrong because they tend to be harmful whenever one engages in them.

It may, for instance, be the case that society has a claim on me to look after my health, to continue living and working, or to develop my talents. For I may be under an obligation to society which is making an effort to have me educated, to pay for adequate health services, and so on. Or it may be that I even have a duty to do so as a soldier or as a trainee. Or certain individuals such as my wife, my children, my aged parents may have claims against me. However, in the absence of such special moral considerations, there would be nothing wrong in itself with these types of conduct.

But suppose someone says that there is nothing wrong with neglecting my talents, either in itself or in any other way. I am not under an obligation to my society or anyone else. The universalization argument does not apply, for most people are only too anxious to develop their talents.[5] Can society create a moral wrong by incorporating in its morality the rule against neglecting one's talents?

There is no doubt that rules of this sort are part of our morality, or were so in the nineteenth century. People certainly believed that this sort of thing was wrong in itself. Duties to oneself were taken very seriously by our Victorian forebears and not only by them. Does 'Develop your talents' become a true moral precept if it is incorporated in the morality of a given society, in the way 'Drive on the left' becomes a true moral precept if it is incorporated in the law of the society? It is not only illegal to drive on the right, it is morally wrong, for it is morally wrong to break the law, and driving on the left is the law. Can we say, it is morally wrong to neglect one's talents when it is part of the moral convictions of a group that it is wrong to neglect one's talents?

---

[5] See above, Chapter Eight, section 6.

The answer is No. There is no parallel between the case of driving on the left and committing suicide. Although there is nothing wrong in itself with driving on the right or on the left, it is dangerous for everyone if people do not uniformly drive on the same side of the road. It is the business of the law to establish such beneficial uniformities. But there is no need for uniformity in the case of taking one's life. No harm is done if some unhappy people commit suicide and others do not.

What, then, is wrong with the law or the morality of a group which includes such rules as 'Don't commit suicide' or 'Develop your talents' even when no harm is done to others by the contravention of the rule? Note, however, that the community may need the labor power, the talents and ingenuity of every one of its members. In such a case, the rights of the community and the rights of individuals would have to be balanced against one another. I am here concerned only with cases where a person's suicide does not affect anyone else's interests at all. If the rule 'Don't take your own life' or 'Develop your talents' is applied to such cases, then the society gives moral backing to a precept which is advantageous merely to every member himself. Society is entitled to exert moral pressure where the interests of some members are threatened by the behavior of others. In our case, it exerts this sort of pressure where the interests of some members are threatened by their own deliberate or careless action. This is meddling in people's own affairs. Society is entitled to do so when people threaten the interests of *others*, for that is its business. But to use moral pressure to make people promote their own interest is not morality, but paternalism. It is treating adults as if they were children, as if they needed to be protected not only from others, but also from themselves.

Ten

The Social Factor in Morality

MORALITY, then, presupposes interaction between people. There is no need for and no point in a morality for solitary individuals on desert islands. But what about society? Granted that one individual is not sufficient, are a lot of individuals enough if they live in a state of nature, outside society? Can there be a morality in such a state? Is it not a fact, and is it not necessarily so, that morality comes into being only when men leave the state of nature and enter society? The question, in other words, appears to be whether morality is prior to society or comes afterwards, whether morality is the parent or the child of society. With this basic question a good many others are linked. Can people be moral by nature or must they be trained to be so by society? Are moral prohibitions dictated by human nature or do they arise out of the needs of society? Are our pangs of conscience and our guilt feelings the natural and untutored consequences of our doing wrong or are they the result of social conditioning? Are there eternal moral truths valid for all societies or are our moral convictions a matter of social convention? The answers to all these seem to follow from the answer to our basic question. But for this very reason, no answer to it is satisfactory.

As usual, a closer examination of the puzzle shows it to be a compound of several smaller questions. Our task is therefore more complex, but less perplexing than it appeared at first. Instead of having to unravel a seemingly insoluble big problem, we have to tackle a great many different small ones which are, severally, quite tractable. And since different answers are required for these minor questions, it is not surprising that no single answer to the major question which contains them all can be satisfactory.

In this chapter, I shall distinguish five minor questions which seem to me to be obscurely at the back of people's minds when they ask whether morality is prior or posterior to society: (a) whether or not there are some types of conduct which must be said to be right (or wrong) whatever changes occur in a given society: as there obviously are no types of conduct which must be said to be customary (or contrary to custom) whatever the changes that occur in the society in question; (b) whether or not there are some types of conduct which must be said to be right (or wrong) even in the absence of any society whatsoever: as there obviously are no types of conduct which can be said to be customary (or contrary to custom) in the absence of any society whatsoever; (c) whether, if there were such types of conduct, anyone could know, in the absence of any society whatsoever, that there were; (d) whether it is possible that people should, by nature, *be* moral or whether being moral involves having been trained to be; (e) whether social changes can have any influence on whether a certain type of conduct *is* right (or wrong) or merely on whether it *is believed* to be.

The Social Factor

The answer to question (d) will enable us to determine the relative importance of human nature and society in man's morals, that is, in the extent to which men conform in their moral practice to what they believe and preach. The answers to questions (a), (c), and (d) will further clarify our understanding of how it is we know what is right and wrong. And the answer to question (b) will throw light on the conditions under which our system of moral concepts properly applies.

1 ABSOLUTE MORAL TRUTHS AND SOCIAL CHANGE

We have already seen [1] that there are some types of conduct, such as killing human beings or cruelty, which are morally wrong whatever the social conditions. As far as these types of behavior are concerned, the collective will of a group, whether expressed through its customs and traditions or through the fiat of its legislator, is not entitled (morally speaking) to dictate in accordance with the desires or the interests of the majority or the group as a whole, but is bound by what is absolutely right.

This has been denied mainly because it was not understood how moral convictions could possibly be true or false. One of the main reasons for this difficulty was the erroneous conception of morality as a sort of law. However, law differs in this respect from morality: law is and ought only to be what the legislator lays down. It is simply the expression of the will of the legislator. There can be no legal truths. It follows from this that, while anyone can ascertain or have his own opinion of what the correct moral precepts or prohibitions are, no one can do so with respect to legal precepts or prohibitions.

It is a corollary of all this (which has already been mentioned [2] that we can distinguish between, say, English middle-

---

[1] Chapter Eight, section 4, pp. 202–204.
[2] Chapter Five, section 3.

class morality and Smith's morality, whereas we cannot distinguish between English law and Smith's law. Smith cannot have his own law in the way in which he can have his own morality. Smith is simply subject to English law in a manner in which he is not subject to English morality. Smith cannot accept or reject English law, neither as a whole nor in part, but he can accept or reject, at least in part, English middle-class morality. And all this follows from the fact that there are moral, but no legal truths. For if there are no legal truths, then obviously no individual can ascertain or even have his own opinion of what they are. If, on the other hand, there are moral truths, then everyone can have his own view of what they are.

It might be objected that this cannot be sound, for law and custom must be on par. Yet it does make sense to speak of Smith's customs as well as of English customs. It must be admitted, in fairness to this objection, that Smith may have his own customs different from those that are prevalent, but here 'custom' is used in two different senses. Smith's own customs are merely his own habits. English customs are not merely Englishmen's habits. For if Smith's customs differ from English customs, then what he does is *contrary to* custom. But if Smith's customs are merely different from the habits of other Englishmen, what he does is not contrary to custom. If Smith's customs differ from English middle-class customs, Smith and other members of the English middle-class need not disagree on what is customary and what is contrary to custom. There is no such ambiguity in 'morality.' If Smith's morality differs from English middle-class morality, then Smith and adherents of middle-class morality disagree on what is right and what is wrong.

There is a further indirect confirmation of the view that there are moral truths. When examining the relationship between the individual and the group, we find the following.

English middle-class morality and Smith's morality are logically on a par: they are the moral convictions of the individuals involved, namely, the members of the English middle-class and Smith, respectively. The morality of the group consists simply of the moral convictions of the overwhelming majority of its members. However, the question whether the group's convictions are correct is as open as whether any individual's are. The individual does not therefore derive his knowledge of what is right and wrong simply by consulting the morality of the group, as he does derive his knowledge of what is legal and illegal by simply consulting the law of the group. On the contrary, the morality of the group is true only if the moralities of its members are.

There can be no reason to doubt, then, that there are absolute moral truths, independent of social changes. Law and custom are social products which, from their nature, change when the "will of society" changes. By contrast, there are moral truths which are not thus logically dependent on the will of society. By 'the will of society' I mean either the will of its representatives entitled to introduce changes (the legislator) or its collective will expressed in what the majority regards as customary.

2 ABSOLUTE MORAL TRUTHS AND THE EXISTENCE OF SOCIETY

Does it follow from the fact that there are moral truths unaffected by social changes that there would be moral truths even if there were no societies at all? Nothing can obviously be said to be customary or contrary to custom, legal or illegal, in the absence of any society whatsoever. Similarly, it might be argued, it would not make sense to say that something was right or wrong where people lived outside society. The question, then, is whether or not any types of conduct could be said to be morally right (or wrong) where people live "outside society," "in a state of nature." The moment the question is raised doubts about its meaningfulness arise. After all, "living in society" and "living outside society" are figurative expressions which we never actually employ. Do we know what we mean by them?

It must be admitted that these phrases sound odd, for we never have occasion to use them. As far as we can tell, people have always lived in societies. We can, however, imagine what it would be like for men to live "in a state of nature." If human beings lived in small, biologically necessary but relatively impermanent groups consisting of one man, one woman, and their dependent offspring, if they had no language or only the most rudimentary forms of one, if they had no fund of knowledge and practical skills to pass on, if they did not inculcate in their young certain uniform rules of behavior, then we would have to say that these people lived "outside" society. To live in a society is to live among men who have a common way of life which they pass on to their children. Societies are "artificial" ways of life, ways of life which go beyond the instinctive or natural and sometimes counter to it.

Our question, then, makes sense. We understand the difference between a state of affairs in which societies exist and one in which none exist. Our question now is whether anything could be said to be right (or wrong) in a state of nature, where no societies exist, as obviously nothing can be said to be legal and customary in such a state. One of the reasons why nothing can there be said to be legal or customary is inapplicable in the case of morality: it is self-contradictory to say, 'In a state of nature killing is illegal or contrary to custom,' but there is nothing self-contradictory in saying, 'In a state of nature it is wrong to kill.' For 'illegal' and 'contrary to custom' imply a reference to a given social system. 'Illegal' means 'illegal in x.' 'Contrary to custom' means 'contrary to custom in x.' There is no such thing as illegality or contrariness to custom apart from a society where it is so. 'Morally wrong' does not carry such implications, hence such remarks involve no self-contradiction.

But while not self-contradictory, claims of the form 'x is wrong in a state of nature' might nevertheless be necessarily false. The reason for this may not be that their contradictories are necessarily true, as in the case of 'Circles are not round,' or that they imply the nonexistence of one of the presuppositions of their being either true or false, as in 'Killing is illegal in the state of nature' (for 'in the state of nature' implies that there is no society, while 'is illegal' presupposes that there is a society). Such claims might be necessarily false because in a state of nature there is no rational justification for the very distinction between morally right and wrong. They might, in other words, be necessarily false because to say that there is a state of nature is to assert the absence of conditions whose presence constitutes the only justification for distinguishing between morally right and wrong.

This, I take it, is Hobbes's contention. In the state of nature, he argues, reason tells us that we would *all* do much better if we *all* followed certain rules, which he calls the laws of nature. At the same time, reason also tells us not to obey these laws in that state because we have reason to think that other people will not follow them and we would do better not to follow them than to be the only ones to do so. Thus, Hobbes's account of the state of nature amounts to the claim that in such a state every statement is necessarily false which claims that some course of action is morally wrong. For to say that something is morally wrong is to imply that one ought not to do it, that to refrain from doing it is in accordance with reason. But it is Hobbes's main contention that in the state of nature to refrain from doing what is "wrong," that is, what is prohibited by the law of nature, is not in accordance with reason.

Is Hobbes's argument sound? What are its steps? The premise is that, in the absence of restrictions imposed by law, men will act either on impulse or in accordance with self-interest. From this Hobbes deduces that there will be perpetual conflict between men. For above everything else, men want to live. Because of the scarcity of resources, one man's luxury means another man's poverty. It is therefore in everyone's interest to secure for himself as great a share of them as possible, to hoard them for future emergencies, to defend them against all possible attacks, to engage in preventive action against others who might become a menace, and so on. In the absence of laws and agencies of law enforcement, there is therefore, and in reason ought to be, a perpetual war of everyone against everyone. As is well known, Hobbes thought that there was only one way out: the formation, by contract among all individuals, of an absolute ruler, a Leviathan, to whom every single man hands over all his rights and powers and who, in return, lays down and rigidly enforces laws. When this Sovereign is established, everybody knows that anyone transgressing the law will be punished. Each individual therefore has reason to obey the law and each, moreover, knows that all the others have reason to obey it, too. Everyone, therefore, has reason to expect that everyone else will obey it.

It has often been pointed out that this argument, as it stands, is unsound. For in a state of nature, the formation of a contract could not have had the desired effect. Between people who act only on impulse or in accordance with self-interest, mutual trust cannot be created by any sort of undertaking. Nor can a Leviathan be created by it. The state cannot come into being when no one can rely on anyone else to act in accordance with the rules, but only on impulse or as it serves his interest. No power could be concentrated in the hands of one person by the device of all others "handing over" their power to him, for power cannot be handed over by words alone. Otherwise the power of the Secretary General of the United Nations would be quite adequate.

However, Hobbes's point can be made in a way not open to this objection. True, a state of mutual trust cannot be brought about, in a state of nature, by the conclusion of a contract, but adequate mutual trust prevails in most societies, whether legal or prelegal, simply because there are established ways of behavior. Some societies do not have even a primitive legal system, but merely a set of customs which establish uniform ways of behavior and sufficient trust between its members. For every member knows that almost every other member will invariably behave in accordance with custom and not always on impulse or as his advantage dictates. Hobbes is merely wrong in thinking that a legal system can come into being by the conclusion of a mutual contract and that only a legal system can provide conditions of mutual trust. Hobbes may be quite right in his main point: only the existence of societies, that is, artificial, common, generally acknowledged, and generally followed ways of life can satisfy all the conditions for the application of moral concepts. Only when there are societies is it correct to say of any line of action that it is morally right or wrong, that one ought to do what is right and refrain from doing what is wrong, and that one ought to satisfy all the other demands of morality.

The question whether Hobbes is right on this point or not cannot be answered in this chapter, but will have to be postponed until Chapter Twelve, section 3.

3 IS KNOWLEDGE OF RIGHT AND WRONG POSSIBLE IN A STATE OF NATURE?

Even if Hobbes's argument is rejected that, outside society, nothing can *be* right or wrong, it might still be maintained that in such a state nothing could *be known* to be so. The most obvious reason for saying this is that, as has been shown, our knowledge of right and wrong depends on our ability to work out in deliberation what is so. Doing so in turn presupposes our ability to survey the facts with a view to determining which of them are moral pros and cons and our ability to weigh them against each other in order to ascertain which are the weightiest reasons. But is it not obvious that this ability requires training, that it presupposes a level of sophistication of which an individual cannot be capable unless he has been helped by the experience of generations? In conditions in which individuals have no cultural heritage to pass on to their children, no common skills, no common knowledge, no common rules of behavior, where language is at best quite primitive, there surely can be no system of reasoning at all, let alone one sufficiently elaborate to allow for specifically moral deliberations.

As already mentioned, the most popular answer to this would be the theory that our knowledge of right and wrong is not a matter of calculation relying on premises which require the experience of countless generations, but a sort of "seeing" or "intuiting" like knowing that something is yellow or that it is soft. Just as we know "immediately" or "intuitively" what is yellow by our eyes and what is soft by our fingers, so we know what is right and what is wrong by our conscience or moral sense. There is no need to worry about the way we learn the words 'right' and 'wrong.' We can discriminate colors before we learn the color words. If we did not, we could never learn them. Similarly, we can discriminate between right and wrong before we learn the words for these properties. Otherwise how could we ever pick up what these words meant?

Dismissing the obvious objection that there is no such moral sense or inner eye, could we not say that our moral sense was a supersensory sense, a sense which did not depend on a sense organ, or perhaps depended on one which we had not yet discovered? We could know whether a man was musical or unmusical even if he had no ears, or artistic even if he had no eyes. All that is necessary is that he should appreciate the right sorts of result. In any case, why postulate a special moral sense, it might be asked. We have one already: reason. Reason is a faculty like sight. As sight enables us to see what color or shape an object has, so reason enables us to see whether an action is right or wrong. We need not be concerned about the objection that if reason were a faculty like sight then there would have to be a corresponding sensory organ. For in the first place there is such an organ: the brain. Cut out the brain or certain portions of it, and you destroy a person's ability to reason, just as you destroy his sight if you cut out his eyes. In the second place, sight is something over and above eyes. Some people have eyes and yet they are blind. Sight works in and through the organ of sight. Similarly reason is something over and above the brain, though it works in and through this organ.

If we accepted this analogy, then an immoral person would merely be like someone who surrounds himself with bad pictures because he lacks artistic discrimination. If the difference between right and wrong were known "naturally" by a moral sense, whether sensory or supersensory, then we would always have to excuse an immoral person, provided only his moral convictions differed from ours or provided he claimed that he had no moral sense, no ability to discriminate between right and wrong, and therefore no moral convictions. We would have to excuse him as we excuse a tone-deaf or a color-blind man for not being able to appreciate music or painting. Some admirers of certain artists have indeed wished to excuse their callous behavior toward their wives and friends by describing them not as immoral but as "amoral," which they construe on the model of unmusicality.

A person who has an artistic sense but nevertheless surrounds himself with trash is simply foolish or perverse. He is like one who, not liking spinach, eats it regularly and for no reason at all. Clever crooks are not foolish or perverse. For despite the Film Production Code crime often pays, and pays handsomely, provided the criminals are clever and ruthless. I am tone deaf and therefore to be pitied. I am deprived of one of the greatest and most deeply satisfying experiences, I am told. I am excluded from a certain sort of refined delight. Crooks are not deprived of any specific experiences, or refined delights. Their self-centeredness and insensitivity to the needs and wishes of others, their callous egoism and brutality are not due to their lack of a specific sense which makes it impossible for them to "see" or "hear" or "savor" or "intuit" the difference between right and wrong.

However, these arguments may not convince a supporter of the theory that reason is a mental faculty. In view of the great popularity of this view, its profound appeal to us, and its great power to confuse people, a detailed refutation of it will be worth the considerable trouble involved.

It is claimed that reason is a mental faculty like sight, that we can "see" moral truths by reason in the way in which we can see visual truths by sight. I wish to show that 'reason' is not the name of a faculty like sight and that seeing that something is right or wrong is no sort of seeing, not even seeing with the inner eye, the eye of the soul, the light of reason, or any other sensory or supersensory organ or faculty.

The mental faculty of sight is a power closely associated with our eyes, a power which enables us to perform certain activities such as picking objects of the same color, telling the distance of things, their shape and size, and so on. (Call these "the activities of sight.") Possessing sight is more than having eyes, for some people have eyes but are blind, and it also is more than the power to perform the activities of sight, for some people might be able to tell the color of things by means of a wavemeter and not by sight.

If reason were a mental faculty, then it, too, would have to be a power closely associated with a certain organ, and a power which enables us to perform certain activities. At first sight it seems to satisfy both these conditions. Reason is closely associated with the brain and it is believed to be a power enabling us to perform certain activities, such as arguing, reasoning, and deliberating. (Call these "the activities of reason.") However, both these views are mistaken. Reason is not logically tied to the brain as sight is tied to the eyes. Nor is it a power enabling us to perform the activities of reason, as sight is the power enabling us to perform the activities of sight.

Take the first point first. We can know that a person possesses reason quite independently of knowing whether he has any particular organs or organ. We know it if we know that he is able to engage in the activities of reason. But we cannot know that a man has the faculty of sight if he does not have eyes. It is not enough to know that he is capable of performing the activities of sight. Hence sight really is a faculty over and above the possession of a power to do certain things and the possession of a certain organ. Reason, on the other hand, is not.

It might be thought that sight was not such a faculty either. For after all, if a man can tell without using any instruments what color a thing is, then surely he must possess the faculty of sight, whether he has eyes or not. Surely he must be able to *see* what color things are. What more is there to possessing the faculty of sight than being able to tell the color, the shape, or the distance of an object put before one without the use of any aids?

Compare two different cases, the man who has lost his eyes in an accident and the man who has never had eyes. The first man, who has learned to use the word 'see' in the ordinary way, knows what it is to see things. If, after he has lost his eyes, he can still tell the color of objects as we can and if he truthfully says that it is just as if he still had his eyes, then we must say that he can still see the color of objects although he has no eyes. And he can *know* with absolute certainty that he can see them.

But if he is born without eyes, then he can never be taught, he can never learn, the use of the word 'see.' For what is its use? There are many information-gathering activities in which we must, or profitably can, use our eyes. We do, for instance, learn to classify or name objects in our environment by, as we say, the use of our eyes, or by sight. In a normally lit room, normal adults can correctly identify tables and chairs, carpets, pieces of crockery, persons, and so on. However, most of them would be capable of doing these things even without the use of their eyes, that is, with their eyes closed or in the dark, namely by touch. So remarks such as 'I saw a mouse in the kitchen,' 'I could tell by the way it felt that it was a jug,' 'It was a jet plane by the sound of it' *indicate how* we managed to identify the things in question. They reveal *on what authority* we are making our main claim, that is, on the basis of which of our senses, sight, touch, or hearing. Such remarks contain a two-fold contention, that there was something of a certain sort in a certain place at a certain time and also that one's contention to that effect was based on the use of a certain sense. This is no less true of 'I saw *him* this morning' or 'I saw *him help her* in the garden' than it is of 'I saw *that* he was drunk.' In all these cases there is the main contention, 'He and I were in the same place this morning,' 'He helped her in the garden,' 'He was drunk,' together with the indication that this claim is based on visual observation.

If a person is born without eyes, he cannot be said to use his eyes and cannot base any claim on that use. Suppose that we put before him various objects and do not allow him to touch them or sniff them or taste them, but tell him what they are. Suppose also that he can identify them later on, that he has no difficulty in finding his way among objects, and that he can tell the color of things without the use of any instrument or code; then we would certainly feel an inclination to say that he must be "seeing" these things even though he has no eyes. This inclination is further strengthened if in his answers there is a close correspondence between the conditions in which he cannot give an answer and what we call 'being too far away to make out,' 'too dark to see,' 'too close to discern,' 'too many things in front of it,' 'too misty,' 'only indistinctly from the corner of my eye,' and so on. Even then, however, we would not *know* whether or not to say he actually saw these things.

One must not misunderstand the nature of the uncertainty. It is not that we are uncertain because we do not know whether, subjectively speaking, his "sensations" are of the same sort as ours. True, I could not know whether his "sensations" were of the same sort as mine, but then this is true also of the "sensations" of two people with working eyes. All we know is that other persons have eyes just as we ourselves do, but that is enough for us to say that they can see provided they can also perform in the appropriate way. Being able to see is being able to perform in a certain way on the basis of *whatever "sensations"* one's eyes afford one. It is from the nature of the case impossible to compare my visual sensations with yours. No conceivable situation could make such a comparison possible.

245

Nothing that anyone could do would ever count toward saying that he had compared his sensations with those of another. But that does not imply that we cannot understand what it would be for two persons to have qualitatively different visual sensations. We can imagine that the visual sensations of insects are very different from those we get, and we can imagine that other people's visual sensations are totally different from ours, that if, *per impossibile*, we had them just now we would have to relearn completely what they are the sensations of, as a man who is wearing left-right, upside-down spectacles has to relearn partially.

Although, then, we always do have this doubt about the qualitative sameness of other people's sensations, this is a factual doubt, not a linguistic, but a metaphysical, that is, practically unsettleable and therefore also unimportant, doubt. It is a doubt equally relevant to the case of the man with, as to the man without, eyes. In the case of the man with eyes, this metaphysical doubt is, however, the only doubt, therefore there is *linguistic certainty*. We know he can see because he can do certain things, such as identifying objects without the use of his hands or instruments or telling what colors they are, and because he has eyes in good working order. 'He can see' means 'He has eyes and they afford him the sensations necessary for him to perform the tasks in question.' It does not mean 'He has sensations of a certain sort, qualitatively the same as mine and those of everyone else who has eyes.' [3] And since it does not mean the latter, it is absolutely certain that very many people can see, although there is the *metaphysical* doubt whether the visual sensations they have are qualitatively the same as those of others.

It might be said that this was all wrong and that its wrongness was shown by the example of the man who once had had

---

[3] Cf. also below, Chapter Eleven, section 1.2.

eyes and could still see after he had lost them. We said that he could see simply because he had visual sensations, and we said (it might be argued) that he had visual sensations because he had sensations of a certain quality of which he alone was the judge. But this is to misunderstand the example. True, we say this man can see because he has visual sensations, but we say he has visual sensations not simply because they are sensations of a certain quality. We say he has visual sensations because (a) he can still perform visual tasks and (b) because he has sensations which enable him to perform them and because (c) these sensations are *qualitatively the same as those previously* afforded him by his eyes. Neither he nor we could know that he had visual sensations if it were not for the fact *that he originally had eyes.*

In the case of the man who is born without eyes, there is a linguistic, in addition to the previously mentioned metaphysical, uncertainty. For here we have a separation of the criteria on the basis of which we normally say that a man can see. Normally, it is only sensations afforded us by our eyes which enable us to perform visual tasks. Here is a person who can perform such tasks on the basis of something afforded him not by eyes but by some other organ. In the other case, there was no real separation of the criteria, for he knows—and we can believe him—that he has qualitatively the same sensations as those previously afforded him by his eyes. In the present case, we have no link with eyes at all. We have to decide whether to include among visual sensations those which satisfy only the first criterion, enabling a man to perform visual tasks, or whether to insist on their being afforded by eyes. Hence the uncertainty about whether a man can be said to be able to see in spite of his not having eyes.

Possession of the faculty of sight is, therefore, logically tied to the possession of eyes. Having the faculty of sight is having visual sensations, that is, sensations which are afforded by a certain sort of organ, or sensations which, though not afforded by eyes, are known to be qualitatively the same. The faculty of sight is logically tied to eyes because if one has never had eyes, one cannot know, nor can anyone else, whether one has the faculty of sight, for it is perfectly conceivable that one should be able to perform the activities of sight without having this faculty. The faculty of sight *is a power which enables one to perform* the activities of sight; not *the power to perform* these activities. Hence the possession of the ability to perform these activities does not entail the possession of the faculty of sight: there might be other faculties equally capable of enabling one to perform these activities.

On the other hand, reason simply is the power to perform the activities of reason. It is inconceivable that a person should be able to perform these activities without having reason. Being able to perform such activities is all that is meant by 'possessing reason.' There is no sensation or feeling which a person must have in order to be able to perform these activities of reason, nor is there any organ affording them. Unlike 'sight,' reason is not, therefore, the name of a mental faculty logically tied to a special organ affording certain characteristic sensations or impressions. Nor, unlike 'sight,' is it the name of *a power which enables us to perform* certain activities, but the name of *the power to perform* these activities.

Therefore, remarks to the effect that reason enables us to "see" what is right and what is wrong can be and have been seriously misleading, for they naturally suggest that reason is a faculty like sight affording us special sensations or nonsensory sensations, sometimes called "intuitions" or "insights" (such as that certain conclusions are false or that killing is wrong), which enable us to perform the activities of reason. In fact, it is the other way round. 'Reason' is the name of the power to perform the activities of reason, which are of the general nature of calculations, the results of which are propositions such as that a certain conclusion is false or a certain act morally wrong. (I have given an account of some of the activities of so-called practical reason in Chapters Two and Three and throughout the book.) It would therefore be better to say that reason is the power *to work out*, rather than the power to "see," the answers to certain questions.

It is now clear that we could not tell, in the state of nature, what is in accordance with or contrary to reason, what we ought or ought not to do, or what is morally right and what morally wrong. For if reason is not the power to "see" this, but the power to work it out in deliberation, then we must have the highly sophisticated skill of deliberating. But it has already been demonstrated that it is practically impossible for a person living outside society to acquire this skill.

4 BEING MORAL BY NATURE

Perhaps it will now be granted that there is no such thing as moral intuition or seeing by reason what is right and wrong. Nevertheless it may be held that we are so equipped by nature as to be able, without having to think, to do what is right and to shun what is wrong. It may not be necessary for us to do anything but to follow nature, impulse, or instinct in order to do right and avoid doing wrong. Nature or God might have implanted in us the promptings of conscience prior to acting and the pangs of conscience and the feelings of guilt when we have disregarded the warnings. In that case we would still know by nature and in a state of nature what is right and wrong. Training in a society would not be necessary. Of course, it would then be a mistake to say that we did certain things because we discovered we ought to do them and refrained from doing others because we found out they were wrong. We would have to say, rather, that we knew that certain things were right and others wrong because our conscience *prompted us* in certain ways, that is, because we were naturally driven to do or to shun certain things.

Can being moral consist simply in following nature? What in any case is meant by 'following nature'? Suppose someone follows his reason—is he following nature or is he not? It is, of course, natural to follow reason and unnatural, perverse, to do what one knows is contrary to reason. On the other hand, in following reason one is not following nature, as one is when following impulse, inclination, or instinct. Following the latter is doing what comes naturally, what one would do naturally, that is, without thinking or deliberating. On the other hand, one cannot follow reason without thinking or deliberating. There is nothing perverse in following reason: it is natural in this sense. But there is nothing spontaneous, unconsidered, unthought-out about following reason: it is not natural in that sense.

In what sense, then, is it maintained that being moral is following nature? It is not claimed in this context that being moral is not perverse, unnatural, against nature, but that being moral is uncritically following the promptings of human nature, without first examining and weighing these promptings, possibly following and possibly resisting them.

We can dismiss without much empirical investigation the theory that all men are always by nature moral. It is a plain fact that many people often are inclined to do what they think or know is wrong and not to do what they think or know they ought to do. This plain fact of our experience is compatible with the present theory only on the basis of a further assumption which is also quite obviously false: the assumption that these immoral inclinations or promptings are *always* due to social influences and never to innate tendencies. Anyone who has ever dealt with children knows how untrue this assumption is.

The alternative to this is no more plausible. It consists in saying that human beings have both moral and nonmoral impulses which may conflict. I mention only one objection to this view: we could never know which were the moral ones and which the others. For how could we distinguish between moral, immoral, and nonmoral promptings if we had only the promptings to go by? These promptings do not come from different places. And even if they did, why should we take any notice of that? Why should we never follow promptings coming from one place and always only those coming from another? Why should we assume that there are promptings with a good origin or status and others with a bad one? How would we distinguish 'higher' from 'lower' promptings if we had only origins to go by?

If it is admitted that we are not always prompted by nature to do what is right and to shun what is wrong, then it must be admitted also that this cannot be the way we know what is right and wrong. In any case, how could we know whether nature *always* prompted us to do what is right and to shun what is wrong unless we already knew, *independently*, what was right and what wrong?

Even if it were true and we could somehow know that we always naturally did what was right and shunned what was wrong, even then the present view would not be tenable. For being moral cannot consist in following nature. If it did consist in this, then animals or robots could be moral, provided only they had the correct natural endowment. In the case of such creatures all the praise and blame must go to the person who has endowed them. We do not praise or blame a digital computer. It acts the way it does because it has been "programed" in this way. If being moral consisted in following nature, our maker would deserve all the credit *and all the blame.* There could not be, in the case of such creatures, any question of resisting or yielding to temptation, of being conscientious or negligent, of making an effort or of being lax. Such people would always, automatically, blindly, and without thinking or trying, do what is right and shun what is wrong.

However, such creatures are not moral beings, and only moral beings can be moral. They are not moral beings because they are incapable of acting contrary to their inclinations or promptings. A moral being must be able to keep his natural impulses in check, to control himself, to do what is required by the weightiest moral reasons, even if this means thwarting the strongest present inclination.

The point is that no creature could be so equipped with natural inclinations that he is guaranteed to do in all possible situations what is required by morality. Killing, stealing, hurting, lying, are indeed wrong, other things being equal. But whether a particular course of action is right or wrong, all things considered, depends on the circumstances in which the person finds himself. It is indeed fortunate that most people have a horror of killing and hurting others, a natural inclination to be kind and to help others in need, for in ordinary circumstances morality will require just these types of action. Quite often, however, the morally required thing will be to kill someone, to hurt someone, or to tell lies. We must attack, perhaps wound and kill, the man who attacks our wife and children or an enemy soldier in wartime. We must not be kind and helpful to a drunkard resisting arrest however much our heart beats for him. The moral man cannot rely on any innate tendency, for he may be in circumstances in which he ought to resist rather than follow it. Everybody must be prepared for this. Of course, those who are badly endowed by nature, such as the homicidally inclined person, must make a particularly great effort and must make it often. But the "well-endowed" person is also sometimes required to make it. He who cannot hurt a fly must overcome his natural tendencies almost as often as the homicidal type his. For societies are often involved in wars, and even in peace we must often refuse, reject, or thwart the demands of others, in the service of justice, in doing our duty, or in keeping our promises. A kindly Vice-Chancellor who cannot say 'No' to anybody is almost as bad as a tough one who says 'No' to everybody. If we were not capable of resisting our kindly tendencies, we would often be unable to satisfy the demands of morality.

5 WHAT SOCIETY ADDS TO ABSOLUTE MORALITY

That the existence of societies is a good thing is beyond all reasonable doubt. Human beings "outside" society can live only the most primitive animallike lives. They have no chance of achieving a full or satisfying life. Without education, without language, without a cultural heritage to draw on, without the division of labor, without skills, without an ordered and settled way of life, existence is a continuous struggle against nature, leaving no time for any of the things that are most worth while.

Not the least important contribution which the existence of a society makes to the life that is worth living is the provision of established patterns of behavior giving everyone confidence and security. It provides institutions and definite rules for the realization of the most fundamental human needs and desires. It makes arrangements about mating and the rearing of children, about the ways individual members of the society may use their talents to earn a living, and the like. Such arrangements give rise to specific injunctions and prohibitions which will be common knowledge among the members of the group.

In view of the great advantages of established ways of behavior, such rules and institutions usually have the backing of the morality of the group. Rules such as 'Thou shalt not steal,' 'Thou shalt not commit adultery,' 'Honour thy father and thy mother,' 'Help the members of your family' are general, society-neutral rules giving moral backing to whatever specific arrangements a given society might make about sex, property, and the family.

Social institutions of this sort introduce a great many differentiations between people. They create social positions and social status, attaching special privileges and duties, thus modifying the otherwise uniform picture of moral relations between members of the group. In addition to the rules arising out of the institutions of the society, there are the special rights and duties arising out of the various patterns of life which a society allows. In order that the various problems confronting each man should be more efficiently met, society arranges for a division of labor, allotting different tasks to different groups and making arrangements guaranteeing that a sufficient number of people is allocated to each task. In some societies, some are born to rule, others to be soldiers, others merchants, craftsmen, or manufacturers, others to till the land, and yet others to be untouchables performing the most menial tasks. In other societies, each individual is free to choose whatever path of life he wishes, free perhaps to change from one pattern to another if he can do so and if he so desires.

Apart from those fixed patterns of life which give rise to special obligations and rights there is in some societies, including our own, an arrangement whereby any individual can enter into special moral ties with other members by voluntary acts, such as promises or contracts.

In every society there are, moreover, special ways of enforcing the rules determining the group's way of life. Some societies have the practice of harming scapegoats, others that of the blood feud, yet others punishment and reward, meted out by special social organs.

All these social arrangements, varying from one society to another, may be subjected to criticism from the moral point of view. The patterns of life may involve social injustice: some impose too many burdens, others grant too many privileges. Even the fundamental institutions of the society may be morally objectionable. It may be that polygamy is unfair to women in the harem or that monogamy and premarital chastity impose too great a strain on human nature. The enforcing arrangements of a given society may violate the principles of retributive justice, as when scapegoats are sacrificed "for" crimes they have not committed. The nature of the penalty may be objectionable on primary moral grounds: it may be too cruel, for example, the chopping off of an arm, or hanging, or it may be too severe for the crime, as when a child is flogged for having stolen some apples.

Lastly, society has to prohibit those courses of action which, because of the particular nature of the social framework, would be harmful if everyone or even if only a few people entered on them. Because of social interaction not foreseeable by ordinary members of the society, some people may suffer harm as the result of a single individual's conduct or as the result of a large number engaging in that sort of conduct. The society is then entitled to prohibit such conduct.[4]

Ideally, then, any given morality would be the application of absolute morality to the special social conditions of the group in question. With regard to any actual way of life, we must therefore ask not only whether it incorporates the rules of absolute morality, but also whether these general rules have

---

[4] Cf. above, Chapter Eight, section 6, p. 211.

been properly applied to the specific social conditions or whether there are any arrangements which are open to criticism from the moral point of view. It is obvious that in hardly any society will the work of applying the principles of absolute morality to individual social conditions have been performed flawlessly. The temptations to which ruling classes are exposed, for example, to impose laws which will be to their own economic advantage, have frequently been noticed. So has the temptation to pass off these self-interested laws as the proper rules of morality. Thrasymachus and Marx are inclined to say that actual moralities are no more than the selfish rules laid down by the ruling class. This is not likely to be true, but even if it were, it would show no more than that actually existing moralities contain a high proportion of, or only, false moral convictions. It does not show that such perversions of morality are all there is to morality.

Eleven

Why are we moral?

HOW, then, can we explain the fact that many people often do what is right and shun what is wrong? In the previous chapter (section 4) it was shown that our nature cannot be responsible for this fact, for a man's morality cannot consist in simply following nature's promptings or his inclinations. It is not merely that we *are* not by nature moral: morality is our second rather than our first nature. It is rather that we *could* not be moral by merely following our nature, whether first, second, or third. The demands of morality and the promptings of our nature may coincide if the circumstances are favorable. But it is a coincidence, not a necessary identity. Hence a person must be capable of working out the demands of morality and of following them even when his natural inclinations pull the other way.

If our nature is not the explanation of our being moral, what is? There would seem to be only two alternatives: either it is an inner force driving us to do what is right and holding us back from doing what is wrong or a force acting on us from the outside. The most obvious candidates are reason and society.

The most striking fact of our moral experience is undoubtedly the conflict between the demands of morality and our desires. A mechanical model of human nature appears to give an adequate account of this. If we say that there are within us two forces, reason and desire, capable of pushing us in opposite directions, and if we say that reason is always on the side of morality, this most striking fact of our moral experience is easily explained. Reason inclines us toward satisfying the demands of morality, desire inclines us the other way. If reason is stronger, we are moral; if desire is stronger, we are immoral.

1 HUME'S DOCTRINE

Hume, as is well known, rejects this popular view. He dismisses as a fallacy what seems a plain fact, the conflict between reason and desire.[1] For, he argues, "Reason alone can never be a motive to any action of the will and it can never oppose passion in the direction of the will." [2] From this he draws the paradoxical conclusion that no human passions or affections or any actions based on them can in any important sense be in accordance with, or contrary to, reason.[3]

'Tis not contrary to reason to prefer the destruction of the whole world to the scratching of my finger. 'Tis not contrary to reason for me to chuse my total ruin, to prevent the least uneasiness of an *Indian* or person wholly unknown to me. 'Tis as little contrary to reason to prefer even my own acknowledged lesser good to my greater, and have a more ardent affection for the former than the latter.[4]

But such a view is plainly absurd. The examples he gives might even be used in teaching someone what is meant by

---

[1] David Hume, A *Treatise of Human Nature*, ed. by L. A. Selby-Bigge (Oxford: Clarendon Press, 1896), bk. II, pt. III, sec. 3, p. 413.

[2] *Ibid.*   [3] *Ibid.*, p. 416.   [4] *Ibid.*

'contrary to reason.' They are stock cases of things that are contrary to reason and are therefore chosen by Hume to drive home his paradoxical and shocking conclusion.

It is not difficult to see how a false conception of the nature of reason has led to these absurd consequences. Hume construes human behavior on the analogy with the movements of the wheels of a machine. After all, human behavior consists in the movement of the limbs which in turn are moved by the nerves and muscles of the body. These in turn must be moved by some energy or power or force inside the person. Since often there appears to be conflict "inside a man," it is fair to assume that there is more than one such force or power at work. The traditional view was that, in addition to the many desires or passions, man has a further force or power inside him, that of reason. Hume's view was that, when we examine the powers of reason, we find that it does not have the force to set the will in motion. Only the passions or desires or the faculty of taste have this power.

Thus the distinct boundaries and offices of *reason* and of *taste* are easily ascertained. The former conveys the knowledge of truth and falsehood: the latter gives the sentiment of beauty and deformity, vice and virtue. The one discovers objects as they really stand in nature, without addition or diminution; the other has a productive faculty, and gilding or staining all natural objects with the colours, borrowed from internal sentiment, raises in a manner a new creation. Reason being cool and disengaged is no motive to action, and directs only the impulses received from appetite or inclination, by showing us the means of attaining happiness or avoiding misery: Taste, as it gives pleasure or pain, and thereby constitutes happiness or misery, becomes a motive to action, and is the first spring or impulse to desire and volition.[5]

---

[5] David Hume, *An Enquiry concerning the Principles of Morals* (Oxford: Clarendon Press, 1894), app. I, p. 294.

The Moral Point of View

The picture is clear enough. If human beings were endowed with reason alone, they would have no motive for doing this rather than that. Reason alone could do no more than apprise them of the facts, of what exists, of what things are like, of what has been, is, and will be going on in this world. It is only because we desire some and abhor other things, because some give us pleasure and happiness, others pain and unhappiness, that we are inclined to behave in one way rather than another. Reason, by telling us what is and will be happening and what are the causes and effects of what, apprises us of what we must do in order to achieve or avoid what, thereby satisfying our desires, achieving happiness, and avoiding misery. Reason can only determine the means, not the ends. Nothing can be in accordance with or contrary to reason, because reason cannot *cause* us to do anything. The real causes of our behavior are our desires.

This conception of reason is false. Reason is not an inner organ, force, or power, like the heart, the kidneys, or the ductless glands. There is no empirical question 'Does reason, or does it not, have the power to move us to action?' as there is the empirical question 'Does the heart, or does it not, have the power to pump the blood through our veins?' We could be mistaken about whether or not the heart pumps the blood through our veins. We can understand the meaning of the word 'heart' and of the expression 'pumping the blood' before we know the answer to the question 'Does the heart pump the blood?' We could not understand the meaning of the expressions 'reason' and 'moving us to action' before we know the answer to the question whether reason can move us to action. The ordinary view of reason expressed in phrases such as 'Desire bade me woo her, reason made me go' could not possibly be erroneous. We *mean* by the word 'reason' something that can make us do things.

Why are we moral?

1.1 Ends and means

How, then, did Hume arrive at this false conception? Perhaps the main reason is the unduly narrow and confused conception of what it is to have and to find reasons. Hume thought that the task of reason was to find reasons, that is, to find what are the appropriate means to our ends. Such a process must, however, come to an end. We can give the means to a preliminary end which, in turn, can be a means to an ulterior end, and so on, but at some stage we reach an ultimate end which is not, in turn, a means to something yet ulterior, but is an end in itself. With regard to these ultimate ends, reason cannot, of course, have anything to say. For, *ex hypothesi*, ultimate ends cannot be supported by way of showing them to be means to yet more ultimate ends.

It appears evident that the ultimate ends of human actions can never, in any case, be accounted for by *reason*, but recommend themselves entirely to the sentiments and affections of mankind, without any dependence on the intellectual faculties. Ask a man why he uses exercise; he will answer, *because he desires to keep his health*. If you then enquire, *why he desires health*, he will readily reply *because sickness is painful*. If you push your enquiries farther, and desire a reason *why he hates pain*, it is impossible he can ever give any. This is an ultimate end, and is never referred to any other object.

Perhaps to your second question, *why he desires health*, he may also reply, that it is *necessary for the exercise of his calling*. If you ask, *why he is anxious on that head*, he will answer because *he desires to get money*. If you demand *Why? It is the instrument of pleasure*, says he. And beyond this it is an absurdity to ask for a reason. It is impossible there can be a progress *in infinitum*: and that one thing can always be a reason why another is desired. Something must be desirable on its own account, and because of its im-

261

The Moral Point of View

mediate accord or agreement with human sentiment and affection.[6]

But is it true that our ends cannot be accounted for by reason? Can we not explain why a man has, and also defend or attack, the ends which he does have? Is it even true that our ends are the things we desire?

What are ends? They are things we can gain or fail to gain. Something which from its very nature cannot be gained, such as the greenness of the grass, the love of a statue, the eradication of all evil, cannot be an end. Ends are necessarily someone's. They do not occur "unowned." They are always yours or mine or ours. The gaining of one's end is a clockable matter, an occurrence at a given point in time, whether measurable in minutes or years. Gaining one's end can consist in bringing something about—the getting of a job, the blowing up of a bridge, the defeat of the enemy—or in preventing it. Preventions are clockable, too. I gained my end today if, because I took my umbrella, I did not get wet all day.

Ends must be distinguished from ideals which, from their nature, are unattainable. The greatest happiness of the greatest number, the relief of all suffering, the eradication of poverty, disease, and ignorance, the raising of living standards, and the like cannot be my ends, because I could never say whether I had gained my end or not. However, they can be my ideals, because we do know the difference between making headway and not making any. We know what it is to come closer to or to drift away from our ideal, while knowing all the time that we cannot reach it. Ends are short-range goals capable of explaining a person's line of action, for example, 'with this end in view (to answer the question whether smoking is one of the causes of lung cancer) I began to study the case histories

[6] *Ibid.*, p. 293.

of 500 lung-cancer patients.' Ideals, on the other hand, are infinitely long-range goals.

Our ends are not the same as what we desire or want.[7] It might be said that they must be, for nothing would be our end if we did not desire or want to gain it. But this sounds so obviously and trivially true only because of an important ambiguity of the words 'want' and 'desire.' It may be my end to track down the murderer although I know that it is my brother and although I dread the moment when I shall succeed. In one sense of 'desire' and 'want,' I do of course desire and want to find him, for it could not be my end to find him if I did not (in any sense) desire or want to find him. But in another, more obvious, more literal sense, I do not want or desire to find him. I abhor, I dread, I hate to think of the moment of success. Nevertheless, I overcome all this in pursuing my end. Or I may have decided to cure myself of my love. This is then my end in many things that I do. But all my desires and yearnings go the other way, and they have constantly to be frustrated and combated.

And what is the ordinary use of the word 'means'? In the first place, we use the expression 'means of . . .' as in 'means of transport' or 'means of payment.' A means of transport, for example, a bus or a plane, is something by its nature capable of serving the purpose mentioned, transportation. Means of payment, for example, a check, a bank note, is something by its nature capable of serving the purpose mentioned, payment. A means of x is something by the use of which we normally achieve our purpose, x.

Secondly, we use the expression 'a means to an end' or, more frequently, '*merely* a means to an end.' Exercise may be merely a means to an end, for example, keeping fit; or it may be an end in itself, when we enjoy it. This use lends weight to the common

---

[7] See also above, Chapter Four, section 1.1, pp. 110–115.

feeling that the ends are important, while the means do not matter: the end is often said to justify the means. Hence people object when they are treated as "mere means to an end." The heiress resents being wooed as a means to an end, to secure her money. She wants to be wooed for her own sake, as an end in itself.

We can now show that it is not true, in any important sense, that reason cannot account for our ends. It is, of course, true that we often explain someone's behavior by pointing out his end, as when we say that he is wooing her *in order to* get hold of her money or that *the reason why* he woos her is that she has a lot of money. But from this it does not follow that our ends are not themselves determined by reason, but always by our desires. A great deal of Jones's behavior, his going on long and dangerous missions, giving many parties, drinking a lot, may be explained by his end: curing himself of his love, which is his strongest and most persistent present sentiment, passion, or desire. Yet, his end is to rid himself of it, and his behavior is explained in terms of the end he is aiming at. Hence, it cannot be his passions which determine his end, for his end is not the satisfaction, but the frustration of his most obtrusive passion.

Moreover, a good deal of a man's behavior is not explained in terms of means to his end. If all were explained in this way, then the contrast between a mere means to an end and an end in itself would be meaningless. On Hume's view, a man who does something as an end in itself cannot have a reason for doing it, for what he does is not a means to an end. Yet, this is obviously false. A man who plays a lot of tennis, not as a means to an end, but for its own sake, as an end in itself, may do so because he enjoys playing tennis. And that is as much a reason for playing tennis as doing it merely as a means to an end, for example, to keep fit or to meet people. We can find

Hume's argument plausible only if we think, wrongly, that the sole type of explanatory reason is the means-end type. As soon as we rid ourselves of this error, we can see that our ends are capable of being accounted for in terms of reasons. I can explain why it is my end to cure myself of my love. My reason may be that the lady is already married or that she does not reciprocate my affections or that she is not worthy of them.

In fact, as soon as we have reached this stage, it becomes clear that, far from being the only type of reason, means-end reasons are only of a provisional and incomplete sort. "I went to the cellar to fetch the kerosene. I then poured some into a jug in order to be able to soak my hand in it. I then struck a match in order to set my hand alight." Here is a perfect chain of means-end reasons all linked to a mad end. We now know why he did what he did, what was his end in doing all these things: his end was to set his hand on fire. But this is not a satisfactory explanation. We want to go on asking, but why on earth did he want to burn his hand? Why on earth should that be his end?

This brings us back to our distinction between explanatory and justificatory reasons.[8] For even when we know one sort of explanation, one reason why he has that end (he has a guilt complex about the things he did with his hand), we still want to say, but that is no reason for setting one's hand on fire. It is an explanation why he did it, but no justification. Sometimes, when we ask for reasons, we do not want explanatory but justificatory reasons. We want to know whether or not reason would give its "Imprimatur." We want to know, not what moved the man, but whether what he did was in accordance with or contrary to reason. Thus, reason can account for some of our ends, not only in the sense of explaining why it is that we have them, but also in the sense of showing that they are

---

[8] See above, Chapter Six, section 2.

in accordance with reason, justified from a rational point of view.

Lastly, reason can account for our ends also in the sense of determining them, making us choose them. When someone asks, 'What shall I do?'—and most of us ask this question quite often—he wishes to choose that end which has the weight of reason behind it. 'Shall I aim at becoming a doctor or an engineer?' is the question of one who is looking for an end backed by reason. If he adopts as his end what he has worked out to have the support of reason, then his end is determined, is accounted for, by reason in the most important sense of that phrase.

1.2 Pleasure not an "ultimate end"

"But you don't understand what Hume is saying," it will be objected. "He is talking about ultimate, not preliminary ends. Preliminary ends may indeed be accounted for by reason, but not ultimate ones. The things you mention are not ultimate ends. Hume gives two examples, the hatred of pain and the love of pleasure. No reason can be given why a man hates pain or why he loves pleasure. Pleasure simply recommends itself to our sentiments and affections, pain does not. Reason does not come into this any more. These are the hooks from which our chains of reasons are suspended. Pleasure is desirable for its own sake, pain hateful for its own sake. What reason could one give or want for loving pleasure and hating pain?"

It is, of course, absurd to ask for a reason why someone hates pain or loves pleasure. But Hume gives the wrong explanation of this absurdity. He thinks it is a case of trying to go beyond the limit. In his view, giving reasons is giving means to an end. Pleasure, he thinks, is an ultimate end, hence we cannot give reasons for it, since that would involve showing pleasure as a means to a yet more ulterior end. Asking why a man loves pleasure is like asking what is the cause of the First or Un-caused Cause.

But pleasure and pain are not ends, hence not ultimate ends. Nor are the pursuit of pleasure and the avoidance of pain ends, hence not ultimate ends. What about pleasure seekers, then? Is not their ultimate end the pursuit of pleasure? No, pleasure seekers have made it *their supreme principle* to do whatever and only what will give them pleasure. Ends are quite different from principles. Ends are what a person is trying to bring about or prevent, principles are rules guiding him in the selection of ends. If a pleasure seeker asks himself the question 'What shall I become?' the choice of his pro-fession (one of the ends he will aim at) will be determined by the pleasure principle. He will have to ask himself what career, what profession, what way of life will yield the greatest amount of pleasure to him.

Ends are the sorts of thing that one can gain or fail to gain. Principles cannot be gained or fail to be gained. They can be adhered to or departed from. When we have gained our end or have failed to gain it, we have done with that end and must pick a new one. When we have adhered to, or broken, one of our principles, this does not terminate our principle. We need not, then, adopt a new one.

It is absurd to ask why men hate pain or love pleasure for the same reason as it is absurd to ask why circles are round or why fathers are male. A person who asks such a question must be said not to know the meaning of the words or the point of 'why questions.' Remarks such as 'I hate pain' and 'I love pleasure' are empty, uninformative, tautologous. They sound like 'I hate tickles and heartburn' or 'I enjoy pins and needles or seeing stars' but they are totally different. When pains and pleasures are construed as specific feelings or sensations such as pins and needles or tickles, and as having a further property, namely, "positive or negative feeling tone" (just as pins and needles have the peculiar property of "bubbliness"), then it seems plausible to say that 'I hate pain' or 'I enjoy pleasure' gives information about my predilections.

This view of pleasure and pain is quite common, even among very sophisticated philosophers. Ryle, for example, seems to hold it, for he says, "It should be mentioned that 'pain,' in the sense in which I have pains in my stomach, is not the opposite of 'pleasure.' In this sense, a pain is *a sensation of a special sort*, which we *ordinarily dislike having*." [9]

However, this view is untenable. 'Pleasure' and 'pain' are not the names of sensations of a special sort. Rather these words and others of the same family are used to indicate how a certain person responds to certain things, such as pursuits, activities, undergoings, experiences, and sensations. In recent years, much has been made of the logical differences between 'pain' and 'pleasure.' I think these have been exaggerated. There are differences, but they are comparatively unimportant.

I begin with the adjectives 'painful' and 'pleasurable.' Epistemologically, the most basic remark we make with these words is, 'I find this painful' or 'I find this pleasant or pleasurable.' The things we can find painful or pleasant are pursuits (physical exercise, philandering), activities (sword swallowing, swimming), undergoings (having an operation, having a shampoo), experiences (a motorcar accident, traveling to the top of a mountain in a ski lift), sensations (sensation of having a tooth drilled, sensation of having one's back scratched).

It is logically possible to be mistaken about whether or not one finds something painful or pleasant, for one may make a mistake about *what* it is that one finds painful or pleasant. A person may think he finds the drilling of his tooth painful, but

---

[9] Gilbert Ryle, *The Concept of Mind* (London: Hutchinson's University Library, 1949), p. 109. My italics.

he may later be shown that the tooth was anesthetized and that what caused the pain was not the drilling but a clip in his mouth that was digging into his gums every time the dentist pressed on the drill. The error is possible because to say, 'I find this painful,' where 'this' refers to a pursuit, activity, undergoing, or experience, is to say, 'This is the cause of a certain sensation or feeling which I find painful.' But when we say, 'I find this painful,' where 'this' refers to a sensation, there is no possibility of a mistake, provided all concerned mean the same sensation.

How is it possible that where sensations are concerned we can immediately give the answer 'I find this painful' or the opposite, and why is it that we cannot be mistaken about this? The reply is simple. Certain pursuits, activities, undergoings, and experiences produce in us certain feelings and certain overt responses such as cries, winces, shrinkings away from the object touching us. Moreover, the feelings produced in us by these things are such as to cause us to respond in these characteristic ways. The feelings are the cause of the characteristic pain behavior. If we did not have these feelings, we would not behave in the characteristic "pain manner."

But how do we know that? Could there not be people who merely respond in the "pain manner" without having these feelings? Could these people ever know that they were lacking in certain feelings? Could they ever detect that they did not really find anything painful, but merely found themselves responding in certain characteristic ways to certain stimuli? Of course, they could find out. Suppose we tap them on the knee in order to produce the patellar reflex. Next we hit them on the thumb with a hammer. We then ask whether they found themselves withdrawing the thumb in the same way as they found themselves jerking the leg when the knee was tapped. If they cannot say that there is a definite difference, namely, that in the case of the knee reflex they *merely* found themselves jerking the leg, whereas in the case of the thumb they found themselves moving away *because* of what it felt like when being hit with a hammer, then they do not really find this painful. And if it is the same in all cases when they produce the "pain responses," then they don't really find anything painful. We have to say of them that they merely manifest pain behavior, but that they do not feel pain.

It is because all (or almost all) people have these feelings and these overt responses that they can learn the current use of the word 'pain.' For parents can tell when their children are in pain simply by their characteristic pain responses. They are justified in assuming that their children feel pain and do not merely show the pain responses, because there are no (or almost no) cases of people who do not have the feelings and because very young children have not learned to simulate pain. They are, therefore, entitled to tell their children when they are showing the pain responses that they are what is called 'in pain.' Children accordingly learn to single out those feelings which cause them to make the characteristic pain responses and to call them 'pains.' Hence children need not, as parents at first have to, read off from their own behavior that they have pains. They can, after all, feel them. In a sense, children know that they are in pain long before they have been taught the use of the word 'pain.' In another sense, they cannot be said to know that they are in pain until they have learned the word 'pain,' for they do not know that what they are in is called 'pain.'

The claim 'I find this painful' must be distinguished from 'This is painful.' The former is personal, subjective, the latter impersonal, objective. The former tells us about someone's predilections or peculiarities, the latter about "the nature of an object." However, the difference comes to only this. 'I find this painful' tells others my particular reaction and implies nothing about other people's. 'This is painful' tells us that *every normal person* finds it so, that a person must be regarded as abnormal if he does not. 'Walking on burning coal is painful' implies (correctly) that anyone who finds it pleasant is abnormal. 'I find walking on burning coal painful' is as overcautious as 'Grass seems to me to be green.'

We can now bring to light the important differences between 'I find this painful' and 'I find this pleasant.' Again, 'this' may refer to pursuits, activities, undergoings, experiences, and sensations. But while to say, 'I find this painful,' was to say either (in the case of pursuits, activities, undergoings, and experiences) that this was something which caused me *sensations* which I found painful or (in the case of *sensations*) that I found this painful, when I say, 'I find this pleasant,' sensations are not necessarily involved. In the case of things one finds pleasant, there is the possibility of the question 'Why do you find it pleasant?' One may, for instance, ask, 'Why do you find hot baths pleasant?' and get the answer 'Because it gives me sensations which I find pleasurable' or 'Because they are soothing' or 'Because they make me drowsy and relaxed and I can go to sleep afterwards.' Only the first of these answers refers to pleasant sensations. The others do not involve any characteristic sensations at all, hence neither pleasant nor unpleasant ones. By contrast, in the case of things we find painful, there is never such a question, 'Why do you find this painful?' For the answer is of necessity always the same: because it causes me, or because it is, *a sensation* which I find painful.

The exact opposite of 'painful' is not, therefore, 'pleasant' but rather 'pleasurable.' For when we say of a pursuit, activity, undergoing, or experience that it is pleasurable, we do normally imply that it is something which causes us pleasant sensations. Here, too, we cannot ask the question why someone finds something pleasurable, for the answer would of necessity always have to be the same: because it causes me, or it is, a sensation which I find pleasant. On the other hand, the exact opposite of 'pleasant' is 'unpleasant'; here, too, we can ask the question why someone finds something unpleasant and might then get the answer 'Because it causes me sensations which I find painful' or 'Because it makes me sick' (also a sensation but not a painful one) or 'Because it makes me ill-tempered' or 'Because it ruins my concentration,' the last two of which are not sensations at all.

However, both the claim that something is (or is found) painful or pleasurable and the claim that it is (or is found) pleasant or unpleasant have this important point in common: they indicate a person's positive or negative response or attitude to something (a pursuit, activity, etc.). What the response or attitude is can be said in general terms. The positive response consists in a tendency to continue, to make efforts to repeat the activity, etc., to be disappointed, sad, or annoyed when it is interrupted, and so on; the negative response is the opposite. What distinguishes the claim that something is (or is found) painful or pleasurable from the claim that it is (or is found) pleasant or unpleasant is the fact that the former implies the occurrence of a characteristic sensation, the latter does not.

There are other words and locutions for making the same claim. Of pursuits, activities, experiences we may say that we find them enjoyable or not, or that they are enjoyable or not, or that we enjoy them or don't, or that we like or dislike engaging in them, doing them, having them, undergoing them, and so on. The expressions 'This pleases me,' 'I am pleased by this,' 'I am pleased with this' don't mean quite the same as

Why are we moral?

'I find this pleasant' or 'I find this enjoyable.' Phrases such as these are used to indicate that certain expectations, hopes, or desires had been satisfied by this.

We can now turn to the nouns 'pleasures' and 'pains.' Here the differences which we have noticed between 'pleasant' and 'painful' are more pronounced. It is correct to say that pains are sensations, namely, painful ones. But it would be quite wrong to say that pleasures were sensations, namely, pleasurable or pleasant ones. Pleasure seekers are not voluptuaries. They are people who pursue only what they find pleasant or pleasurable, what they enjoy doing, undergoing, or experiencing. What makes them objectionable is that they will neglect their moral obligations, their duties and responsibilities, whenever they do not enjoy discharging them. People who spend all their time and money at race meetings, at summer or winter resorts, at casinos, at hunt balls, at the opera, at concerts, at plays, in art galleries may be pleasure seekers as much as gluttons or philanderers. They simply find different things pleasant.

But while it is true to say that pains are sensations which we find painful, it is misleading to say that they are sensations which we *ordinarily* dislike having. For this implies that it is merely an empirical and not a necessary proposition that we dislike having the sensations which we call pains. True, we might have liked and disliked different sorts of sensations from the ones we actually like and dislike, but whatever sorts of sensations we like and dislike, we only call pains those which we dislike. And if there are sensations which we ordinarily dislike but on some occasions like having, then we do not call them pains on those occasions on which we like having them. Suppose we ordinarily dislike having a sensation (as of having our ears bitten) to such an extent that we would be prepared to say that we found that sensation painful; then if on a particular occasion we do not dislike having that sensation, we cannot say that we are in pain or that we are having a pain.

What about martyrs? They sometimes like or even rejoice in their pains. The answer is that what they like having and rejoice in is the experience of martyrdom or the fact that they are being martyred, not the painful sensations involved in this. They like, or rejoice in, *having the experience* for what it is, the testimony of their courage, the proof of their true love of God, or the promise of rewards in the afterlife. They do not like, or rejoice in, *having the sensations*. For there is all the difference in the world between these two. We could not have *the experience* of flying, of coming out of a faint, of having our head massaged, of having a tooth drilled, of going down in a lift without actually doing these things, but we could have the corresponding *sensations* while sitting in our armchair, doing nothing. So singled out, sensations are simply the "inner aspects" of our experiences.

It should be obvious that the martyr does not like or rejoice in having the sensations. He rejoices in these experiences and even in these not for their own sakes, but for what they imply. If he merely had the sensations, he would not be pleased, for they alone count for nothing. It is, moreover, plain that the martyr must have sensations which he dislikes having or else what he goes through are not pains, else he is not undergoing torture, not laying up credit in heaven.

If we say that pains are sensations of a certain sort, then we cannot go on to specify the sort by saying that they are of a sort which we ordinarily dislike having. For it is not an open question whether a person who has a pain likes or dislikes having *that sort* of sensation. We learn what a pain is only when we have experiences which we show every sign of disliking. Let us remind ourselves briefly of the way we learn the characteristic pain talk. On certain occasions, the baby cries, winces when a certain spot on his body is touched, shrinks away from the touching hand, shows signs of relief when an ointment is applied, and so on. It is on occasions like these that the baby is introduced to the characteristic "pain" talk. His natural "complaint behavior," crying, wincing, shrinking away, and so on, develops into the linguistic complaint 'I have a pain in my knee.' At the same time he learns that that feeling which makes him cry, wince, etc., is called 'a pain' and that he can complain about it or at least report it with the words 'I have a pain.' Thus, the occasions on which he naturally manifests pain are the natural occasions for learning the conventional pain complaints. *Whatever* he feels on the occasions when he naturally manifests pain, he will learn to call 'pain.' And since he learns the word on the occasions when he feels something which he wants to stop, reduce in intensity, of whose return he is afraid, etc., the very meaning of 'a pain' will be 'something which I dislike,' 'something which I do not enjoy.'

The reason why many people find this so hard to accept is that they have in mind two other ways of classifying sensations, two other kinds of sorts of sensation. We have already come across the first kind of sort, for example, in 'the sensation as of going down in a lift' or 'the sensation as of having one's soles tickled.' When we classify sensations in this way, then it is indeed an open question whether we dislike having them or not. Some people like, others dislike, having them. If a pain were a sensation of this kind of sort, then it might be true that pains are sensations of a sort which we ordinarily dislike having, but perhaps on special occasions don't dislike having. If one does not keep the two kinds of sort of sensation apart, one may be inclined to think that whether one likes or dislikes having one's pains is an empirical question.

There is yet another way of classifying sensations, one that is particularly popular with philosophers. Suppose both you and I are in pain. Let us say that we both have an inflamed and pussy thumbnail, and we have throbbing pains under the nail. We both have sensations we dislike having, but have we the same sensations? I can remember that when I had an inflamed and pussy thumbnail before, I had exactly the same sensations as I have now. I would recognize that feeling immediately even if I could not diagnose it or say of what experience (having a pussy thumbnail) it is the "inner aspect." But I do not know whether in that sense you have the same sensation as I have. And of course I can never know. All I can know is that you have the feeling you always have when you have pussy thumbnails or similar experiences and also that you have a feeling of a sort which you dislike having. But suppose for a moment that I had the sensation which you now have and which you would immediately recognize to be the sensation as of having a pussy thumbnail: would I recognize it to be that, as I immediately recognize the sensation I have to be the "inner aspect" of that experience? [10]

Even so, it might be objected, 'I love my beloved' is tautologous, yet 'Why do you love your beloved?' is not absurd. Similarly, even though 'I love pleasures' be a tautology, it cannot follow from this that 'Why do you love pleasures?' is an absurd question. But this is to forget that 'beloved' is a word which is used both to refer to a person and to imply a certain relation between myself and that person, whereas 'pains' and 'pleasures' do not refer to persons or things. 'Why do you love your beloved?' means 'Why do you love *that person* (whom you love)?' and the answer *cannot* be, 'Because I love persons of that sort, that is, persons whom I love, beloved persons.' If 'Why do you hate pains?' is interpreted to mean 'Why do you hate sensations of this sort?' the answer *must be*, 'Because I find them painful.' 'Why do you love your beloved?' makes sense because the answer can refer to her qualities other

---

[10] See also Chapter Ten, section 3, p. 246.

than her being loved. 'Why do you hate pains?' does not make sense because the answer cannot refer to any properties other than being hated.

I conclude that Hume's arguments for saying that reason cannot account for our ends, that none of our ends can in any important sense be in accordance with or contrary to reason, that our ends are determined by our passions or desires or affections are unsound.

2 KANT'S DOCTRINES

Kant shares Hume's conviction that our ends are determined by our desires, and our desires by our empirical nature. He agrees that it is the function of reason to work out the best means to our ends. Hence, in that respect, reason can and ought only to be the slave of the passions. But this implies that no man can be responsible for his behavior, hence there can be no right and wrong. If there is to be any morality at all, men must be capable of choosing and pursuing ends which are not determined by the desires but by reason. Reason must be, at least at times, the master and not merely the slave of the passions. But how can this be possible?

Kant explains how it is possible by means of a more complicated mechanical model of human nature than that used by Hume. Instead of regarding man as a machine driven by the desires alone, he thinks of him as being moved by two different and frequently opposed "forces" or "engines," desire and reason. These forces are connected to one central executive wheel or lever or arm, the will, which they can set in motion.[11] In what we call strong-willed persons, reason is the stronger engine, hence such a person will be able to act in accordance

---

[11] Immanuel Kant, *The Fundamental Principles of the Metaphysics of Ethics*, trans. by T. K. Abbott (London: Longmans, Green & Co., 1946), pp. 19, 78–86, for example.

with reason, that is, in the direction in which reason "pushes," and contrary to desire. In weak-willed persons, desire is stronger, hence such a person will tend to act contrary to reason.

Kant can thus explain what Hume simply denied could occur, the conflict between reason and desire and the possibility of acting in accordance with or contrary to reason. The felt conflict between reason and desire is now explicable on the analogy with the movement of a wheel subject to two opposing forces and consequently turning in the direction of the greater. Responsibility is explained in terms of this conflict. There can be no morality in the case of a creature which is subject to only one force, for then there is no conflict. Such a creature is "moral" by nature, without effort, without having to resist any temptation, without even having to think. Hence a being whose will is subject to reason alone, who has a "holy will," cannot be moral, for it cannot be under an obligation; it does automatically what reason dictates. Nor, of course, can a will be moral which is subject only to the causality of desire, since it is incapable of doing what is in accordance with reason.[12] Even a creature who is subject to both reason and desire can be moral only if and when his reason is stronger than his desire.

How, then, does reason "work on" the will? It does so by issuing to it certain rules or principles or laws or commands. These are expressed in formulas containing the word 'ought,' which Kant calls 'imperatives.' Any will which from its subjective constitution can be, but is not solely, determined by such rules of reason is under an obligation, for an obligation *is* the relation of an objective law of reason to such a will.[13]

This mechanical model of human nature enables Kant to draw a distinction between two different tasks performed by practical reason, thus combining the convictions of common

---

[12] *Ibid.*, pp. 36–37. [13] *Ibid.*, pp. 35–36.

sense with the doctrines of Hume. For the reason of such a twin-engined creature can issue two entirely different sorts of commands or imperatives, hypothetical and categorical. It can recommend a course of action as a means to an end determined by desire, a hypothetical imperative, or it can command a course of action as an end in itself, an end determined not by desire at all, but by pure reason alone. In issuing hypothetical imperatives, reason is indeed the slave of the passions, for its recommendations then hang on an empirical condition, on the fact that the person in question desires the end to which the recommended course of action is a means. As far as hypothetical imperatives go, Hume's claims about practical reason are quite true. Reason is here merely aiding the desires. It does not really issue laws or commands but only rules or counsels or principles. The force of these recommendations does not come from reason but from the fact that certain ends are desired by the person. Such recommendations are contingent and conditional, they vary from person to person and from time to time. They cannot be universally valid, "since whatever is only necessary for the attainment of some arbitrary purpose may be considered as in itself contingent, and we can at any time be free from the precept if we give up the purpose." [14]

But reason has another task, the issuing of laws or commands which are not conditional or contingent. In this employment, reason is not the slave of the passions, but an independent force which can come into conflict with the passions and can overrule them. When reason issues categorical imperatives, we cannot free ourselves from the precept by giving up the purpose, for we are commanded to have the purpose as well. "The unconditional command leaves the will no liberty to choose

---

[14] *Ibid.*, p. 44.

the opposite; consequently it alone carries with it that necessity which we require in a law." [15] Moral imperatives, says Kant, cannot be hypothetical but must be categorical.

2.1 Hypothetical and categorical imperatives

Kant's case against Hume rests on his distinction between the two different roles of practical reason but, as we shall see, it is untenable. It not only confuses a great many different distinctions with one another, but none of the separate distinctions of which it is confusedly compounded has anything to do with the distinction between moral and nonmoral imperatives.

To begin with, Kant gives an inaccurate account of the use of 'ought' sentences. They are ordinarily used in arguments designed to prove, or give reasons for, answers to the question 'What shall I do?' or 'What ought I to do?' or 'What should I do?' Such practical arguments, as we have seen,[16] are of the following forms:

(A) (i) One ought to sow early after a wet spring.
     (ii) The spring is wet.
     (iii) Therefore I (you, we, etc.) ought to sow (or: have reasons for sowing) early.
(B) (i) A wet spring is a reason for sowing early.
     (ii) The spring is wet.
     (iii) Therefore I (you, we, etc.) ought to sow (or: have reasons for sowing) early.

Forms (A) and (B) are equivalent. The same alternative conclusions can be derived from either major premise. There is, therefore, no difference between saying, 'One ought to . . .' and 'There is reason for . . . .' It is not surprising, then, that someone who says, 'You ought to do x,' is expected to offer a reason for it, that if he claims he has none or that there is

---

[15] *Ibid.*   [16] Chapter Three.

none we would have to answer that he did n̶o̶t̶ know what he was talking about.

'Ought' sentences can occur in the major premises or in the conclusions of such arguments. When they occur in the major premises, they are no more than rules of reason to be employed, together with facts, in order to yield imperatives, in Kant's sense. As major premises, they do not apply to particular persons or to particular situations. They are employed by particular persons in particular situations in order to ascertain which facts are relevant to the problem. But it is only the conclusions of such arguments which are imperatives in Kant's sense.

The reasons for these imperatives are to be found in the minor premises of the practical arguments. They are the facts which, together with the major premises, entail the conclusions. What makes them reasons for the conclusions, for the imperatives, is the fact that, together with the major premises, they entail the conclusions. That the spring is wet is a reason for *saying that you (or he or I, etc.) ought* to sow early only because of the major premise, that a wet spring is a reason for sowing early.

Next, we notice that some imperatives are preceded by an 'if' clause, others not. Let us call the former "if imperatives," the latter "bare imperatives." Thus, 'You ought to feed them calcium *if* the shells are too thin' and '*If* the painters come, you ought to cancel your dentist's appointment' and '*If* you want to lose weight, you ought to eat less' are "if imperatives." 'You ought to wear corsets, dear' and 'You ought to clean your teeth after every meal' or 'You ought to go and see a doctor immediately' are "bare imperatives."

Kant distinguishes between two different employments of "if imperatives," which he calls assertorial and problematical imperatives, respectively. The former recommend a course of action as a me⬤ to an end which is actually someone's, the latter as a means to an end which merely might be someone's. Happiness is actually everyone's end, hence imperatives recommending a course of action as a means to happiness are assertorial. Curing someone or poisoning someone is a possible end, hence imperatives recommending a course of action to these possible ends are merely problematical.

Kant claims that all hypothetical imperatives are conditional upon the end, as a means to which (and because it is one's end) they recommend a certain line of action. Hence, he argues, such imperatives are supported by means-end reasons. Hence they do not bind absolutely but only on condition that we desire the end which is their condition. However, moral imperatives must be absolutely and universally binding, independent of all empirical and contingent conditions. 'If you want to cure Jones, you ought to give him aspirins' and 'If you want to poison Jones, you ought to give him cyanide' are practically equally necessary, equally binding. They bind on condition that the person addressed desires the end mentioned in the 'if' clause. If he does not want to cure Jones, but to poison him, he ought not to give him aspirins, but cyanide. 'You ought to give Jones cyanide' is supported by a means-end reason, namely, the one stated in the protasis, that you want to poison, not to cure him. If you want that end, then reason recommends that course of action.

However, this must be rejected. In the first place, reasons for imperatives can never be stated in their 'if' clauses, for reasons must be stated in 'because' clauses or their equivalents, for example, 'since' clauses. If I ask *why* I ought to feed him cyanide, I cannot be told, '*If* you want to poison him, you ought to . . . .' That is not a reason, but a repetition of the recommendation. The answer can only be, '*Because* (or since) you want to poison him.' 'If' clauses state the *eventualities for which*, not the *reasons why* recommendations are made.

Kant overlooks this point because he does not see that what he calls problematical imperatives are not imperatives at all. He fails to distinguish conditional recommendations from mere statements of necessary connections. The confusion is all the more understandable as there is one use of 'must' in which it means very much the same as 'ought.' There are utterances containing 'must' in which this word could be replaced by 'ought' without changing their meaning. 'If you want to supervise the painters, you *must* cancel your dentist's appointment' simply states a little more strongly the same thing as 'If you want to supervise the painters, you *ought* to cancel your dentist's appointment.' But, sometimes, the word 'must' is used in utterances which are not imperatives at all, but merely statements of a necessary connection, a means-end relationship. 'If you want to lose weight, you *must* eat more fruit' does not recommend to you to eat more fruit. It merely states the fact (if it is a fact) that in order to lose weight one must eat more fruit, that eating fruit is a necessary condition of, an indispensable means to, losing weight. Such utterances state the necessary condition of something, namely, gaining an end.

In remarks of this sort, 'must' cannot be replaced by 'ought' without changing the meaning of the sentence. 'If you want to lose weight, you *must* eat more fruit' means something different from 'If you want to lose weight, you *ought* to eat more fruit.' The former can be verified by an investigation of people who do and people who don't eat fruit. The latter cannot be verified in this way. For even if it is true that one *must* eat more fruit (than a certain quantity) *if* one wants to lose weight, it may still not be true that *if* one wants to lose weight one *ought* to eat more fruit. For there may be counterreasons.

It may be wrong (when there is a shortage and all the fruit is reserved for the troops or the children), or it may be unhealthy to eat more fruit. What one ought to do in a given situation may depend on a great many factors, some of which may be more important than one's end, to lose weight. In that case, it is not true that one ought to do what is a necessary means to that end.

This failure to distinguish between the use of 'ought' and one of the uses of 'must' leads naturally to another confusion, that between two quite different uses of "if imperatives" which in their protasis refer to the possible end of the person addressed, for example, 'If you *want* to lose weight, you *ought* to eat more fruit.'

Such imperatives may, in the first place, be used to make a conditional recommendation (to eat more fruit) in the event that the person addressed should wish to lose weight and is prepared to take steps to gain his end. No reason for the recommendation is either stated or alluded to. The reason might, for instance, be 'because if you lose weight your resistance will be lowered and the fruit will build it up.' In that case the reason for the recommendation is a means-end reason, but the end is not referred or alluded to in the protasis. It is an end which the person addressed may be presumed to have, namely, the safeguarding of his health which will be threatened if he pursues the end stated in the protasis.

Alternatively, this "if imperative" may be used to make an entirely different claim where the reason for the recommendation is alluded to (not stated) in the protasis. Stated more fully, its meaning would be, 'You ought to eat more fruit *since* you want to lose weight and since you *must* eat more fruit *if* you want to lose weight.' A full statement of the reason would run '*because* you want to lose weight and because you *must* eat more fruit *if* you want to lose weight.' Here the reason is a means-end reason, and the means-end relationship is stated in the second half of the explicit statement of the reason. But the recommendation as a whole is unconditional. What is now *unconditionally* recommended, for a means-end reason alluded to in the protasis, is the eating of more fruit.

The three things which Kant fails to distinguish could be fully stated as follows:

(A)   If one wants to lose weight, one must eat more fruit.

(B)   (i) One ought to do what is necessary to achieve what one wants.

      (ii) If one loses weight, one's resistance is lowered. *If* one does not want one's resistance lowered, one must eat more fruit.

     (iii) You don't want your resistance lowered.

     (iv) Therefore, *if* you want to lose weight, you ought to eat more fruit.

(C)   (i) One ought to do what is necessary to achieve what one wants.

      (ii) If one wants to lose weight, one must eat more fruit.

     (iii) You want to lose weight.

     (iv) Therefore you ought to eat more fruit.

(A) simply states a necessary connection between eating more fruit and losing weight. It states that one is a necessary condition of the other, that one is a means to the other. It is not an imperative. The word 'must' cannot, without a change of meaning, be replaced by 'ought.'

(B) and (C) are two alternative interpretations of the imperative 'If you want to lose weight, you ought to eat more fruit.' (B) takes it to be a conditional recommendation, (C) an unconditional one. In (B), it is not stated among the reasons for the conclusion that the person wants to lose weight, hence the conclusion is conditional upon that fact. In (C) it is stated among the premises that the person wants to lose weight, hence this is one of the reasons, therefore the conclusion cannot be conditional upon that fact. (B) interprets 'If you want to lose weight, you ought to eat more fruit' as a conditional recommendation, the conclusion of a practical argument, the reasons for which are not even alluded to in the original imperative. (C) interprets the original imperative as an unconditional recommendation the reason for which is a means-end reason that is alluded to in the protasis. (B) takes the protasis of the imperative to be part of the conclusion; (C) takes it to be an elliptical version of the reasons, a full statement of which is given in premises (ii) and (iii). On interpretation (B) the fact stated in the protasis (your wanting to lose weight) cannot be among the *reasons for* the conclusion, since it forms *part of* the conclusion. On interpretation (C) that fact cannot be part of the conclusion, since it constitutes one of the reasons. Kant did not keep the two interpretations apart, hence he thought that the facts stated in the protasis of an "if imperative" were both parts of and the reason for the conclusion. But this is impossible.

Kant's account of hypothetical imperatives is therefore untenable. The problematical imperatives which he calls imperatives of skill,[17] for example, 'If you want to cure him, you must (ought to) give him aspirins,' are either mere statements of means-end relationships, therefore not imperatives at all, or genuine imperatives, in which case they must be interpreted as conditional imperatives the reasons for which have not even been alluded to in the protasis. *That* you want to cure him is not, as Kant thought, the reason why you ought to give him aspirin. True, you ought to give him aspirins *only if* you want

---

[17] Kant, *Fundamental Principles*, p. 38.

to cure him, but in that case no reason has been mentioned *why* you ought to give him aspirin. For if it is said that the reason surely is *that* you want to cure him, then the recommendation cannot contain that condition. We cannot in one and the same breath imply *that* you want to cure him (by giving that as our reason for our recommendation) and also imply that you might or might not want to cure him (by making our recommendation conditional upon your having that end).

What Kant calls assertorial imperatives,[18] for example, 'If you want to be happy, you must give up drink,' must be interpreted as recommendations which in their protasis allude to the reason for the recommendation, in our case 'because you want to be happy and because if you want to be happy you must give up drink.' But, as was pointed out, such recommendations are quite unconditional.

In the light of all this, we can see that, instead of Kant's single molar distinction between categorical and hypothetical imperatives, we are left with six different molecular distinctions. We also see that the six distinctions do not coincide. They are different and independent distinctions, and they give us no help in bringing to light what is characteristic of and peculiar to moral judgments. Here is a summary of them.

(i) "Bare imperatives" such as 'You ought to wear corsets, dear' and "if imperatives" such as 'If you want to please Joan, you ought to invite Jack.'

(ii) Problematical imperatives such as 'If you want to please Joan, you ought to invite Jack' and conditional recommendations such as 'If it does not rain today, then you ought to water the flowers to-night.' In the latter case, a recommendation is made for a certain eventuality, that it does not rain during the day. In the former case, the

---

[18] *Ibid.*, pp. 38–39.

recommendation is made for an eventuality of a certain sort, namely, that the person addressed wishes to achieve a certain end, to please Joan.

(iii) Conditional imperatives in which the protasis alludes to the reason for the recommendaton made, such as 'If you want to please Joan, you ought to invite Jack,' where the reason alluded to is 'you want to please Joan,' and conditional imperatives in which no allusion is made to the reason, such as 'If you want to supervise the painters, you ought to cancel the dentist's appointment,' where the reason might be anything from 'because it would be inconsiderate not to tell him' to 'because you will have to pay for it if you don't cancel it.'

(iv) Conditional imperatives which are supported by means-end reasons, such as 'Since you want to please Joan, you ought to invite Jack' (and since you *must* invite Jack *if* you do not want to displease her), and conditional imperatives which are supported by other kinds of reason, such as 'Since you want to supervise the painters, you ought to cancel the dentist's appointment.'

(v) Problematical imperatives such as 'If you want to please Joan, you *ought* to invite Jack' and statements of necessary connections such as 'If you want to please Joan, you *must* invite Jack.'

(vi) Moral imperatives such as 'You ought to cancel the dentist's appointment, since it would be very inconsiderate to let him keep the time for you when he could fit in others' and nonmoral imperatives such as 'You ought to cancel the dentist's appointment or else he will charge you for it.'

The distinction between moral and nonmoral imperatives cuts across all the other distinctions. Moral imperatives may be conditional, for example, 'If the painters come, then you ought to cancel the dentist's appointment because he is definitely keeping the time for you,' or unconditional, for example, 'You ought to cancel the dentist's appointment since he is definitely keeping the time for you.' They may be problematical imperatives, for example, 'If you want to supervise the painters, you ought to cancel the dentist's appointment,' or conditional recommendations, for example, 'If the painters come, you ought to cancel the dentist's appointment.' They may allude to the reasons for the imperative, for example, 'If you want to be a man of your word, then you ought to keep your appointment with the dentist,' or they may not allude to the reason, for example, 'If you want to supervise the painters, you ought to cancel the dentist's appointment.' They may be supported by means-end reasons, for example, 'You ought to go now because you ought to keep your appointment (and because you must go now if you want to keep your appointment),' or by other kinds, for example, 'You ought to cancel your appointment because it would be inconsiderate not to turn up without letting him know.' Of course, moral imperatives cannot be statements of necessary connections, since these are not imperatives at all. But this does not help us to understand the difference between moral and nonmoral imperatives, for nonmoral imperatives cannot be statements of necessary connections either.

2.2 Is reason the master of the passions?

"Just the same," it might be objected by someone, "what have you said to disprove Kant's point that, insofar as an imperative recommends a course of action as a means to an end, the force of this imperative depends on our wanting this end, that, in Kant's words, 'We can at any time be free from the precept if we give up the purpose'? [19] Could moral imperatives

[19] *Ibid.*, p. 44.

be contingent, dependent, conditional, hypothetical in this sense? If they were, would not that show that reason was merely the slave of the passions? And is it not clear that if there is to be any morality, reason must be their master?"

My point in drawing the distinctions of the previous section was to break down the sharp division between the two operations of reason, between the field in which reason is merely the slave of the passions and that in which it is their master. I tried to show that means-end reasons are related to the imperatives which they support in exactly the same way as any other type of reason. That one can make out a case for saying that reason is the slave of the passions and also for saying that it is their master is not due to the fact that there are two quite different types or employments of reason, namely, means-end and moral reasons. It is due rather to the fact that there are two quite different senses of 'slave of the passions' and 'master of the passions.' These two senses apply equally to all types, means-end as well as moral reasons.

Note first that not only moral reasons, but means-end reasons as well, may conflict with the passions. If my end is to regain the affections of Susie, then I ought to do anything that is a good or necessary means to that end. I may further know that if I want to regain her affections I must for a time treat her with indifference, flirt with other women, etc. I know that in such a situation I have a (means-end) reason (prima facie, of course) to treat her with indifference. And if there are no other overriding reasons dictating another course, then I *ought*, all things considered, to treat her with indifference, even though my passion for her may oppose this course dictated by (means-end) reasons. In such a case, reason may be the slave of my passions or their master, in a perfectly straightforward sense. I may yield to my inclinations and treat Susie lovingly: in that case reason is the slave of my passions. Or I may treat her with indifference: in that case, reason is their master. Obviously, whether reason is master or slave of the passions will depend on the person and the circumstances. One can give no a priori answer to this question.

There is, however, another sense of being 'the master (or the slave) of the passions,' in which we can give an a priori answer to it. Both Hume and Kant, however, have given the wrong answer. For Hume claims that reason is and ought only to be the slave of the passions, and Kant maintains that, as far as means-end reasons are concerned, reason is and ought only to be the slave, but as far as moral reasons are concerned, reason may and ought to be the master of the passions. The true answer is that in this sense reason is and ought to be the master of the passions whatever kind of reason is considered. The sense I have in mind is that of 'being *by its nature* the master (or slave) of the passions' or 'having *the function of* controlling (or being controlled by) the passions.' We have already demonstrated that whatever types of reason are involved, a man ought always to follow reason, that is, reason ought always to be the master of, it is always the function of reason to overrule, the desires.

It was therefore only because of a muddle that Kant was puzzled about the possibility of the categorical imperative. He thought that in the case of means-end reasons it was easy to explain why we always obeyed reason. He thought it was because there could be no conflict between reason and desire, since reason merely worked out the means to our desired ends, hence in following reason we always necessarily followed desire anyway. However, there was a difficulty in explaining how it is that we can follow reason in the case of categorical imperatives, for there we must often or always act in the face of opposing desires. The truth is that the two cases are exactly analogous. For as was shown above, our desires may conflict with reason even in the case of means-end reasons. The very desire for the love of Susie yields a means-end reason for treating her with indifference, which is opposed to the way I desire to treat her. The problem is the same in all cases, namely, how we are able to follow reason when it conflicts with our strongest present felt inclinations. But we have already dealt with this question in Chapter Six.

The distinction between hypothetical and categorical imperatives seemed to Kant to solve yet another problem, because he failed to keep it apart from the one just discussed. We have rejected Kant's solution of the problem how reason can "determine," that is, *bring about*, right conduct. His solution was that in following hypothetical imperatives we are really driven by desire, while in following categorical imperatives we are really driven by reason. We must now reject his solution of the problem how reason can "determine," that is, *ascertain*, right conduct. His solution is that in hypothetical imperatives reason relies on experience, on human nature, on conditions varying from person to person, and that therefore there are no universally valid answers to what a man ought (hypothetically) to do. If moral imperatives are to be universally binding, they cannot be hypothetical, they must be categorical, that is, independent of all conditions and of all experience, based on pure reason alone.

But this argument overlooks the difference between saying that an individual must be able to determine what is right and wrong irrespective of what *he* desires and saying that he must be able to determine what is right and wrong irrespective of what is *human nature*, that is, what human beings universally desire. Kant cannot draw a distinction between these two claims because he thinks of reason as a faculty of the same sort as, though higher and more authoritative than, desire. He thinks that an individual's reason can come into conflict not only with *some* of his desires, not only with all of *his* desires, but with "all *our* propensions, inclinations, and natural dispositions," [20] that is, even with the most basic and universal desires and needs of *human nature*.

But this is to misconceive reason. Reason is not a nobler, higher, more authoritative desire. We can think of a person without this or that desire, even without any desires. We can also think of a person with desires, but without practical reason. We are therefore inclined to construe reason on the model of a single, separate desire, only on a higher plane. But it is nonsense to think of a creature without desires though endowed with practical reason. A creature could not possess practical reason without possessing desires. Kant's notion of a holy will is nonsensical. When in asking, 'What shall I do?' we invoke reason, we are not invoking a higher-order desire, but we are simply taking an over-all view of the desires, our own and other people's, present and future. In following reason, we are not following one separate, though higher, finer, and more authoritative desire, but we are following an ordinary common desire, namely, one that we have weighed in a certain way and crowned as the one most deserving satisfaction, whether it is present or future, one of our own or someone else's. The peculiar authority of reason is based not on the peculiar nature of the desire it represents, but on the fact that it brings before us those other claims which are not directly felt now. Reason reminds us of the offers of other buyers elsewhere, still to come, which fortify us against the entreaties of the buyers who are with us in the office now. But reason is not itself another buyer. It enables us to turn down the present buyer though not because it has made a better offer. It merely tells us of better offers which will probably or certainly be made.

---

[20] *Ibid.*, p. 52.

It is true that practical reason involves what we normally call 'the will.' It is also true that it is our ideal to have a will which always obeys reason. But that does not mean that our ideal is a holy will, one which, from its nature, can only follow practical reason, for such a will is a contradiction in terms. By 'the will' we normally mean our ability to resist a present strong inclination and to follow a course contrary to it. *Will power* is the ability to pursue a certain line of action, determined upon for certain reasons, in the face of bodily fatigue, pain, fear, and the like. *Strength of will* consists in the ability to pursue such a course in the face of temptations, such as the expectations of pleasure, gain, honor, fame, as well as in the face of threats and other forms of psychological pressure.

Kant was quite justified in almost identifying the will and practical reason,[21] for the main exercise of our will, that is, our ability to resist inclination, occurs when we follow reason in opposition to desire. But his conception of the will as a sort of arm capable of being moved by two kinds of muscle, reason and desire,[22] is quite untenable. For reason and desire are not separate muscles at all. A creature could not have a will or practical reason if it did not have desires. For practical reason is the ability to deliberate, to give answers to the question 'What shall I do?' and where there are no desires, there can be no deliberation, no weighing of pros and cons, since there could then be no pros and cons.

The realization that practical reason is inseparable from the desires enables us to distinguish between the claim that what is right and wrong is independent of what a particular individual wants or desires on a particular occasion and the claim that what is right and wrong is independent of what all normal human beings desire. When employed from the moral point

---

[21] *Ibid.*, p. 35.   [22] *Ibid.*, p. 19.

of view, reason rejects killing, but it does so only because it is part of human nature to want to live and because life is a presupposition of the satisfaction of every other desire. If human nature were constituted differently, reason might not have to reject the taking of life.

In order to have an objective, universally valid morality, it is not necessary that there should be courses of action which are right or wrong for all possible creatures endowed with practical reason. We need not agree with Kant that

If a law is to have moral force, i.e. to be the basis of an obligation, it must carry with it absolute necessity; that, for example, the precept 'Thou shalt not lie,' is not valid for men alone, as if other rational beings had no need to observe it; and so with all other moral laws properly so called; that, therefore, the basis of an obligation must not be sought in the nature of man, or in the circumstances in the world in which he is placed, but *a priori* simply in the conceptions of pure reason.[23]

The only requirement is that, in working out what is right or wrong on a particular occasion, a man should not have to consider merely what are his strongest desires. Of course, in working this out he only determines what would be right and wrong for any *human* being in just the situation in which he finds himself. Nothing follows from it about other kinds of rational creatures, if there are any. Morality is anthropocentric, but why should that matter, as long as it is not egocentric or a matter of social convention? We need not be upset because the categorical imperative is impossible, for it is unnecessary.

3 WHY ARE WE MORAL?

We can now turn to the question why we are moral. It should be pointed out that, in ordinary contexts, this is not

---

[23] *Ibid.*, preface, p. 4.

a question that calls for explanation. On the contrary, that people are moral is taken as "natural," as not requiring explanation. Many philosophers who have argued that it is natural to be moral have probably merely wished to assert that such behavior is not strange, odd, foolish, perverse, and therefore in need of explanation. This point is well taken. A person who is moral need not justify his behavior, or explain it. On the contrary, it is immorality that stands in need of justification and, other things being equal, of explanation.

However, when we are not concerned with explaining the behavior of this or that person, but are concerned to examine human behavior, we may reach a stage at which being moral calls for explanation. If we regard as not being in need of explanation merely instinctive, impulsive, or conditioned behavior, then morality calls for explanation. For as was previously stated, morality cannot consist in following first, second, or third nature. Unlike animals, human beings act in ways which require a different type of explanation, namely, explanation in terms of *their* reasons for doing things.

It was already noted that human beings, in addition to having natural propensities, inclinations, instincts, or desires and in addition to behaving in ways which result from the conditioning of these, can also act *after and in accordance with deliberation.* We have seen that human beings inherit a system of working out what is the best course of action open to them and also the ability to follow the results so obtained (the will), even when this means acting contrary to the strongest felt desire.[24]

When this has been understood, there is no longer any mystery in why we are moral—those of us who are. For being moral is simply a special case of following reason, namely, the weightiest moral reasons. The explanation of why it is

---

[24] See above, Chapters Three and Six.

that we follow them is correspondingly simple: we have been trained to regard moral reasons as superior to all others, and we have accepted that. Or rather, I should say, most of us have accepted it and most of us act on it on most occasions, though some of us have, like Thrasymachus, rejected morality altogether, and many of us often merely pay lip service to it.

Twelve

Why should we be moral?

WE are now in a position to deal with the various problems we shelved earlier. In Chapter Three we had to postpone the examination of how we verify those fundamental propositions which serve as major premises in our practical arguments. We must now deal with this. The examination of the prevailing consideration-making beliefs used at the first stage of our practical deliberations leads naturally to the examination of our rules of superiority used at the second stage. This in turn involves our investigating whether moral reasons are superior to all others and (a question mentioned in Chapter One) whether and why we should be moral. That opens up the most fundamental issue of all, whether and why we should follow reason.

1 THE TRUTH OF CONSIDERATION-MAKING BELIEFS

Let us begin with our most elementary consideration-making belief: the fact that if I did x I would enjoy doing x is a reason for me to do x. There can be little doubt that this is one of

Why should we be moral?

the rules of reason recognized in our society. Most people would use the knowledge of the fact that they would enjoy doing something as a pro in their deliberations whether to do it. When we wonder whether to go to the pictures or to a dinner dance, the fact that we would enjoy the dinner dance but not the pictures is regarded as a reason for going to the dinner dance rather than to the pictures. We are now asking whether this widely held belief is true, whether this fact really is a reason or is merely and falsely believed to be so.

What exactly are we asking? Is our question empirical? Obviously it cannot be answered by direct inspection. We cannot see, hear, or smell whether this belief is true, whether this fact is a reason or not. The nature of our question becomes clearer if we remind ourselves of the function of consideration-making beliefs, namely, to serve as major premises in practical arguments. These arguments are supposed to yield true answers to questions of the form 'What shall I do?' or 'What is the best course of action open to me?' Premises of an argument are true if the argument is valid and the conclusion is true. We can infer that the premise is true if the argument is valid and if it is true that the course of action recommended in the conclusion of the argument is the best course open to the agent. The matter is considerably simplified by the fact that, at this point, we are dealing merely with prima-facie reasons. In order to determine the truth of the conclusion, we have only to find out whether the recommended course of action is the best, *other things being equal*, that is, whether it is better than its contradictory or its contrary.

Our practical argument runs as follows:
(i) The fact that if I did x I would enjoy doing x is a reason for me to do x.
(ii) I would enjoy doing x if I did x.
(iii) Therefore I ought to do x (other things being equal).

Hence our consideration-making belief (i) is true (since the argument is valid) if our conclusion (iii) is true. As pointed out above, our conclusion is true if the course recommended is the best, other things being equal, that is, if it is better than its contrary and its contradictory—better than (iv), I ought *not* to do x, and (v), it is *not* the case that I ought to do x.

The problem of the truth or falsity of consideration-making beliefs is thus reduced to the question whether it is better that they, rather than their contraries or contradictories, should be used as rules of reason, that is, as major premises in practical arguments. How would we tell?

It is not difficult to see that the contrary of our rule of reason is greatly inferior to it. For if, instead of the presently accepted belief (see above (i)), its contrary became the prevailing rule, then anyone trying to follow reason would have to conclude that whenever there is something that he would enjoy doing if he did it then he ought *not* to do it. "Reason" would counsel everyone always to refrain from doing what he enjoys, from satisfying his desires. "Reason" would counsel self-frustration for its own sake.

It is important to note that such an arrangement is possible. To say that we would not now *call* it 'following reason' is not enough to refute it. We can imagine two societies in which English is spoken and which differ only in this, that in one society, (i) is accepted, in the other the contrary of (i). It would then be correct to say in one society that doing what one would enjoy doing was following reason, in the other society that it was acting contrary to it. The "tautologousness" of the first remark *in our society* is not incompatible with the "tautologousness" of the contrary remark *in another society*. From the fact that the proposition 'Fathers are male' is analytic, we can infer that 'fathers are male' is necessarily true. But this is so only because we would not correctly *call* anything

'father' that we would correctly call 'not male.' And it is
perfectly in order to say that in any society in which English
was spoken but in which the words 'father' and/or 'male' were
not used in this way those words did not mean quite the same
as in our society. And with this, the matter is ended, for we
are not concerned to settle the question which verbal arrangement, ours or theirs, is the better. Nothing at all follows from
the fact that a society has our usage of 'father' and 'male' or
theirs. But in the case of the use of 'reason,' much depends on
which usage is accepted. The real difficulty only begins when we
have concluded, correctly, that the word 'reason' is used in a
different sense in that other society. For the practical implications of the word 'reason' are the same in both societies, namely,
that people are encouraged to follow reason rather than act
contrary to it. However, *what* is held in one society to be in
accordance with reason is held to be contrary to it in the other.
Hence, we must say that in practical matters nothing fundamental can be settled by attention to linguistic proprieties
or improprieties.

What, then, is relevant? We must remember what sort of a
"game" the game of reasoning is. We ask the question 'What
shall I do?' or 'What is the best course of action?' Following
reasons is following those hints which are most likely to make
the course of action the best in the circumstances. The criteria
of 'best course of action' are linked with what we mean by
'the good life.' In evaluating a life, one of the criteria of merit
which we use is how much satisfaction and how little frustration there is in that life. Our very purpose in "playing the
reasoning game" is to maximize satisfactions and minimize
frustrations. Deliberately to frustrate ourselves and to minimize satisfaction would certainly be to go counter to the very
purpose for which we deliberate and weigh the pros and cons.
These criteria are, therefore, necessarily linked with the very

purpose of the activity of reasoning. Insofar as we enter on that "game" at all, we are therefore bound to accept these criteria. Hence we are bound to agree that the consideration-making belief which is prevalent in our society is better than its contrary.

But need we accept that purpose? Is this not just a matter of taste or preference? Could not people with other tastes choose the opposite purpose, namely, self-frustration and self-denial rather than satisfaction of desires and enjoyment? The answer is No, it is not just a matter of taste or preference. Whether we like or don't like oysters, even whether we prefer red ink to claret, is a matter of taste, though to prefer red ink is to exhibit a very eccentric taste. Whether we prefer to satisfy our desires or to frustrate them is not, however, a matter of taste or preference. It is not an eccentricity of taste to prefer whatever one does *not* enjoy doing to whatever one does enjoy doing. It is perverse or crazy if it is done every now and then, mad if it is done always or on principle.

It might be objected that these people would merely be *called* mad by us—this does not prove that they really are, any more than the fact that they might well call us mad proves that we are. This objection seems to take the sting out of the epithet 'mad.' However, it only seems to do so, because it is misconstrued on one of the following two models.

(i) 'They are called artesian wells, but that's only what we call them in this country.' In this case, the distinction is between what we all, quite universally but incorrectly, call them in this country and what they really are, that is, what they are properly and correctly called. The difference is between an established but incorrect usage, and the correct but possibly not established usage. However, people who prefer whatever they do not enjoy doing to whatever they do would not merely generally (though incorrectly) but quite correctly be called mad.

(ii) 'When two people quarrel and call each other "bastard," that does not prove that they are bastards.' On this model, it might be argued that the word 'mad' has no established usage, that we use it only in order to insult people who are not average. But this is untenable. Admittedly we often use the word 'mad' to insult people who are not mad, just as we use the word 'bastard' to insult people who were born in wedlock. But we could not use these words for these purposes unless they were correctly used to designate characteristics generally regarded as highly undesirable. When a person is certified insane, this is done not just because he differs from average, but because he is different in certain fundamental and undesirable respects. To prove the undesirability of these differences, it is enough here to point out that no one *wants* to become mad. Our conclusion must be that there is a correct use of the word 'mad' and that people who prefer whatever they do not enjoy doing to whatever they do differ from normal people in just such fundamental and undesirable respects as would make the word 'mad' correctly applicable to them.

The contradictory of our most fundamental consideration-making belief is also less satisfactory than *it* is. If it were to be believed that the fact that one would enjoy doing x was not a reason for doing it (a belief which is the contradictory of our most fundamental consideration-making belief), then people wishing to follow reason would be neither advised to do what they would enjoy doing nor advised not to do it. Reason would simply be silent on this issue. Never to do what one would enjoy doing would be as much in accordance with reason (other things being equal) as always to do it. In such a world, "following reason" might be less rewarding than following instinct or inclination. Hence this cannot *be* following reason, for it *must* pay to follow reason at least as much as to follow instinct or inclination, or else it is not reason.

To sum up. People who replace our most fundamental consideration-making belief by its contrary or contradictory will not do as well as those who adhere to it. Those who adopt its contrary must even be said to be mad. This seems to me the best possible argument for the preferability of our fundamental consideration-making belief to its contrary and contradictory. And this amounts to a proof of its truth. I need not waste any further time on examining whether the other consideration-making beliefs prevalent in our society are also true. Everyone can conduct this investigation for himself.

2 THE HIERARCHY OF REASONS

How can we establish rules of superiority? It is a prima-facie reason for me to do something not only that *I* would enjoy it if *I* did it, but also that *you* would enjoy it if *I* did it. People generally would fare better if this fact were treated as a pro, for if this reason were followed, it would create additional enjoyment all round. But which of the two prima-facie reasons is superior when they conflict? How would we tell?

At first sight it would seem that these reasons are equally good, that there is nothing to choose between them, that no case can be made out for saying that people generally would fare better if the one or the other were treated as superior. But this is a mistake.

Suppose I could be spending half an hour in writing a letter to Aunt Agatha who would enjoy receiving one though I would not enjoy writing it, or alternatively in listening to a lecture which I would enjoy doing. Let us also assume that I cannot do both, that I neither enjoy writing the letter nor dislike it, that Aunt Agatha enjoys receiving the letter as much as I enjoy listening to the lecture, and that there are no extraneous considerations such as that I deserve especially to enjoy myself there and then, or that Aunt Agatha does, or that she has special claims against me, or that I have special responsibilities or obligations toward her.

In order to see which is the better of these two reasons, we must draw a distinction between two different cases: the case in which someone derives pleasure from giving pleasure to others and the case where he does not. Everyone is so related to certain other persons that he derives greater pleasure from doing something together with them than doing it alone because in doing so he is giving them pleasure. He derives pleasure not merely from the game of tennis he is playing but from the fact that in playing he is pleasing his partner. We all enjoy pleasing those we love. Many of us enjoy pleasing even strangers. Some even enjoy pleasing their enemies. Others get very little enjoyment from pleasing their fellow men.

We must therefore distinguish between people with two kinds of natural make-up: on the one hand, those who need not always choose between pleasing themselves and pleasing others, who can please themselves *by* pleasing others, who can please themselves more by not merely pleasing themselves, and, on the other hand, those who always or often have to choose between pleasing themselves and pleasing others, who derive no pleasure from pleasing others, who do not please themselves more by pleasing not merely themselves.

If I belong to the first kind, then I shall derive pleasure from pleasing Aunt Agatha. Although writing her a letter is not enjoyable in itself, as listening to the lecture is, I nevertheless derive enjoyment from writing it because it is a way of pleasing her and I enjoy pleasing people. In choosing between writing the letter and listening to the lecture, I do not therefore have to choose between pleasing her and pleasing myself. I have merely to choose between two different ways of pleasing myself. If I am a man of the second kind, then I must choose between pleasing myself and pleasing her. When we have eliminated all possible moral reasons, such as standing in a special relationship to the person, then it would be strange for someone to prefer pleasing someone else to pleasing himself. How strange this is can be seen if we substitute for Aunt Agatha a complete stranger.

I conclude from this that the fact that I would enjoy it if *I* did *x* is a better reason for doing *x* than the fact that you would enjoy it if *I* did *x*. Similarly in the fact that I would enjoy doing *x* if I did it I have a reason for doing *x* which is better than the reason for doing *y* which I have in the fact that you would enjoy doing *y* as much as I would enjoy doing *x*. More generally speaking, we can say that self-regarding reasons are better than other-regarding ones. Rationally speaking, the old quip is true that everyone is his own nearest neighbor.

This is more obvious still when we consider the case of self-interest. Both the fact that doing *x* would be in my interest and the fact that it would be in someone else's interest are excellent prima-facie reasons for me to do *x*. But the self-interested reason is better than the altruistic one. Of course, interests need not conflict, and then I need not choose. I can do what is in both our interests. But sometimes interests conflict, and then it is in accordance with reason (prima facie) to prefer my own interest to someone else's. That my making an application for a job is in *my* interest is a reason for me to apply, which is better than the reason against applying, which I have in the fact that my not applying is in *your* interest.

There is no doubt that this conviction is correct for all cases. It is obviously better that everyone should look after his own interest than that everyone should neglect it in favor of someone else's. For whose interest should have precedence? It must be remembered that we are considering a case in which there are no special reasons for preferring a particular person's interests to one's own, as when there are

Why should we be moral?

no special moral obligations or emotional ties. Surely, in the absence of any *special* reasons for preferring someone else's interests, *everyone's* interests are best served if *everyone* puts his own interests first. For, by and large, everyone is himself the best judge of what is in his own best interest, since everyone usually knows best what his plans, aims, ambitions, or aspirations are. Moreover, everyone is more diligent in the promotion of his own interests than that of others. Enlightened egoism is a possible, rational, orderly system of running things, enlightened altruism is not. Everyone can look after himself, no one can look after everyone else. Even if everyone had to look after only two others, he could not do it as well as looking after himself alone. And if he has to look after only one person, there is no advantage in making that person some one other than himself. On the contrary, he is less likely to know as well what that person's interest is or to be as zealous in its promotion as in that of his own interest.

For this reason, it has often been thought that enlightened egoism is a possible rational way of running things. Sidgwick, for instance, says that the principle of egoism, to have as one's ultimate aim one's own greatest happiness, and the principle of universal benevolence, to have as one's ultimate aim the greatest happiness of the greatest number, are equally rational.[1] Sidgwick then goes on to say that these two principles may conflict and anyone who admits the rationality of both may go on to maintain that it is rational not to abandon the aim of one's own greatest happiness. On his view, there is a fundamental and ultimate contradiction in our apparent intuitions of what is reasonable in conduct. He argues that this can be removed only by the assumption that the individual's greatest happiness and the greatest happiness of the greatest number are

---

[1] Henry Sidgwick, *The Methods of Ethics*, 7th ed. (London: Macmillan and Co., 1907), concluding chapter, par. 1.

both achieved by the rewarding and punishing activity of a perfect being whose sanctions would suffice to make it always everyone's interest to promote universal happiness to the best of his knowledge.

The difficulty which Sidgwick here finds is due to the 'fact that he regards reasons of self-interest as being no stronger and no weaker than moral reasons. This, however, is not in accordance with our ordinary convictions. It is generally believed that when reasons of self-interest conflict with moral reasons, then moral reasons override those of self-interest. It is our common conviction that moral reasons are superior to all others. Sidgwick has simply overlooked that although it is prima facie in accordance with reason to follow reasons of self-interest and also to follow moral reasons nevertheless, when there is a conflict between these two types of reason, when we have a self-interested reason for doing something and a moral reason against doing it, there need not be an ultimate and fundamental contradiction in what it is in accordance with reason to do. For one type of reason may be *stronger* or *better* than another so that, when two reasons of different types are in conflict, it is in accordance with reason to follow the stronger, contrary to reason to follow the weaker.

3 THE SUPREMACY OF MORAL REASONS

Are moral reasons really superior to reasons of self-interest as we all believe? Do we really have reason on our side when we follow moral reasons against self-interest? What reasons could there be for being moral? Can we really give an answer to 'Why should we be moral?' It is obvious that all these questions come to the same thing. When we ask, 'Should we be moral?' or 'Why should we be moral?' or 'Are moral reasons superior to all others?' we ask to be shown the reason for being moral. What is this reason?

Why should we be moral?

Let us begin with a state of affairs in which reasons of self-interest are supreme. In such a state everyone keeps his impulses and inclinations in check when and only when they would lead him into behavior detrimental to his own interest. Everyone who follows reason will discipline himself to rise early, to do his exercises, to refrain from excessive drinking and smoking, to keep good company, to marry the right sort of girl, to work and study hard in order to get on, and so on. However, it will often happen that people's interests conflict. In such a case, they will have to resort to ruses or force to get their own way. As this becomes known, men will become suspicious, for they will regard one another as scheming competitors for the good things in life. The universal supremacy of the rules of self-interest must lead to what Hobbes called the state of nature. At the same time, it will be clear to everyone that universal obedience to certain rules overriding self-interest would produce a state of affairs which serves everyone's interest much better than his unaided pursuit of it in a state where everyone does the same. Moral rules are universal rules designed to override those of self-interest when following the latter is harmful to others. 'Thou shalt not kill,' 'Thou shalt not lie,' 'Thou shalt not steal' are rules which forbid the inflicting of harm on someone else even when this might be in one's interest.

The very *raison d'être* of a morality is to yield reasons which overrule the reasons of self-interest in those cases when everyone's following self-interest would be harmful to everyone. Hence moral reasons are superior to all others.

"But what does this mean?" it might be objected. "If it merely means that we do so regard them, then you are of course right, but your contention is useless, a mere point of usage. And how could it mean any more? If it means that we not only do so regard them, but *ought* so to regard them,

309

then there must be *reasons* for saying this. But there could not
be any reasons for it. If you offer reasons of self-interest, you are
arguing in a circle. Moreover, it cannot be true that it is always in my interest to treat moral reasons as superior to reasons
of self-interest. If it were, self-interest and morality could never
conflict, but they notoriously do. It is equally circular to argue
that there are moral reasons for saying that one ought to treat
moral reasons as superior to reasons of self-interest. And what
other reasons are there?"

The answer is that we are now looking at the world from
the point of view of *anyone*. We are not examining particular
alternative courses of action before this or that person; we are
examining two alternative worlds, one in which moral reasons
are always treated by everyone as superior to reasons of self-
interest and one in which the reverse is the practice. And we
can see that the first world is the better world, because we can
see that the second world would be the sort which Hobbes
describes as the state of nature.

This shows that I ought to be moral, for when I ask the
question 'What ought I to do?' I am asking, 'Which is the
course of action supported by the best reasons?' But since
it has just been shown that moral reasons are superior to reasons of self-interest, I have been given a reason for being moral,
for following moral reasons rather than any other, namely,
they are better reasons than any other.

But is this always so? Do we have a reason for being moral
whatever the conditions we find ourselves in? Could there
not be situations in which it is not true that we have reasons
for being moral, that, on the contrary, we have reasons for
ignoring the demands of morality? Is not Hobbes right in
saying that in a state of nature the laws of nature, that is,
the rules of morality, bind only *in foro interno?*

Why should we be moral?

Hobbes argues as follows.

(i) To live in a state of nature is to live outside society. It is to live in conditions in which there are no common ways of life and, therefore, no reliable expectations about other people's behavior other than that they will follow their inclination or their interest.

(ii) In such a state reason will be the enemy of co-operation and mutual trust. For it is too risky to hope that other people will refrain from protecting their own interests by the preventive elimination of probable or even possible dangers to them. Hence reason will counsel everyone to avoid these risks by preventive action. But this leads to war.

(iii) It is obvious that everyone's following self-interest leads to a state of affairs which is desirable from no one's point of view. It is, on the contrary, desirable that everybody should follow rules overriding self-interest whenever that is to the detriment of others. In other words, it is desirable to bring about a state of affairs in which all obey the rules of morality.

(iv) However, Hobbes claims that in the state of nature it helps nobody if a single person or a small group of persons begins to follow the rules of morality, for this could only lead to the extinction of such individuals or groups. In such a state, it is therefore contrary to reason to be moral.

(v) The situation can change, reason can support morality, only when the presumption about other people's behavior is reversed. Hobbes thought that this could be achieved only by the creation of an absolute ruler with absolute power to enforce his laws. We have already seen that this is not true and that it is quite different if people live in a society, that is, if they have common ways of life, which are taught to all members and somehow enforced by the group. Its members have reason to expect their fellows generally to obey its rules, that is, its

311

religion, morality, customs, and law, even when doing so is not, on certain occasions, in their interest. Hence they too have reason to follow these rules.

Is this argument sound? One might, of course, object to step (i) on the grounds that this is an empirical proposition for which there is little or no evidence. For how can we know whether it is true that people in a state of nature would follow only their inclinations or, at best, reasons of self-interest, when nobody now lives in that state or has ever lived in it?

However, there is some empirical evidence to support this claim. For in the family of nations, individual states are placed very much like individual persons in a state of nature. The doctrine of the sovereignty of nations and the absence of an effective international law and police force are a guarantee that nations live in a state of nature, without commonly accepted rules that are somehow enforced. Hence it must be granted that living in a state of nature leads to living in a state in which individuals act either on impulse or as they think their interest dictates. For states pay only lip service to morality. They attack their hated neighbors when the opportunity arises. They start preventive wars in order to destroy the enemy before he can deliver his knockout blow. Where interests conflict, the stronger party usually has his way, whether his claims are justified or not. And where the relative strength of the parties is not obvious, they usually resort to arms in order to determine "whose side God is on." Treaties are frequently concluded but, morally speaking, they are not worth the paper they are written on. Nor do the partners regard them as contracts binding in the ordinary way, but rather as public expressions of the belief of the governments concerned that for the time being their alliance is in the interest of the allies. It is well understood that such treaties may be canceled before they reach their predetermined end or simply broken when it

suits one partner. In international affairs, there are very few
examples of *Nibelungentreue*, although statesmen whose countries have profited from keeping their treaties usually make
such high moral claims.

It is, moreover, difficult to justify morality in international
affairs. For suppose a highly moral statesman were to demand
that his country adhere to a treaty obligation even though
this meant its ruin or possibly its extinction. Suppose he were
to say that treaty obligations are sacred and must be kept
whatever the consequences. How could he defend such a policy?
Perhaps one might argue that someone has to make a start in
order to create mutual confidence in international affairs. Or
one might say that setting a good example is the best way of
inducing others to follow suit. But such a defense would hardly
be sound. The less skeptical one is about the genuineness of
the cases in which nations have adhered to their treaties from
a sense of moral obligation, the more skeptical one must be
about the effectiveness of such examples of virtue in effecting
a change of international practice. Power politics still govern
in international affairs.

We must, therefore, grant Hobbes the first step in his argument and admit that in a state of nature people, as a matter
of psychological fact, would not follow the dictates of morality.
But we might object to the next step that knowing this
psychological fact about other people's behavior constitutes a
reason for behaving in the same way. Would it not still be
immoral for anyone to ignore the demands of morality even
though he knows that others are likely or certain to do so, too?
Can we offer as a justification for morality the fact that no
one is entitled to do wrong just because someone else is doing
wrong? This argument begs the question whether it *is* wrong
for anyone in this state to disregard the demands of morality.
It cannot be wrong to break a treaty or make preventive war

if we have no reason to obey the moral rules. For to say that it is wrong to do so is to say that we ought not to do so. But if we have no reason for obeying the moral rule, then we have no reason overruling self-interest, hence no reason for keeping the treaty when keeping it is not in our interest, hence it is not true that we have a reason for keeping it, hence not true that we ought to keep it, hence not true that it is wrong not to keep it.

I conclude that Hobbes's argument is sound. Moralities are systems of principles whose acceptance by everyone as overruling the dictates of self-interest is in the interest of everyone alike, though following the rules of a morality is not of course identical with following self-interest. If it were, there could be no conflict between a morality and self-interest and no point in having moral rules overriding self-interest. Hobbes is also right in saying that the application of this system of rules is in accordance with reason only in social conditions, that is, when there are well-established ways of behavior.

The answer to our question 'Why should we be moral?' is therefore as follows. We should be moral because being moral is following rules designed to overrule self-interest whenever it is in the interest of everyone alike that everyone should set aside his interest. It is not self-contradictory to say this, because it may be in one's interest *not* to follow one's interest at times. We have already seen that enlightened self-interest acknowledges this point. But while enlightened self-interest does not require any genuine sacrifice from anyone, morality does. In the interest of the possibility of the good life for everyone, voluntary sacrifices are sometimes required from everybody. Thus, a person might do better for himself by following enlightened self-interest rather than morality. It is not possible, however, that *everyone* should do better for himself by following enlightened self-interest rather than morality. The best possible life *for everyone* is possible only by everyone's following the rules of morality, that is, rules which quite frequently may require individuals to make genuine sacrifices.

It must be added to this, however, that such a system of rules has the support of reason only where people live in societies, that is, in conditions in which there are established common ways of behavior. Outside society, people have no reason for following such rules, that is, for being moral. In other words, outside society, the very distinction between right and wrong vanishes.

4 WHY SHOULD WE FOLLOW REASON?

But someone might now ask whether and why he should follow reason itself. He may admit that moral reasons are superior to all others, but doubt whether he ought to follow reason. He may claim that this will have to be proved first, for if it is not true that he ought to follow reason, then it is not true that he ought to follow the strongest reason either.

What is it to follow reason? As we have explained, it involves two tasks, the theoretical, finding out what it would be in accordance with reason to do in a certain situation, what contrary to reason, and the practical task, to act accordingly. It was shown in Chapter Three how this is done. We must also remind ourselves that there are many different ways in which what we do or believe or feel can be contrary to reason. It may be *irrational*, as when, for no reason at all, we set our hand on fire or cut off our toes one by one, or when, in the face of conclusive evidence to the contrary, someone *believes* that her son killed in the war is still alive, or when someone is *seized by fear* as a gun is pointed at him although he knows for certain that it is not loaded. What we do, believe, or feel is called irrational if it is the case not only that there are conclusive or overwhelming reasons against doing, believing, or feeling these things, but also that we must know there are such reasons and we still persist in our action, belief, or feeling.

Or it may be *unreasonable*, as when we make demands which are excessive or refuse without reason to comply with requests which are reasonable. We say of demands or requests that they are excessive if, though we are entitled to make them, the party against whom we make them has good reasons for not complying, as when the landlord demands the immediate vacation of the premises in the face of well-supported pleas of hardship by the tenant.

Being unreasonable is a much weaker form of going counter to reason than being irrational. The former applies in cases where there is a conflict of reasons and where one party does not acknowledge the obvious force of the case of the other or, while acknowledging it, will not modify his behavior accordingly. A person is irrational only if he flies in the face of reason, if, that is, all reasons are on one side and he acts contrary to it when he either acknowledges that this is so or, while refusing to acknowledge it, has no excuse for failing to do so.

Again, someone may be *inconsistent*, as when he refuses a Jew admission to a club although he has always professed strong positive views on racial equality. Behavior or remarks are inconsistent if the agent or author professes principles adherence to which would require him to say or do the opposite of what he says or does.

Or a person may be *illogical*, as when he does something which, as anyone can see, cannot or is not at all likely to lead to success. Thus when I cannot find my glasses or my fountain pen, the logical thing to do is to look for them where I can remember I had them last or where I usually have them. It would be illogical of me to look under the bed or in the oven unless I have special reason to think they might be there. To say of a person that he is a logical type is to say that he always does what, on reflection, anyone would agree is most likely to lead to success. Scatterbrains, people who act rashly, without thinking, are the opposite of logical.

When we speak of following reason, we usually mean 'doing what is supported by the best reasons because it is so supported' or perhaps 'doing what we think (rightly or wrongly) is supported by the best reasons because we think it is so supported.' It might, then, occur to someone to ask, 'Why should I follow reason?' During the last hundred years or so, reason has had a very bad press. Many thinkers have sneered at it and have recommended other guides, such as the instincts, the unconscious, the voice of the blood, inspiration, charisma, and the like. They have advocated that one should not follow reason but be guided by these other forces.

However, in the most obvious sense of the question 'Should I follow reason?' this is a tautological question like 'Is a circle a circle?'; hence the advice 'You should not follow reason' is as nonsensical as the claim 'A circle is not a circle.' Hence the question 'Why should I follow reason?' is as silly as 'Why is a circle a circle?' We need not, therefore, take much notice of the advocates of unreason. They show by their advocacy that they are not too clear on what they are talking about.

How is it that 'Should I follow reason?' is a tautological question like 'Is a circle a circle?' Questions of the form 'Shall I do this?' or 'Should I do this?' or 'Ought I to do this?' are, as was shown (in Chapter Three), requests to someone (possibly oneself) to deliberate on one's behalf. That is to say, they are requests to survey the facts and weigh the reasons for and against this course of action. These questions could therefore be paraphrased as follows. 'I wish to do what is supported by the best reasons. Tell me whether this is so supported.' As already mentioned, 'following reason' means 'doing what is supported by the best reasons.' Hence the question 'Shall (should, ought) I follow reason?' must be paraphrased as 'I wish to do what is supported by the best reasons. Tell me whether doing what is supported by the best reasons is doing what is supported by the best reasons.' It is, therefore, not worth asking.

The question '*Why* should I follow reason?' simply does not make sense. Asking it shows complete lack of understanding of the meaning of 'why questions.' 'Why should I do this?' is a request to be given the reason for saying that I should do this. It is normally asked when someone has already said, 'You should do this' and answered by giving the reason. But since 'Should I follow reason?' means 'Tell me whether doing what is supported by the best reasons is doing what is supported by the best reasons,' there is simply no possibility of adding 'Why?' For the question now comes to this, 'Tell me the reason why doing what is supported by the best reasons is doing what is supported by the best reasons.' It is exactly like asking, 'Why is a circle a circle?'

However, it must be admitted that there is another possible interpretation to our question according to which it makes sense and can even be answered. 'Why should I follow reason?' may not be a request for a reason in support of a tautological remark, but a request for a reason why one should enter on the theoretical task of deliberation. As already explained, following reason involves the completion of two tasks, the theoretical and the practical. The point of the theoretical is to give guidance in the practical task. We perform the theoretical only because we wish to complete the practical task in accordance with the outcome of the theoretical. On our first interpretation, 'Should I follow reason?' means 'Is the practical task completed when it is completed in accordance with the outcome of the theoretical task?' And the answer to this is obviously 'Yes,' for that is what we mean by 'completion of the practical task.' On our second interpretation, 'Should I follow reason?' is not a question about the practical but about the theoretical task. It is not a question about whether, given that one is prepared to perform both these tasks, they are properly completed in the way indicated. It is a question about whether one should enter on the whole performance at all, whether the "game" is worth playing. And this is a meaningful question. It might be better to "follow inspiration" than to "follow reason," in this sense: better to close one's eyes and wait for an answer to flash across the mind.

But while, so interpreted, 'Should I follow reason?' makes sense, it seems to me obvious that the answer to it is 'Yes, because it pays.' Deliberation is the only reliable method. Even if there were other reliable methods, we could only tell whether they were reliable by checking them against this method. Suppose some charismatic leader counsels, 'Don't follow reason, follow me. My leadership is better than that of reason'; we would still have to check his claim against the ordinary methods of reason. We would have to ascertain whether in following his advice we were doing the best thing. And this we can do only by examining whether he has advised us to do what is supported by the rest reasons. His claim to be better than reason can in turn only be supported by the fact that he tells us precisely the same as reason does.

Is there any sense, then, in his claim that his guidance is preferable to that of reason? There may be, for working out what is supported by the best reasons takes a long time. Frequently, the best thing to do is to do something quickly now rather than the most appropriate thing later. A leader may have the ability to "see," to "intuit," what is the best thing to do more quickly than it is possible to work this out by the laborious methods of deliberation. In evaluating the qualities of leadership of such a person, we are evaluating *his ability to perform correctly the practical task of following reason* without having to go through the lengthy operations of the theoretical. Reason is required to tell us whether anyone has qualities of leadership better than ordinary, in the same way that pencil and paper multiplications are required to tell us whether a mathematical prodigy is genuine or a fraud.

Lastly, it must be said that sometimes it may be better even for an ordinary person without charisma not to follow reason but to do something at once, for quick action may be needed.

Index

Absolute morality, 183

Advice, 74, 86, 153

Approval, 26-29; moral, and disapproval, 33, 41, 42, 50; nonmoral, and disapproval, 27, 33

Arguments, practical, 281, 286, 298, 299

Austin, J. L., 79

"Bare imperatives," 281, 287; see also Imperatives

Being moral, 249 ff.; cause of, 257 ff.; following the weightiest reasons, 252; justification of, see Morality, justification of; not following nature, 250

Beliefs, consideration-making, 94-99, 106, 170, 171, 298, 302; function of, 299; the most fundamental, 298, 303, 304; truth of, 300

Broad, C. D., 215, 216

Calculative rationalism, 24; see also Rationalism

Canons, 123-126 *passim*

Carritt, E. F., 216

Categorical rationalism, 25; see also Rationalism

Celibacy, 210, 211

Commands: distinguished from laws, 136-139; Hare's view of, 79

Conformity with reason, 89-91, 140-144, 147, 149, 160, 249, 250, 259, 300, 301, 306, 315; acting in, 315; Hume's view of, 258 ff.; morality in the state of nature and, 315 ff.; whether "worked out" or "seen" by reason, 248-249

Conscience, 13, 17, 23, 113, 211, 231, 240, 249, 250

Consideration-making beliefs, see Beliefs, consideration-making; Rules of reason

Considerations: legal, 100, 134; moral, 134, 169, 229; of self-interest, see Self-interest, reasons of

321

Index

Index

Implication, presumptive, 102
Inconsistency, 316
Individual initiative, the morality of, 212, 213
Interest: conflict of, 190; long-range, 99, 106; of everyone alike, 202, 203, 209; one's, our, etc., *see* Self-interest; real, 117-118; short-range, 99, 106
Intuition, 23-24, 171, 172, 189, 190, 192, 240, 248, 249
Intuitionism, 22-24
Irrationality, 315

Justice, 207, 255
Justification, 13, 105, 112, 133, 148-156, 157, 167, 212, 265; of being moral *and* of morality, *see* Morality, justification of

Kant, Immanuel, 9, 15, 25, 183, 191, 192, 199, 200, 209, 211, 277-295

Law, 99; as model of morality, 178, 179, 233; of nature, *see* Natural law
Law theory, 18, 20
Legal system, 127, 128, 130, 133, 134, 174, 178, 179, 201, 239
Luther, Martin, 13

Macdonald, Margaret, 51, 53
Man of good will, 32, 169, 185, 186
Martyrs, 274
Marx, Karl, 256
Mathematical prodigies, 23
Maxims, 9, 10, 25, 123-126, 188, 195, 199, 200, 209
Means, 263; to our ends, 140, 263, 279, 280, 281, 286
Model: means-end, of reasons, 87-88; of human nature, 277-278
Moore, G. E., 21, 30, 48, 155
Moral: approval and disapproval, 33, 41, 42, 50; balance, 204-207; blindness, 22; convictions, *see*

Convictions, moral; credit and debit, 205; desert and merit, 206; equilibrium, 204-207; feelings, 20; grounds, 27, 28, 33, 178, 255; properties, 19; reasoning, *see* Reasoning, moral; reasons, *see* Reasons, moral; relations to oneself, 214; relations to others, 254; rules, *see* Rules, moral; rules, criteria of, *see* Criteria, of moral rules; sense, 22, 240, 241; skepticism, *see* Skepticism, moral; terms, 19; truths, 234; truths, absolute, 235-239; utterances, 35, 38
Moral fact theory, 18, 19, 21, 22
Moralities, 99, 174, 182, 193, 197, 199, 200, 202, 211, 213, 215, 257; and society, 253; compared with legal systems, 179-180; contrasted with morality as such, 181; demands of, 258, 313; distinguished from absolute morality, 183; nature of, 314; truth of, 183, 256
Morality, absolute, 183; and international affairs, 312-313; justification of, 10, 313; *raison d'être* of, 309; truth of, *see* Moralities, truth of
Morally impossible rules, 197-200 *passim*
Moral sense theory, 22
Mores, 123-129 *passim*
Motivation, theories of, 14
Motives, 153, 258; distinguished from reasons, 156-162
'Must,' some uses of, not interchangeable with 'ought,' 283; *see also* 'Ought'

Natural law, 122, 139, 177, 237, 238, 310
Necessary connection, statements of, *see* Statements of necessary connection

323

Index

Index

Reasons (*continued*)

terest, *see* Self-interest, reasons of; on balance, 103, 104, 120; other-regarding, 121; other-regarding, inferior to self-regarding reasons, 306; other things being equal, or prima facie, 103, 104, 105, 120; presumptive, 103-105; sans phrase, 103; self-regarding, 119, 121, 202; self-regarding, superior to other-regarding reasons, 306; short-range, 121; ultimate and preliminary, 223

Recommendations, 282, 287, 288; conditional, 283-289 *passim*; distinguished from statements of necessary connection, 283; imperatives used as, 282; unconditional, 286, 287

Regularities, 123-126

Regulations, 123-127

Response theory, 18, 19, 20, 26-33

Reversibility, 202, 203, 211

Ross, Sir David, 21, 103, 146 n., 171, 216

Rule, Golden, 202, 203

Rules: of priority, *see* Priority, rules of; of superiority, *see* Superiority, rules of

Rules, moral, 139, 192-203 *passim*, 310, 314; designed to overrule rules of self-interest, 309; of duty and of supererogation, 205, 206; primary and secondary, 204-206

Rules of reason, 94 ff., 107, 193, 278, 299; individual, 107-121; moral, 107, 170, 171; social, 122-139

Ryle, Gilbert, 109, 268

Sanctions, 8, 124, 129, 131, 133

Self-defeating rules, 197, 200

Self-frustrating rules, 196, 197, 200

Self-interest, 6, 8, 13, 98, 101, 115-118, 170, 171, 184, 185, 187, 188;

morality and promotion of, 230; moral reasons compared with reasons of, 308-310; reasons of, 99, 100, 106, 170

Sensations, 267, 271, 274; distinguished from experiences, 274; various kinds of classification of, 274, 275, 276; visual, 245-248 *passim*

Sense: moral, 22, 240, 241; of duty, 12, 17, 119

Sidgwick, Henry, 189, 307, 308

Sight: a power enabling us to perform the activities of, 243, 248; logically tied to eyes, 142; logically tied to visual sensations, 247-248; the activities of, 243; the mental faculty of, 241-248

Skepticism, 15, 18, 224; moral, 14

Slave of the passions, *see* Passions, slave of the

Social pressures, 124-132 *passim*

Sophists, 12

Standards, 35, 60, 61, 63, 67, 68, 84

Statements of necessary connection, 283 ff.

State of nature, 132, 231-239 *passim*, 310; the result of the supremacy of reasons of self-interest, 309

Stevenson, C. L., 36, 38, 43, 44, 77, 90

Suicide, 210, 211, 214, 228, 230

Summum bonum, *see* Ends, ultimate

Supererogation: rules of, 205, 206; works of, 206

Superiority: principles of, 101; rules of, 99, 170-172, 298, 304 ff.

Taboos, 174

Tasks: practical, 142, 144, 145, 315; theoretical, 142, 144, 145, 147, 315; visual, 247

325

Index

Taste, faculty of, 259
Theory, *see* Emotive theory; Impact theory; Motivation, theories of; etc.
Thrasymachus, 200, 256, 297
Toulmin, S. E., 23, 48

Ultimate end, 87, 261
Universalizability, 209, 210, 212
Unreasonableness, 316
Urmson, J. O., 83
Utilitarians, 11, 192, 203

Validation, 75, 80, 82
Value questions, 85
Visual: sensations, *see* Sensations, visual; tasks, *see* Tasks, visual

Wants, 114 ff.
Will, 16, 258, 279, 296; holy, 278; in relation to desire, 278; Kant's view of, 277; Kant's view of, non-sensical, 293, 294; power of, 294; strength of, 294